An award-winning writer and broadcaster, **HOWARD JACOBSON**'s novels include *The Mighty Walzer* ~~~~ of the Bollinger Everyman Wodeh~~~~ *~~~~ry Now?* (both longlisted for the ~~~~ ~~~~ker Prize-winning *The Finkler Q~~~~ ~~~~ne.* Howard Jacobson lives in Lo~~~~

Praise for *Whatever It Is, I Don't Like It*

'An acutely observed collection of occasional pieces that pick at absurdist life and reveal him to be a cultural critic gifted with precise comic timing' *The Times*

'The no-nonsense tone, coupled with a coherent defence of truth, even in uncomfortable circumstances, shows the essayist as natural comedian' Philip Hensher *Prospect*

'If there is a Booker for collections of occasional pieces, this latest book should be immediately Bookered ... I read it with something like love for its author . . . [reveling] in reading the language of a man who revels in writing it' *Canberra Times*

'A collection of enduring value ... [Jacobson] is, too, the master of the brilliant observation ... this is a book with a sly grin and the odd, raucous guffaw' *Glasgow Herald*

'Jacobson is certainly thoughtful and emotional but, like Mark Twain, can jolt you with laughter when you least expect it. Rich and flavorful – best ingested in small amounts so the savory pleasures linger' *Kirkus*

'A brilliant wordsmith whose command of language and irony leaps off every page' *The Saturday Age*

BY THE SAME AUTHOR

Fiction

Coming From Behind
Peeping Tom
Redback
The Very Model of a Man
No More Mister Nice Guy
The Mighty Walzer
Who's Sorry Now?
The Making of Henry
Kalooki Nights
The Act of Love
The Finkler Question
Zoo Time

Non-fiction

Shakespeare's Magnanimity (with Wilbur Sanders)
In the Land of Oz
Roots Schmoots: Journeys Among Jews
Seriously Funny: From the Ridiculous to the Sublime

WHATEVER IT IS, I DON'T LIKE IT

Howard Jacobson

B L O O M S B U R Y

LONDON • NEW DELHI • NEW YORK • SYDNEY

First published in Great Britain 2011
This paperback edition published 2012

Bloomsbury Publishing Plc
50 Bedford Square
London WC1B 3DP

www.bloomsbury.com

Bloomsbury Publishing, London, New Delhi, New York and Sydney

A CIP catalogue record for this book is available from the British Library

ISBN 978 1 4088 2242 5

10 9 8 7 6 5 4 3 2 1

Typeset by Hewer Text UK Ltd, Edinburgh

Printed in Great Britain by Clays Ltd, St Ives plc

Mixed Sources
Product group from well-managed
forests and other controlled sources
www.fsc.org Cert no. SGS-COC-2061
© 1996 Forest Stewardship Council
FSC

For Ziva

Groucho Marx: I've got something here you're bound to like.
  You'll be crazy about it.
Chico Marx: No, I don't like it.
Groucho Marx: You don't like what?
Chico Marx: Whatever it is, I don't like it.

A Night at the Opera

CONTENTS

Contents

INTRODUCTION

What follows is a selection of the columns I have been writing for the *Independent* since 1998. The title, *Whatever It Is, I Don't Like It*, might be asking for trouble, as it suggests a querulousness which I don't in all honesty lay claim to. There is a great deal that I do like. But it isn't in my nature to be non-confrontational, and these columns have, I hope, been amicably provocative from the start – picking a fight with those who make the world more sanctimonious, more foolish and, in every sense, more impoverished than it needs to be, while at the same time expecting to be read in a spirit of good-hearted amusement. It matters to me to be entertaining. Some would say it matters too much. But I don't have any story to break or any information to convey; I am a stranger to the current affairs agenda; and I don't see myself as an opinion former.

Novelists are not here to have opinions; our job is to submit opinion to the comic drama of ambiguity and contradiction, and I have all along conceived these pieces as more like little novels than articles – flights of fancy, tales of misadventure, character sketches, pauses for reflection, eulogies to those I admire and farewells to those I have loved. Some read like conversations, assuming a commonality of seriousness and exasperation between the reader and the writer that underlies whatever laughter we share.

I have been guided in my choice of which columns to reprint by no principle other than pleasure – the pleasure I recall taking in the writing of them and the pleasure I was assured they gave to those who read them. It is for this reason that I have not dated them or – except in the case of a small number that were written when I was travelling in Australia – grouped them according to subject or chronology. Each stands or falls on its own merits, self-revelatory, requiring neither context nor explanation.

Though some of the pieces are intimate – I do not conceal, for example, my passion for mafiosi shirts – this is not a memoir in another form. But a lot happens to a man in thirteen years. Thus the wife whose father's ashes I helped scatter into the West Australian sea he loved is not the wife who, in a more recent piece, I feared was about to leave me for Richard Wagner. And some of the friends I wrote about in 1998 are no longer here in 2011.

To emphasise that these are celebratory no less than angry or satiric pieces, the collection begins with an account of a mechanical elephant taking over the streets of London: an event which I witnessed and recorded with nothing short of rapture.

Howard Jacobson

2011

THE SULTAN'S ELEPHANT

We are entranced. We have not stopped smiling or looking dreamy for days. If you didn't know us better you'd say we were in love, except that we are not suffering any of love's unease. Not a condition we admit to very often in this column. As a rule we come to bury wonder not to praise it. In a childish world someone has to do the dirty business of growing up. But this week we have rediscovered the child in our self (that's if you can rediscover what you never were) and are aquiver with enchantment. The Sultan's Elephant is the cause. The mechanical contrivance, some fifty feet in height, complete with tusks and trunk and elephantine sadness, which roamed the streets of London for a weekend and stills roams the imaginations of those who saw it.

You will appreciate how beside our normal self we are when I say that we very nearly, for the duration of the elephant's stay, got the point of Ken Livingstone. Loose of tongue, slack of jaw, lumbering of attitude and posture, careless of whoever gets in his way, and dangerous to lose one's footing in the vicinity of – this is Livingstone I'm talking about, not the elephant – he nonetheless had the foresight to close central London to traffic for as long as it took the elephant to enjoy the city and the city to enjoy him, and for this, when he is consigned for all eternity to hell, I hope they give him the occasional cooling weekend off. Well, not weekend exactly; maybe half-hour. And not *too* cooling. A man whose brain boils with the impetuosity of prejudice does not deserve in the next life the temperateness he declined in this. But then again, he did let us have the elephant.

Central London without traffic is a marvellous place. Elephant or no elephant, it would be good, now we have seen how well it works, to close London to traffic one day a week. The motor car is a neurosis not a necessity. Millions of people still found a way of getting in. Shops stayed busy, cafes still spilled their customers on to the streets, but the difference this time was that you could stroll the city rather than have to dodge it, and it's only when you stroll a city that you truly enjoy its dimensions – the breadth of its boulevards, the plenty of its amenities, its rooftops, its vistas, and the easy companionableness, if you will only give them opportunity to express it, of its citizens.

If there was trouble on the weekend the Sultan's Elephant came to London I didn't see it. No one was competing with anybody: that helped. There was no trophy at stake. No tribe squared up to tribe. And no one plied us with liquor. But of course it was the elephant, ultimately – its pure, purposeless presence among us; street theatre without street theatre's usual agitating agenda – that soothed the savage breast. All those other considerations helped, but what made humanity benign for an hour was the grandest toy any of us had ever seen.

There is something about an elephant that brings out the best in people, ivory collectors apart. It's the size partly. As with whales and dinosaurs, the thought that life can fill up such a big space, that we share hearts and lungs with creatures built on such a scale, somehow aggrandises us. We want there to be life on Mars because we want Creation to be limitless. Looking at elephants or whales might not make believers of us, but we glimpse the grandeur of a creative impulse in them. What immortal hand or eye, and all that.

But an elephant isn't only majestic by virtue of its scale, it is also tragic because of it. Or at least it seems so to us. It looks hard to be an elephant. We know how difficult it is to drag around our own tenements of flesh and we accept existence on the understanding it will not get easier. Elephants look old in body from the moment they are born. Their every step is weary. Hence, I suppose, the fantasies we weave about their inner life: each elephant a Proust in his own right, recalling his life history before he goes to sleep, retracing in his imagination his peregrinations from waterhole to waterhole, unable to bear the sight of ancestral bones when by chance he comes upon them, and reburying them with all due ceremonials and formalities, including, for all we know, elephant eulogies and hymns. Elephants break our hearts.

Why a toy elephant should have the same effect is hard to explain. The brainchild of Royal de Luxe, a theatre company based in Nantes, the Sultan's Elephant – the idea for which is taken from a Jules Verne story, though narrative seemed beside the point – is an exquisitely conceived and manufactured puppet. It is entirely non-Disneyesque, not in the slightest cute or anthropomorphic, and postmodern in the sense that no attempts are made to hide its workings. Indeed, the Lilliputian-liveried men who pull its strings and drive its motors, and who are revealed within the elephant as it moves, are integral to what we feel about it. Emotionally as well as mechanically they serve the elephant's inexplicable purpose. It is they who flap his suede ears, open and close his tired eyes, and twist his sinister, reticulated trunk. But what ultimately fascinates us about the Sultan's Elephant is the part of him over which they have no control – his sense of being, as though the soul of living elephant has migrated into this wooden one.

Yes, yes, I know. But the truth of it is that I, like everyone else come out to have a quick look, felt bound to stay to have a second, and a third. In order to see him advancing towards us again we had to run ahead or find a short cut, nipping down alleys that connected New Regent Street to Haymarket, or Jermyn Street to Piccadilly, places we normally frequent only to buy shirts, then there he'd be, marvellous in his grave impassivity, as though the spoils of Empire had returned unconquered to reclaim the offices and citadels of imperial power. We watched as in a dream.

Don't ask me what the children thought. Mainly, they cried when the elephant showered them with water, and otherwise, as far as I could tell, feigned delight because they knew delight was expected of them. Wasted on children, wonderment. You have to know why life is serious to know why sometimes it must be a toy. They marvel best who marvel least.

THE EFFING ICELANDIC VOLCANO

Heartbreaking tales all week of people trapped in their hotel swimming pools for up to five days. They say you could hear the wailing in the Givenchy Spa at Le Saint Geran, Mauritius, from as far away as the beach at Sandy Lane where word had got out – good that something had got out – that supplies of iced strawberries were running dangerously low. I can no longer watch the news on television, so heartbreaking are the scenes of couples reuniting who have not seen each other for seventy-two hours.

Yesterday, at the bar of the Groucho Club, I was embraced tearfully by an old friend I'd last talked to at the bar of the Groucho Club the week before.

'I'm back,' he told me.

I told him I didn't know he'd been away.

'Christ, man,' he said, 'the word "away" doesn't get it.'

I wondered what word got it.

He told me what had happened. He'd been in Torremolinos with his family. When he said 'family' his eyes welled up. Had I not known his family I'd have pictured a tottering mother on a Zimmer frame, a wife already made weak by bulimia nervosa, and genius but fragile twins desperate to get back to a Mensa interview in London. In fact, his mother runs a major charity single-handed, his wife has completed six marathons this year, and his two boys had joined him after making their third successful assault on Everest without breathing equipment. He'd been in Torremolinos with them, anyway, paragliding, when he heard that no planes were leaving Malaga for the UK. He rang up Willie Walsh who was a personal friend, but Willie said there was nothing he could do, the effing Icelandic volcano having grounded BA more effectively than all the effing cabin stewards in effing Christendom.

I'm not saying this is how Willie Walsh actually speaks, only that this was how my friend reported him.

The barman at the Groucho asked us to tone down the swearing as other members of the club were offended by it. 'Christ,' my friend said, 'do you know where I've been for the last four days?'

The barman shook his head, but when he heard Torremolinos he apologised. 'Swear away,' he said.

Unable to fly out of Malaga, my friend had shepherded his little family into a hire car for which the shysters were charging a thousand euros a day. For a Smart!

'Christ!' I said.

He put a hand over my mouth. 'You haven't heard the worst of it yet,' he said. 'We were told there were ferries leaving from Algeciras to Tangier, from where we could get a trawler to Lisbon, where a cargo ship was said to be leaving for La Coruña from which local fishermen were rowing stranded passengers to Roscoff from where light aircraft which could fly below the ash cloud were taking people to Cork . . .'

'So what happened when you got to Cork?' I asked.

'Cork! Who said we got to Cork? The car broke down five kilometres outside Malaga. Do you know much it cost to get towed back to Torremolinos?'

I guessed a thousand euros an hour.

And back in Torremolinos? I expected him to say they wind-surfed to Ibiza where they caught a pirate ship to Monaco where they hijacked a train heading for Luxembourg before terrorists attacked it in the Massif Central and kidnapped his mother. But only the windsurfing was right. Back in Torremolinos they had to go back to their villa and resume their effing holiday.

'Christ!' the barman said.

So I told them my story. Setting sail from Troy, I ran into a fierce north-easterly which carried me across the Aegean Sea to Libya where I'd heard there was a travel company called 'Lotos' which, while it couldn't guarantee to get you out made you very comfortable in the time you were there. Having a column to write in London, I went in search of other Englishmen as anxious to escape as I was, only to encounter a one-eyed giant called Polyphemus – I know, I know, but that's foreign travel for you: you never know who you're going to run into – whom I had in the end to blind to get away from. What happened next, to keep it brief, was that I managed to locate a tramp steamer headed for the Island of Dawn where I met the enchanting Circe with whom I am ashamed to admit I had a bit of a fling. Aware I could not afford to stay – her rates were a thousand euros a minute without kissing, and that was if she liked you – she pointed me in the direction of home, warning me to watch out for the Sirens, a sort of Girls Aloud of the Ionian Sea, though thankfully I was no more into their music than David Cameron, whatever he says to the contrary, is into Take That. Anyway, anyway, we all have our troubles, and mine finally ended when I arrived home, a little the worse for wear, after ten years of being away, and was able to massacre my wife's suitors.

Ten years, mark! Ten years, not five days. What's happened to our idea of what constitutes an arduous journey?

Don't mistake me. We make light of no one's travails in this column. Hell is other countries, airports are vile places, and I don't doubt that many a stranded passenger had pressing reasons to be back. But if you want to experience real travel nightmare try getting from Soho to Swiss Cottage. The horror of the London Underground has been well documented – if you're not blown apart by jihadists, or pushed on to the rails by homicidal maniacs on day release, or trampled by bored French schoolkids, you suffocate – and the overground is worse. Despite Boris Johnson's promise to bring back buses fit for humans to travel on, they remain the Legoland suspensionless boneshakers they were, with nowhere to sit unless you go upstairs and you can only get upstairs if you're a gymnast. London roads are now an obstacle course: if you can find a road that isn't closed for the installation of new water pipes or Crossrail, you can be sure it will be potholed, or made impassable by bumps they have the effrontery to call traffic calmers. What's calming about driving over hummocks? What's calming about breaking your spine? Has anyone met a calm London cabbie? London at this minute is in the grip of a road-induced collective nervous breakdown, and yet people are being winched aboard Royal Navy Chinooks in order to get back. Explain that to me, someone.

LIBRARIES

Several years ago, when the the British Library was housed in the British Museum – which meant that you could always while away the odd hour looking at ancient Greek or Indian erotica if you didn't feel like work – I had cause to ask to be delivered to my desk *The One Hundred and Twenty Days of Sodom* by the Marquis de Sade. Today it's freely available in print, for all I know at a reduced price in Tesco's; but twenty years ago you had to sign for it, your signature being an assurance that you required the book for purposes of serious scholarship only, that you would not deface or remove it from the library, that you would not divulge to anyone what it contained, and that you would think clean thoughts.

I've invented some of those stipulations, but not all. Before the British Library would entrust a volume of such gross indecency to your safe keeping, it did indeed insist you complete a form promising not to reveal a word of what you'd read. Since I was researching de Sade for a novel about someone who was researching de Sade I didn't see how I could honour this under-taking, and for months after my novel was published I would start whenever the doorbell rang, fearing that the British Library

9

Police had come for me. What they did to people who reneged on their assurances and put the contents of restricted literature into the public domain I had no idea, but given that this was not any old restricted literature, but *The One Hundred and Twenty Days of Sodom*, I didn't see how the punishment could fail to measure up to the chastisements adumbrated in that work. Embuggery, amputation, dismembering, slitting, slicing, cleaving, the rack, the cross, the guillotine, flogging with a bull's pizzle while being forced to kiss a nun's . . . But there I go, blabbing again.

What has brought these hours of innocent study in the British Museum back to me after all this time is the suspension last week, pending investigation, of Ceri Randall, librarian at Pyle Library, near Bridgend in South Wales. Under investigation is whether Ceri Randall was within her rights to evict a person demonstratively doing porn on one of the library computers. What constitutes fit material for a public library – that is the question.

Just about nothing that's in it these days, is my first response. Call me a pedant, but I think of a library as a place that houses books. Books which educated opinion deems us to be the better, intellectually and spiritually, for having read. If you wonder who should be given the responsibility of deciding which those books are, wonder no more. I will do it. So call me paternalistic as well.

It amazes me that we have to insist on this. The idea of a free library presupposes the value, to the individual and to society, of reading, and the value of reading presupposes the value of books. If we fill a library with potboilers and that genre of contemporary literature described as crossover because it crosses us over from maturity to infancy, we abandon the grand educative function which libraries were philanthropically invented to serve. First the serious books give way to footling books, then the books give way altogether to something else. Records, tapes, CDs, DVDs, and now computers.

Don't mistake me for a puritan. I like the lunacy of libraries. I like the tramps pretending to be immersed in newspapers, and the people who have been swindled of their inheritances trying to put together lawsuits from the only law book on the shelves, and the would-be aristocrats searching family trees, and the general-knowledge freaks memorising every entry in the *Encyclopaedia Britannica*, and the mutterers and the snorers and the wild laughers and the rheumy old men who are here every day, from nine in the morning to six at night, shouting 'Shush!' at anyone who coughs. Libraries attract nutters – it's the flipside of their grand educative function – and it's proper that whoever haunts books should be kept in mind of the fragility of reason. Books sometimes make you wise, and sometimes send you mad. But the detritus of popular entertainment, which leads neither to wisdom nor to madness, only to terminal triviality, and from which any good library should be a refuge, is something else again. Don't give libraries a penny, I say, until they present themselves once more as palaces of bookish learning, for the behoof of the studious and the deranged alike.

So Ceri Randall is a bit of a hero to me, by simple virtue of the fact that she has been prepared to make a value judgement in a library. What you are doing here is low and inappropriate. It was not for swapping indecencies in an Internet chat room that libraries were built. Get out!

All I hope now is that she keeps her job and starts evicting any adult she catches reading Harry Potter.

But then I remember my library experiences with the Marquis de Sade, and the look of utter distaste which crossed the librarian's face when I asked whether the ban on telling anyone what I was reading extended to my wife. My wife? I would speak of embuggery to my wife? For a moment she made me feel I had befouled a sanctum – no, two sanctums, the sanctum of marriage and the sanctum of scholarship.

There is a difference, of course, between de Sade and a chat room. One is literature – oh yes it is, forcing us to re-examine 'the true relation betweeen man and man', in the words of Simone de Beauvoir – and the other is the mere vacant rubbing at an itch. I would like Ceri Randall, as she prepares her defence, to be very clear about this. Filth isn't the issue. Filth can be art and art belongs in libraries. The issue is the trivialising of the human soul.

And libraries aren't for that.

THE PART OF ME THAT IS
FOREVER COSA NOSTRA

There's a shop I seem to keep passing at the moment. No matter where I'm going or what manner of transport I am using, there it always is, somewhere between X and Y, a constant irritation to my senses, not because I don't like the shop and what it sells, but because I do. I am not going to describe its location exactly, partly for the reason that I am not certain myself, and partly for the reason that I don't want other people to know of its existence. Once everybody knows, it will have lost its allure. Enough that it's in London, in the vicinity of New Bond Street.

Generically, it's a shop you will recognise at once. A gentlemen's outfitters, as such were once called – though, of course, no man now thinks of himself as a gentleman nor goes along with the concept of being fitted out – expensively Mediterranean, of the sort always named after a famous Italian composer, Puccini, Verdi, Mascagni, Monteverdi, Donizetti, Morricone, though you suspect the owner, like the majority of his clients, is actually from the Levant.

The clothes, meanwhile, whoever buys and sells them, are definitely Italian. Southern Italian is how I think of them. From Naples or Bari or Taranto. Or maybe even more southern still

– Sicily, say. Mafia clothes, that's what I'm saying. Clothes to meet other members of the Mob in. Which is presumably why I am drawn to the place, why I keep seeing it from the top of a bus, or from the window of a speeding taxi, or out of the corner of my eye when I am running to get to the chemist before it closes. There is a part of me that is forever Cosa Nostra. Nothing to do with violence or extortion. I wouldn't hurt or take money from a fly. It's an aesthetic thing, that's all. It's about dressing. I hanker to dress like a Sicilian-born Mobster.

I sat next to someone from the Mafia once, in a swing club in New York. He was tall for an Italian, with a long pale face and beautifully tapered fingers. He wore a treble-breasted grey silk suit, shot through with filaments of platinum, and the softest of soft white shirts, with long pointed collars and cuffs lined with swansdown. I admired the way he sat at the head of the table dispensing favours, buying the most expensive Armagnacs, choosing cigars for everyone, including the women, and permitting, with a slow inclination of the head, those who wanted to get up and dance to do so. He was, of course, above dancing himself. Personal dancing is not what you do if you're Mafia.

The other thing I liked about him was the way he kept smiling at me. It's possible that he was coveting my clothes as much as I was coveting his. A blue linty blazer worn over a button-down Viyella Tory shirt, yellowish corduroys and Chelsea boots. There weren't, after all, many other people accoutred as I was that night. But what I think he really saw in me was Mob material. Someone who might, in other circumstances, have been useful to him, maybe his bag carrier, maybe his sidekick, who knows – maybe even his Godfather. When my father drove taxis in Manchester they called him the Godfather. So it's in my genes.

A couple of days ago, anyway, I finally found myself, with half an hour to spare, outside the very window I'd been speeding past for weeks. Pavarotti, I think the place was called. Or Lanza. I can't remember. What I do remember, though, and with great vividness, was a powder-blue ensemble – powder-blue blouson with navy leather elbow patches, powder-blue trousers with navy leather piping round the pockets, and powder-blue canvas yacht shoes, laced with dyed rope of the deepest indigo. All very well, but what shirt do you wear with that?

Then I saw it, high in the collar as is the vogue all over Italy at the moment, two buttons at the throat, the collars edged tastefully in steel, the cuffs sawn away at a diagonal, so that you can show off your diamond watch at the same time as your diamond links, and the colour – this being the best part – a peacock blue which seemed to change its hue according to the angle from which you viewed it, now azure, now violet, now as crimson as spilt blood. So there would be economy in buying such a shirt, as it goes with everything in your wardrobe.

Did I mention that the shop was also one of those where you have to ring the bell and say 'Luigi sent me' before they let you in? They looked me over a couple of times, through the grille, then must have seen what the mafioso saw in New York, and unlocked. I wasn't in there long. Just long enough to ascertain that the incarnadined pigmy buffalo belt for the trousers alone was £850. 'Nice,' I said, not showing alarm. 'But I was looking for something a little more ostentatious.'

I don't like being unable to afford things. Foolish, I know, but I feel that not being able to afford things is a sign of personal failure. Had I organised my life better, become the surgeon my grandma wanted me to be, or better still a footballer, I could have bought ten powder-blue blousons edged in navy leather with my earnings from a single missed penalty.

No doubt that's who Pavarotti's fits out – footballers with the aesthetic of the Mob. But who am I to disapprove? I studied English literature with F. R. Leavis and can barely quiet the Mafia in my soul. What right do I have to expect better of men with

CSEs in the three Rs of rapping, raping and roasting? Give any of us too much money and regard and we'll act like fools.

My single consolation as I leave Respighi's empty-handed: thank God I belong to a profession that keeps me too poor at least to *look* a prat.

JUICING

Just occasionally a column should be a two-way thing. The small distraction I provide from rage and sorrow every week I provide without expectation of reciprocity. A job's a job. But today I'm the one in need. Help me, somebody. How do you juice? But don't rush to answer until you have fully grasped the question.

I have the necessary equipment. I have more gadgets for juicing than anyone I know who doesn't own a juice factory. Mixers, masticators, macerators, extractors, blenders, squeezers, juicerators, pressers, citrus reamers – you name them, I have them. Loose me into a kitchen shop and I buy a machine for juicing. Perhaps it's the word. *Juice.* I think I must hear the secret of life itself in it.

Every year at about this time I begin to emerge from a personal winter of extreme catarrhal discontent, and experience a deep longing for juice. It could be atavistic. Long ago in the primeval swamp my ancestors either survived on citrus fruits or *were* citrus fruits. It can be no accident, anyway, that I live in an area where the only shops that don't sell sex sell health foods. Hot ginger zingers to the left of me, siriguela spicer to the right, and those are not the names of lingerie or aphrodisiacs. Sensing sunshine and the promise of a new beginning last week, I made it to the nearest of these health delis and by pointing – for I am voiceless after a long winter – got them to juice me up some orange, apple, ginger and lime.

Normally you must stipulate precisely what you want – 'So is that a wild acai berry sparkadula or an all-night boogie-woogie banana nirvana and watermelon nog?' – or they won't serve you. But in this instance they wanted me out of the shop fast; I am not, after all, a good advertisement for their produce. I drank it in a single swallow and ordered two more, the bill coming to a watermelon pip short of twenty smackers. At that rate, I calculated, I'd be out of my life savings – however worthless – by nightfall. So I did what I always do on exactly the same date every year and that was buy everything I needed to make my own juice and in the process surprise my wife by my initiative.

I don't know how other people retrieve their blenders from the cupboards in which they've been stored all winter, but I do it sideways on and blind, relying on feel rather than visual recognition. I found what I was after eventually but cut my finger on the rotary blade which I am always at pains to remove from the machine itself when I put it away, mindful that the majority of fatalities take place in the kitchen. Now I am not one to complain of injury – broken nail, grazed knuckle, paper cut: I bear them all with equanimity – but the juice of lime stings a cut finger beyond endurance. The juice of orange ditto. And I am messy with an orange, never having mastered that rococo single-movement peel of which our grandmothers were capable. My way is to squeeze the orange with one hand and then to make lunges at it with the other, not unlike Jack Nicholson hacking at the bathroom door in *The Shining*. Why I don't simply call that juicing, suck my fingers and have done I cannot explain. I must like the mechanical process more.

By this time, anyway, it was necessary for me to wash the

citrus out of my stinging cut and apply plasters to it – one to go round the finger left to right, the second to go over the top and secure the first, and the third to go round the finger right to left to secure the second. How the first plaster got into the blender I am again unable to explain. But in seeking to extract it I accidentally pushed a button named PULSE – a button which until now I'd never seen the purpose of unless you are meant to feel it to check whether you are still alive. In the confusion caused by this sudden throbbing, I failed to secure the lid on the blender, as a consequence of which enough juice for a small kindergarten erupted volcanically, some of it landing on the kitchen ceiling, some of it landing on my wife's cookery books, but most of it landing on me.

Except that you couldn't by any stretch of the imagination call this juice. Juice runs. Juice flows. This moved, since we are talking horror films, like the Blob. These are mere interim questions, but why was this more like soup or purée than juice? Why, though it had two whole witch-twists of ginger in it, didn't it taste remotely of ginger? And whatever it tasted of and looked like, would you, reader, consider it permissible – hygienically, and from a culinary point of view – to soak up the spillage with a sponge, squeeze it back into the blender and serve it to your wife pretending nothing had happened?

All hope of getting anything that could be called a drink out of this having fled, I set about cleaning up. Not only were the jackets of the cookery books covered with a tacky pith, the pages were already glued together. I didn't dare put them in the sink. I couldn't dry them on myself because I was tackier than they were. In the end the only thing I could think of doing was to lick them clean. Which raises another question: do you tell your wife you've licked her cookery books? And if she asks why, do you explain?

Unable to lay hands on a tea towel (they spoil the look of a kitchen, my wife believes), I took off my shirt – a silky two-tone

Brioni slim-fit with blue piping on the inside of the collar; not a shirt to juice in, I accept, but I like to work in the kitchen in unsuitable clothes in the same way some men like to bungee-jump in three-piece suits – and mopped the mess up with that. It wasn't inevitable that I should slip on the shirt, but I did. In the act of keeping my balance I pulled over the blender, cracking a tile and damaging three more fingers. The blender itself, of course, is finished – finished in the mechanical and the reputation sense. But that's not the worst of it. After four washes I am still unable to get the bitter-smelling confetti of sticky orange and lime pulp off my Brioni shirt.

So here's my question. How do *you* juice?

BOOKS ARE BAD FOR YOU

Callooh! Callay! It's World Book Day. Or at least it was on Thursday. You must have noticed – pages falling out of the sky, libraries festooned with publishers' catalogues, writers on every corner, words flowering on wintry trees.

As a writer of books myself, I am almost hysterically in favour of anything that ministers to their consumption. 'Read, read, you little bastards!' was one of my suggestions for a World Book Day slogan, the exhortation to be delivered by a masked flagellator sent to every school in the land. A proposal the organisers rejected, presumably on the grounds that 'little bastards' contains too many syllables for the little bastards to read.

My other suggestion, also rejected, was for a poster campaign likening a book to a packet of cigarettes, with the words 'Reading is Bad for Your Health!' or 'Literacy Kills!' splashed in blood-red letters across the jacket. This would have had the advantage of enticing into reading those children who need to feel they're doing something dangerous with their time. It would also have had the advantage of being true.

Books are bad for us. Books are murder.

If you don't believe me, read what books say. Of whom was

it written, that 'Coming later to Sir Walter Scott, she conceived a passion for the historical, and dreamed about oak chests, guardrooms, minstrels . . . She studied descriptions of furniture in Eugène Sue, and sought in Balzac and George Sand a vicarious gratification of her own desires'? Scott and Sand and Balzac, note – literature! So by modern standards, at least, we're talking about a rather classy reader here, a woman with more grown-up books under her belt by the age of sixteen than most kids leaving school today will have read before they're sixty.

'*Elle avait lu* Paul et Virginie, *et elle avait rêvé la maisonette de bambous* . . .' The French is a clue, if you didn't pick it up already in Balzac and George Sand. *Elle avait rêvé* . . . Dreaming, dreaming, dreaming, 'of love and lovers, damsels in distress swooning in lonely lodges . . . gloomy forests, troubles of the heart, vows, sobs, tears, kisses, rowing boats in the moonlight, nightingales in the groves, gentlemen brave as lions and gentle as lambs . . . weeping like fountains'. The very stuff of the imagination, members of the jury, the very education of the heart. And her name? And her fate? Emma Bovary, Miss French Provincial Page Turner herself, killed by the non-fulfilment of expectations planted in her heart by literature, choking on her own book-fuelled yearnings, destroyed by the brain-rot which is unchecked reading!

The next time someone recommends you a book with the promise that you won't be able to put it down, just murmur 'Madame Bovary' and walk away. And the next time you see a person devouring whole chapters on a bus or train, dreaming of rowing boats in the moonlight, and never once loosing their eye from the page, tell them that you are being cruel only to be kind, and put their book down for them.

Unputdownability is not a virtue in a book. Any book worth reading will have you arguing with it by the bottom of page one, will have you reaching for your pencil and your notebook by page two, or will have you so astonished that you must set it aside every couple of minutes to consider what you've read. Anything less is vacancy, not reading. What we call devouring books is no more than that torpor of the mind to which the world has given the name Bovarysme.

Flaubert was by no means the only novelist to write about the catastrophic effect of novels on readers ill-equipped to handle them. Fear of the disease of reading fuelled the nineteenth-century novel. *Northanger Abbey* is a relatively frolicsome satire on Gothic reading (and make no mistake, all unchecked reading is Gothic at heart), but by the time we get to *Persuasion* Jane Austen is in more sombre temper. Anne Elliot's remonstrance with Captain Benwick in the matter of his incontinent reading, making so bold as to 'hope he did not always read only poetry' as it was 'the misfortune of poetry, to be seldom safely enjoyed by those who enjoyed it completely', should be an example to us all. Never mind civil liberties. Never mind the reader's human right to read what and how he likes. If we care for those we love, it is our duty to save them from the perils of vacant irreflectiveness if we can.

Captain Benwick would have said he was 'moved' by what he read. Being 'moved' was big in the feeling-drenched late eighteenth and early nineteenth centuries, and is back with a vengeance. In the list of popularly inane words we use to describe books, 'moving' is second only to 'readable', and any civilised country would make calling a book 'readable' a capital offence. Readable! The instructions on a sauce bottle are readable! *Mein Kampf*, when you settle down to it, is readable. But 'moving' is more insidious because it makes a heartless brute of those affected otherwise. It also presupposes the desirability of an emotion which most of the time is but a vicarious satisfaction of our own desires – the self walled up in a lonely lodge, weeping like a fountain.

In our pulpy times, the blurb 'Didn't move me at all' would be praise indeed. Along with 'I put it down every thirty seconds'.

And 'So good I could barely read it'. Because that surely is the truth of it. When a book is painful it is difficult, not easy to read. The last hours of Mme Bovary are so unremittingly agonising we approach the pages that tell of them with great reluctance. Ditto, in an entirely different spirit, the pages which deliver felicity to Anne Elliot at last. So much happiness, so nearly missed, hurts the heart, and we can barely entertain it.

Which is more or less how I feel about World Book Day. When books no longer empower thought or sense, we might as well not have them.

THE TWENTIETH CENTURY? TOSH

Is it possible that the twentieth century was from start to finish tosh? Forget the wars, the murderous nationalisms brewed in the souls of common men, the even more murderous ideologies brewed in the souls of intellectuals, the mendacities, the invasions, the appropriations, the bombings, the camps, the refugees, the genocides, the casual slaughter not just of others but of our own, the betrayals of every idea worth living by (our fault, yes, for thinking we could live by ideas in the first place), the disappointments, the diseases, the astonishing technological advances which gave us *I'm A Celebrity – Fill in the Rest*, and the wherewithal to rape by Internet – forget all that, it's culture I'm thinking about, high culture, the stuff of modernist poets and painters. Is it possible that, viewed culturally, the twentieth century was from start to finish tosh?

It's going to the Kirchner exhibition at the Royal Academy that has made me ask this question. I like Kirchner. Sometimes I believe I get German Expressionism, sometimes I don't – depends how disgusted I am feeling with my fellow men – but Kirchner I go on admiring. He isn't a towering twentieth-century genius like Picasso, or even, to my mind, a near-towering twentieth-century genius like Beckmann or Dix. But that's precisely why I like him. He doesn't quite give the age what the age demanded. He has the decency to go ghostly on it, to let it swallow him at last. Whereas the towering geniuses won't let go, hanging on in the hope the age will expire before they do. Such sycophantic exponents of the contemporary they are, too, such spaniels to their times, such tireless pleasers. Kirchner, finally, was neither pleased nor pleasing. He painted those women in the streets of Berlin wearing spears for feathers, drew himself into corners, a voyeur in the dark, fetishising breasts and gloves, and let the times bleed him of his vitality. Pity more don't learn from his example.

But all that said, it was in the act of entering his milieu that I felt the twentieth century – *my* century, after all – suddenly turn ridiculous on me. Partly the fault of the gallery notes, I accept. Read notes on gallery walls and you wish you'd never been born. Everything so neat and understood. Every mystery solved. Every inconsistency ironed over. The age, the man: these the ideas in the air, those the painter's gifts, now behold them hand in hand. And all in that icy academician prose, mirthless, well schooled and well behaved, rendering precise that which was once tumultuous.

Remember the schoolmistress Miss Peecher in *Our Mutual Friend*? Schooled and schooling 'in the light of the latest Gospel according to Monotony'. Miss Peecher whose official residence was furnished with 'its little windows like the eyes in needles, and its little doors like the covers of school-books', who 'could write a little essay on any subject, exactly a slate long, beginning at the left-hand top of one side and ending at the right-hand bottom of the other, and the essay should be strictly according to rule'. Is it her they call in to cobble the curator's notes whenever there's an exhibition in the offing? Probably not. She was buxom and shining, Miss Peecher, and the schoolmistresses who write the little essays we read on every gallery wall the length and breadth of this great art-loving nation are certainly not buxom, neither do they shine. Eaten away with ambition and intellectual obedience they are, black of dress, pale of finger, gaunt of face, swallowers of light not emitters of it, whichever gender they happen to inhabit. But the spirit of Miss Peecher, if not the body, lives on, compressing everything you need to know into a slate-size essay.

Tough on the twentieth century, I acknowledge, to blame it for the sins of Miss Peecher. It isn't the age that says of itself such things as 'only by acting instinctively could one counteract the calculating material values that dominated modern society'. And it certainly wasn't Kirchner who said of himself that he 'regarded sex as a vital, liberating force'. But you can't blame Miss Peecher for all of this either. Even if we ignore the little essays, there, in Kirchner's chosen subject matter and preoccupations, are the same twentieth-century clichés we encounter whenever we pay homage to modernism.

You know the ones. Nudism, Russian dance, Japanese theatre, exotic carvings showing African or South Sea Island influences, free love, free sex, more nudism, nudes in hats, nudes with dressed men, nudes with undressed men, nudes in hats with Russian dancers, cancan dancers either in a line or one at a time, either with pants or without, because the cancan originally blah blah, black women as symbols of primitive sexuality, drugs, alcohol, street walkers under phosphorescent lamps, courtesans in drawing rooms, infidelity, troilism, troilism involving girls a little younger than they ought to be, more nudism, jealousy as pick-me-up, jealousy as depressant, spiritualism, table rapping, table-rapping nudes, bathing, boys bathing, circuses – oh God, circuses! – nudes on horseback, clowns, the artist as clown, the artist as tragic clown . . .

Must I go on?

All just routine bohemianism of course, the attempt some of us feel bound to make in every age to break the mould, to live simultaneously within and without society. We do not hold with banking or politics so we embrace nudism and the Japanese theatre. I'm not against it. But we fool ourselves if we think vitalism of whatever sort is any less an orthodoxy than the ones it thumbs its nose at. No sooner do we fight authority than we create another version of it. Our fate: never to be free.

Already, barely into a new century, we are at it again, only this time our heroes in the struggle against 'material values' and the imposition of governmental lies are human rights lawyers, anti-Blairites, marchers, Michael Moore. Myself I'd prefer going nude bathing in a hat or gazing up at cancan dancers (with or without). But that's just me. Either way, it's tosh, all of it.

THE CHATFIELD PANT

To the growing list of crimes against humanity ascribed to the United States of America, may I add a further? The Chatfield Pant. Let others, more familiar with the Ralph Lauren range of casual clothes for angularly rangy types of all ages, rail against The Keating Pant and The Andrew Pant. I rest my case on The Chatfield Pant.

That The Chatfield Pant is a traditional, zippered, flat-fronted chino, clean-fitting, classically perpendicular, of a military design, with not too much roominess in the rise, seat and leg, you hardly need me to tell you. Ditto that it comes in navy, nubrick and black, the nubrick winning it hands down for me every time. Whether you do as Ralph Lauren suggests and wear it with an Oxford Blake shirt for 'pure Polo style' is a matter entirely for your own conscience, but I wouldn't have you in my house if you did. Not that you would come if I invited you. If I have never hit it off with people who wear The Chatfield Pant, it must in all honesty be said that they have never hit it off with me.

All this, of course, is no less true of Ralph Lauren clothes in general. It takes a particular kind of man to want an embroidered polo player astride his left nipple. Occasionally, when I am tired and emotional, or consumed with self-dislike, I try to imagine myself as someone else, a wearer of Yarmouth shirts and fleecy sweats, of windbreakers and rugged Tyler shorts, of baseball caps with polo players where the section of the brain that concerns itself with aesthetics is supposed to be. But the hour passes. Good men return from fighting Satan in the wilderness the stronger for their struggle, and so do I.

The Chatfield Pant, however, offends against more than mere style. The Chatfield Pant is a language violation of a peculiarly American sort. Why the definite article? When a man goes into his wardrobe to decide how he would like to look, he does not say I think will wear The Levi Jean today, together with The Brogue Shoe, The Pantella Sock and The Silk Tie. Nor will he, I suspect, remember to apply the definite article to The Chatfield Pant once it has passed into his possession. So why the The at the time of marketing?

Let's stop beating about the bush. It all comes down to American ignorance of the arts of civilisation. Lacking assurance in such matters as adorning the human body, Americans do one of two things: either they dress like Scotsmen, or they seek refuge in grammar, hoping that the definite article will make them definitive. The two are probably related. Think the malt whisky that calls itself The Macallan. If you have never visited America and would like a picture of the place, picture this – 200 million Americans standing on their tartan carpets (The Tartan), all in The Chatfield Pant, all drinking The Macallan.

Absurdity piles upon absurdity. Once you employ the definite article, you are lumbered with the singular noun. You cannot, can you, have The Chatfield Pants. But what you sometimes give to grammar, you often take from euphony and sense. A pant is preposterous. Only a nation with no ear would buy a pant. But then only a nation with no ear would study math. There is no point in arguing this. Maths is right, math is wrong. You hear it or you don't. Your lookout. Ask yourself this question, though: do you really want to follow into war a country that thinks that math sounds right?

As for the Chatfield element of The Chatfield Pant, I am not able to shed light. I have unearthed a Thomas Chatfield of Ditchling, in Sussex, active in the second half of the fifteenth century, but whether he was active designing flat-fronted chinos with not too much roominess in the rise, I cannot say. The Chatfield family motto – *Pro aris et focis* – does sound as though it could have something to do with trousers, but it turns out to mean 'For altars and hearths', which would have helped us only had we been looking for a maker of candles and fire furniture – The Chatfield Wick, say, or The Chatfield Tong. Pursue it further yourself, if genealogy's your thing.

There is evidence that Thomas Chatfield's descendants made their way to America, and who's to say they were not the founding fathers of the towns of Chatfield in Arkansas, Minnesota, Oregon and Texas, tight-in-the-rise chino-wearing places without a doubt. My own guess is that Chatfield is meant to sound aristocratic, suggesting Chatsworth, Chatham, chateau and chateaubriand, with a field thrown in for striding through. The usual woeful purloining, in other words – as in American high art, so in American low fashion – of the cultural associations of others.

Better, anyway, if we must part from America, that we do so over The Chatfield Pant, not its foreign policy. Trust the small things, I say. Burdened with the information that his uncle had murdered his father in order to get into his mother's pants – pants, note, not pant – Hamlet loses himself in meditation. But let him find Polonius behind the arras, listening in, and he can act swifter than an arrow. Snooping we know what to do with. Murder and incest are more difficult. So goes the world around. In the end, we leave the enormities to God.

This, in the light of the hysterical abuse being heaped by the day now on America. 'The current American elite is the Third

Reich of our times,' thunders John Pilger, picking up the vogue for calling everyone you disagree with a Nazi. But then Pilger always was more Timon than Hamlet, his speciality the big crime. Without doubt, Pilger's apocalyptic prose has served us well in the past; the trouble is, it of necessity grows hungry by what it feeds on. Now a bigger crime, and now a bigger still, until there is no differentiation left.

Forget the Third Reich. Be guided, rather, by The Chatfield Pant.

'KEEP SMILING' – FRANZ KAFKA

Of the pains and sorrows incident to the life of man, the publication of a book ought not to be the most excruciating. Since everybody has a book out now – a self-help manual, a children's book, a self-help manual on the writing of a children's book, a memoir of the time you tried to write a children's book, a self-help manual on how to write a memoir of the time you tried to write a children's book – the anticlimax of publication is common knowledge. But some writers still manage to rise to the occasion. Myself – and if you think this is a roundabout way of announcing the appearance of my new novel, you are right – I find the whole thing hell. Nothing to do with reviews or sales. It's book-signing that upsets me, not the having to do it but the being unable to do it – the mess I make. I don't know how other authors fare, but every book I sign I deface.

My pen is always wrong. Wouldn't you think I would know by now to be sure I have a decent pen on me? I used to swear by fountain pens, but the last time I used one I leaked all over the title page and in the act of apologising profusely – you know the style: head thrown back, arms waving – I leaked all over the people queuing for my signature. Is there a greater crime an author can commit on publication day than to blot his readers?

So it's been a ballpoint ever since. But even ballpoints can smudge. Last week at Hay I smudged about twenty pages. Horrible globules of sticky ballpoint ink on the first and final flourishes of my signature. In panic I tried faking hay fever, hoping that a surreptitious handkerchief would serve as blotting paper, but you soon discover that your readers are no keener on having bits of tissue sticking to their books than they are on your sneezing into them. There might be professions where fans will take anything from their idols, a filthy paper handkerchief included, but novel writing isn't one of them. Thereafter, whenever a blob or gloop of inky gunk appeared I just smiled and closed the book abruptly. With a bit of luck the pages will have stuck together by now.

I am also illegible. Other novelists note the time it takes me to finish a signing session, supposing that I must have twice as many readers wanting my book signed as they have. In fact, the length of my queue is to be explained by the number of people coming back a second or a third time to get me to decipher what I wrote for them originally. As if I knew! 'How do you expect me to remember that?' I ask them. 'We're not asking you to remember,' they say, 'we're just asking you to read it.' I have to explain to them that I'm a writer not a reader. 'So what was it you wrote?' they want to know. 'I'm the wrong one to ask,' I tell them, 'I'm illegible. But it's probably my name.'

In fact, it's never *just* my name. I am temperamentally incapable of writing *just* my name. I don't do legible and I don't do brief. While we were at Hay my partner got John Updike's signature. 'To Jenny, with best wishes and cheers.' Imagine being able to do that! 'Best wishes and cheers.' You might ask why 'Best wishes' *and* 'cheers', but still and all, such pithiness! I've never managed anything so economical in my entire career. Even the 'To' I can't pull off. I always think it should be 'For', implying that the book was written with this very reader in mind, or that I am making a gift of it, which of course I'm not. But most times I no sooner write 'For' than I realise it is inappropriately personal and might conceivably cause the reader problems, especially if she's a woman and her husband sees it, so I cross it out and write 'To' instead. Add the crossing-out to the blobs of ink and strips of tissue and that's not a pretty page they're left with.

After which I can't just toss off a 'Best wishes', can I? I've got a first-edition Kingsley Amis that says 'Hi!' Such a disappointment. You hand over your book to a master of the language and he writes 'Hi!' Call me foolish but I feel I owe my readers more than that – more in the way of words and, quite frankly, more in the way of feeling. As the book, so the inscription, surely. If your subject is the horror of the human condition you must convey a flavour of that in your message. Line up to get your *Brothers Karamazov* signed and you're not going to be satisfied with 'Have a good one! – Fyodor Dostoevsky'.

And yet the last time I wrote 'Man that is born of woman hath but a short time to live, and is full of misery – Kind regards, Hay, 2004' I got the distinct impression that the recipient was unhappy. Seeing what had happened, the next person in the queue was very firm in her directions. 'Make it to Ann,' she said, 'without an e.' Simple, you'd think. 'To Ann.' But no. 'To Ann without an E,' some demon made me write. 'With love, with an E, from the author' – and then what was I going to say? – 'with an A.' For which blather I had next, still writing in her book, to apologise. 'Forgive this nonsense – with two Es,' I went on, before it dawned on both of us that this would end only when I had defaced every page.

I got the shop to give the poor woman her money back at the finish. I gave them all their money back. That's another of the reasons I dread publication. I end up thousands of pounds out of pocket.

RIGOLETTO

Just blown the best part of two hundred smackers staring into the back of someone's bald head. This is called going to the opera. More precisely going to the Royal Opera House in Covent Garden. I visit Covent Garden infrequently for this very reason: if I'm going to spend my children's inheritance on a seat, I believe I should at least be able to see something from it.

I can just about reconcile myself to the cost. Seats for a coming Madonna concert at the O2 Arena are said to be changing hands on eBay for £700, which makes an upside-down bucket with your back to the stage of the Royal Opera House cheap at half a million. In fact, I'm lying when I say I can reconcile myself to the cost. I am of the generation that believes paying £100 for anything is irresponsible. I grew up in a house that cost half that. For £100 my parents were able to feed and clothe three children from the moment of our birth to our leaving home eighteen years later. And have enough left for a celebration party when we'd gone. Like everyone else I eat at expensive restaurants – what choice do I have? – but I still find any bill over £20 for two (three courses, champagne, Shiraz, but no dessert wine) criminally exorbitant,

Rigoletto

whereas people under forty we dine with consider anything under ten times that amount a snip.

But all right, opera's different. You're paying for more than a night out. You're paying to be reconnected to civilisation and, if laziness and too many dinners have stopped you listening to the music you loved when you were young, you're paying to be reminded of who you once were, what you once felt, the melodious idealism which once made your heart flutter like a caged bird. And the building is exhilarating. And the bar is good. And people make more of an effort with their appearance than when they go to any old theatre, though still not a sufficient effort in my view. Grand opera requires that the audience too be grand. Dinner jackets should be mandatory. Would you want to be Rigoletto howling for his daughter in a sack while looking out at an audience in jeans and cardigans?

All the more reason, then, when you've gone to the trouble and shelled out more than a banker earns in thirty seconds, to expect a view of something other than the bald head of the person in front of you. I know there are seats in the Royal Opera House from which you can see the singers, but these, like a place at Eton, have to be bought for you before you're born. I exaggerate only slightly. Turn up at the box office a month before a production expecting a seat you can see from and they look at you as though you're insane. So how is a man with a life to lead supposed to know where he is going to be a month from now? Opera itself teaches that our lives change from happy to sad, from purposeful to pointless, in the course of half an aria. But the decent seats at Covent Garden are bagged years in advance by people prepared to bank a) on their continued existence, b) on their precise whereabouts, and c) on the music they're going to be in the mood to listen to.

Couldn't they reserve a few good seats for opera's natural audience – the existential chancers and cultural vagabonds of our dull society? And couldn't they, at the same time, insist that anyone over six foot three – actually, five foot three is where I'd draw the line – sits in row Z?

The bald man in front of me is, I would guess, six feet dead. I know I should thank my lucky stars he is bald. At the opera you get many a shock-headed person trying to look like Simon Rattle – half the time, for all I know, it *is* Simon Rattle – which means you can see neither over him nor past him. But as it happens there are two shock-headed people in front of the bald man, so although I can twist in my seat to see either side of him, all I get to see is them, twisting in their seats to see round the Simon Rattles in front of them.

I tell myself I'm here for the singing not the acting. I spend a quarter of any opera I like with my eyes closed anyway, so what the hell – just spend it all like that. But this is a notoriously raunchy production that's been kicking round the repertoire for years – a *Rigoletto* that's all humping (the pun is not mine) – and I want to see if it's as naff as it's been made out. The sexing up of opera rates as one of the great absurdities of our time. See an opera in Germany and it's invariably set in a fetish club and sung in shiny leather sado-shorts. Even Mozart's *Requiem*. But this is London where we are meant to have a keener sense of the ridiculous. Only not on this occasion. Naff it decidedly is – fellatio and cunnilingus to music, or at least I think what they're doing is fellatio and cunnilingus, but given how far back from the stage I am and how many impediments to seeing anything there are, it might just be a more than usually excitable bridge evening at an old persons' home in Pinner.

And now, of course, it becomes positively unseemly, my bouncing about in my seat, craning my neck, lifting myself up by the roots of my hair, to ascertain whether those really are bare breasts on the serving wenches, or just flesh-coloured bodices. Do I care? Does it matter if that's a nipple or a brooch? Thwarted, whether it matters or not, I fall to counting the hairs on the bald man's head, all 117 of them. Three warts. Four liver spots. And a bruise, sustained, I imagine, the last time he ruined an orgy at the Opera House for someone less sweet-tempered than me.

And yet in the end, somehow, somehow, the music works its magic. By the time we reach the magnificent quartet, mixing mellifluousness with cynicism, answering hope with desolation, tempering rage with love, I have forgotten where I am and it is worth it after all. Art doing what it's supposed to do – making life supportable. But must there always be these obstacles to refined emotion? Does sublimity have to be quite so bloody expensive, uncomfortable and fatuously staged?

PIE PELLICANE

A pelican crossed my path on Boxing Day. Not in flight, on foot. And not in Queensland or in Florida but in London. You feel there should be superstitions associated with such an event. When a pelican crosses your path on Boxing Day it means you're going to go on a long journey, or inherit a fortune, or lose your heart to a beautiful feathery white woman with a big mouth and an inordinate appetite for fish. Unless pelicans materialise vengefully on Boxing Day in a spirit of bird solidarity with the turkey you stuffed and ate the day before. When a pelican crosses your path on foot on Boxing Day you know that the next time you gorge on flightless fowl you'll choke on it.

Whatever the auguries, I was out strolling in St James's Park with my wife, enjoying the wintry sunshine, relieved to be walking off the previous day's excesses, when a pelican cut across us. We were approaching the Blue Bridge in a westerly direction, and he was approaching it in a easterly direction, on foot, as though he'd just come from the Palace. Since he wasn't going to pause, we did, allowing him to get on to the bridge without obstruction. It is a strange experience meeting a pelican, pedestrian to pedestrian, and it must have been even stranger for those already on the bridge observing him coming towards them. You don't expect to meet a pelican on a bridge.

In fact, I know this pelican. He's the sociable one who sometimes joins you on a bench in St James's Park and tries to eat your mobile phone while you're filming him with it – though I'm sure he does that only because he knows it makes a better photograph. Even by pelican standards he has a piercing eye and a wonderfully Italianate beak, all distressed umbers and citric yellows and patina'd verdigris. He also has more pink in his feathers than you expect of a white pelican – as though a flamingo long ago sneaked in between one of his forebears' sheets. Some consciousness of his individually fine deportment, despite the inherited absurd appearance of his species, must explain his conviviality. Food has nothing to do with it. He perambulates more like a human than a bird, in order to be seen and admired.

It is, in general, a wonderful thing to run into any of the large birds as long as they don't mean ill by you. You wouldn't want to find yourself alone on a bridge with a cassowary, for example, on account of his penchant for ripping out your stomach with his big toe. And even the most flirtatiously feather-boa'd emu always looks as though she will turn on you if you read her signals wrong. But there is something benign about a pelican. On his own territory, fishing on a lonely beach or sitting folded and uncomfortable, as though buggered, on a pole, he will cast an idle but protective eye your way. They say a dolphin will save a swimmer who gets into trouble in the water, but a pelican offers more existential assistance. He teaches the virtue of imperturbability and absurdism. On our territory, however, that something benign about him is increased a hundredfold. Have a pelican amble towards you in St James's Park and you believe a kindly hand is ordering the universe after all.

There wasn't anyone on that bridge, no matter what language they spoke, no matter what kind of Christmas Day they'd had, who didn't laugh to see him. Though he is a show-off and even a bit of a bully when it comes to right of way, he inspires, in humans at least, an unconditional joy.

So why is that? Because he is out of place, partly. Because we don't expect to see a pelican strolling through the park on Boxing Day as though he too needs to walk off a heavy dinner from the day before. And because, though he chooses our company, he comes from a world we can't begin to understand. But most of all, I think, because he isn't beautiful. He is grand but it is the grandeur, as it were, of adversity overcome. Fancy managing to look good when you have all that extraneous bulk and a floppy throat pouch to carry around. A flamingo approaching us on the bridge would also have had us reaching for our cameras. But she would not have inspired the affection the pelican did. Too graceful. Too naturally the thing she is.

It's for the same reason that the fast bowler Darren Gough won this year's Christmas Day *Strictly Come Dancing* champion of champions dance-off, easily beating the beauteous Alesha Dixon who had triumphed in the competition proper only the week before. When Darren Gough dances he defies probability. Dancing is not a skill we feel can be, or should be, locked away inside a man of such lumbering machismo. And when he releases lightness from his giant frame it is as though he is refusing the limits placed on flesh itself. For a moment, anything is possible for anyone. This, after all, is why we surrender to the programme despite all that nice to see you to see you nice drivel – not to applaud someone born airy like Alesha merely being herself, but to watch great albatrosses of men and women find elegance in their earthbound ungainliness.

There was a way in which this was true of Alesha also. She did not, of course, have physical bulk or an inappropriately comic personality to transcend, but she did have a clumsy assumption about herself to overcome: the assumption that as a thoroughly modern girl – a pop singer with a round red mouth and a lean hot body – she would do best when her dresses were brief and she was free to jive or salsa. In fact, she most moved the judges and the voting public when she waltzed. Bounce we knew she had; the surprise was to discover she could do old-fashioned grace.

There is a fancy abroad that we are all in pursuit of ourselves. It is a commonplace of the self-improvement business that once we learn to act in accord with who we really are we will be happy. In *X Factor* dross-speak, we have a dream we must make true. Bad advice, all of it. It's who we are that keeps us miserable. Rather than find ourselves we need to find someone who isn't us at all. Release the person you didn't know was there, I say. Learn from the pelican. Be who you're not. Don't fly when flying is expected of you – walk. Don't be beautiful, be strange.

BEST GIG IN EDINBURGH

Just back from trundling my wares in Edinburgh, where, among other trials, I had consented to be thrown, as sacrificial pompous pundit, to a bunch of carnivorous comedians. A radio thing, which was why I couldn't say no. Now that television is wall-to-wall children's programming with the word sex (or the promise of the word sex) thrown in – *Dating in the Kindergarten, Sex and the Hobbit, A History of Sex and Homework* – you can't ever say no to radio. But I was more than usually tense on the morning of the event, to take my mind off which I spent many hours in a cemetery close to the Scottish National Gallery of Modern Art. As a rule I prefer graveyards to gigs at festivals: at least there they know they're dead.

Next to God and my country I revere comedians and in the main get on with them. But ever since I wrote *Seriously Funny: An Argument for Comedy* they have been inclined to treat me as a sort of composite Rosencrantz and Guildenstern figure, a false friend who has dared to pluck the heart out of comedy's mystery. So I knew in my bones what was going to happen. The comedians would make gags about academic jargon and other *Start the Week*ery and I would accuse them of philistinism.

Stirred by the unevenness of the contest – for laughter always has the beating of learning in a crowded place – I would liken their reluctance to discuss what they do, or have others discuss what they do, to a doctor's refusing to examine hearts on the grounds that he would thereby interfere with the mystery of vitality. I would argue that to think about joking was not to usurp the joke itself and install pedantry in its place, but simply to take a hand in our pleasures – to try to understand, in tranquillity, why we are like we are. In a scientific and humanistic age we throw open everything to the light; why should comedy, alone with religious fundamentalism, be exempt? Persuaded by my simple honesty, the studio audience would roar on every word I spoke, leaving the comedians to slink away like so many Goliaths felled by the sweet-tongued David. All this I anticipated, and all this, between ourselves, gentle reader, was exactly what transpired; but I still needed my prepatory morning among the memorials to the dead.

It is a very fine cemetery, this one. Not one of your exquisitely retiring country graveyards where you yearn to be laid, when your time comes, under a sad cypress, rolled round in earth's diurnal course, a thing of faded lettering and quiet nature yourself now, all your striving to be anything else put finally to rest. No, although it is solemnly shaded, a step or two back from the clamour of the living, Dean Cemetery is an urban, even a civic burial place, bristling with verbose Victorian tombstones, elaborate sarcophagi, neoclassical tablets set into the walls, busts, sculptures, obelisks, even pyramids. Where a country churchyard is a grateful relinquishment of the clamour of life, Dean Cemetery is a celebration of it. Here are soldiers, sailors, statesmen, surgeons, painters, zoologists, critics (I encountered no comedian) – all still active in this wordy commemoration of their worldly genius.

But it was one stone in particular which caught my attention. It read:

SACRED TO THE MEMORY
OF
ARCHIBALD McGLASHAN
TEACHER OF ENGLISH
DIED 14 MARCH 1881
AGED 36 YEARS
'A MAN GREATLY BELOVED'.

Had I not had comedians to put right later in the day, I believe I could have loitered by this stone until the sun went down. And what was it in particular that struck me? Everything. Every single word.

Died aged thirty-six years, of course; died aged anything other than forty years older than whatever age you happen to be, is always enough to make you stop and think. Longevity is what you like to read about in graveyards, doughty souls who gave up the ghost at ninety-eight and then only because they couldn't think what else to do, not people cut off before their prime. And thirty-six is particularly cruel: just when you're getting going, just when you've outgrown stand-up and tele-vision, just when you are getting your first glimpse of what it all might be about.

Except that Archibald McGlashan seemed already to know. Teacher of English. As bald as that. Not linguistician or phil-ologist. Not lecturer in liberal and media studies, nor professor of ideological piety, nor doctor whose speciality is whichever humanities happen to be thought relevant at whatever political moment. Not even Teacher of English with no offence meant to non-English-speaking minorities. Just Teacher of English, enough said. Simple words etched into plain stone.

Tempting, in these fractiously ambitious times, to view such a measured memorial sadly. Here lies some mute inglorious Milton, died soon and died obscure. If only Archibald McGlashan had shared in our twentieth-century advantages he might have got somewhere, become famous like Sting, had his own series on telly – *Sex in the Grave* – at the least made it on to *Big Brother*. Never mind that he's dead; even alive, Teacher of English is too modest an achievement for us to contemplate without melancholy. The poor bastard, we think, forgetting that it wasn't all teenage junkies with abusive parents in the 1870s. The poor bastard, forgetting that you were allowed to enthuse your pupils once, that there was an exhilaration in passing on the baton of learning and enquiry, enfranchising young minds with the best of thought and feeling, because 'best' wasn't then an unacceptable and outmoded elitist concept.

For which favour, conscientiously bestowed – and I take this to be the logic of the epitaph – you became 'A Man Greatly Beloved'. Not honoured, lettered, knighted, prize-laden, bestselling and all the rest of it, just greatly beloved. We don't even need to be told by whom. By humanity, naturally.

Best gig in Edinburgh – Archibald McGlashan, Dean Cemetery, any time you're free, dead in the earth.

ALL AT SEA

Today I buried my father-in-law at sea. Buried is probably not the word for it. There was no body. What we did was cast his ashes to the four winds.

I've never seen a person's ashes before. I suppose I'd unthinkingly assumed that 'ashes' was only a way of speaking, that what we burn down to is some sort of odoriferous powder, finer and sweeter perfumed than talcum, and somehow still animated by soul. But we don't. We make the same sort of ash as a bonfire makes. Grey and grainy and unspiritual. Plenty of it, too. A whole plastic flaskful, which can take a fair bit of shaking out. Especially if your hands aren't steady.

I don't fancy being burned myself. I'm too worried about the possibility of a mistake. Imagine lying inside that highly flammable wooden lozenge and listening to it crackle while you're still alive, still able to hear the congregation singing 'Jerusalem'. Imagine the condition of your mind. Illogical, I know, given that you can be buried alive just as easily. But then I've never fancied the soil option either. Earth, water, air, fire – let those who are happy to live in the elements, die in the elements. I'm not. I keep hoping I can hold out long enough for someone to

48

discover some new and more suitable medium for my expiry. Something less natural. Evaporation through abstruse sentence, say. Interment in metaphor.

Scatter me in words, O my beloved.

My father-in-law was lucky in that the elements spoke directly to him. He was a gardener, a garlic grower, a pisser on to the roots of lemon trees, a maker of barbecues and fires, and a waterman – that's to say he swam, fished, sailed, and therefore understood and loved the capriciousness of the wind. What a bore he could be on each and all of those subjects! When he expatiated on boats to me, I thought I was dead already. He showed me nautical charts. He talked knots to me. Tides. Reefs. Rips. Sandbars. Fathoms. Channels. Fish. Masts. Sails. The lives of Dutch navigators, for Christ's sake! He clogged my brain with seaweed. He picked my bones clean with maritime minutiae.

But at least he knew how he wanted to be disposed of. Burned to soulless ash and scattered on to the waters of the Indian Ocean off Rottnest, the paradisal people's isle a half nautical hour from the port of Fremantle. And let the winds and tides and fish and fathoms do as they wished with him.

So that was where we repaired to do his bidding – his widow, his daughter, his old fishing and camping friend Eric the ferryman, Eric's wife Dot, and me. There is always farce associated with the disposal of ashes: so of course we left him on the boat and had to run back for him, and of course we weren't able to open the plastic canister that contained him until his daughter found a way of breaking into it with a car key, and of course the wind blew half of him back into our faces. Life is three-quarters farce; it is only fitting that death should be the same.

'There is a willow grows aslant a brook . . .' Nothing to do with Rottnest but it's a great line when you're thinking about watery graves. There is, though, a wooden jetty which gives out into Thomson Bay and we sat on the end of that like urchins looking for jellyfish and watched the water discolour with our husband and friend and father. We threw flowers after him – camellias from Dot's garden, and wild flowers, white and green and yellow everlastings, which his daughter had picked illegally from the roadside a thousand miles north of here. And so we made a floating memorial park for him.

Then we sang. Then they sang. No words, just a tune. 'The Swan', by Saint-Saëns. They'd been a quartet when they were young. Dot the singer, Joy on the piano, Eric on the violin, and the man who was now a faint discoloration of the Indian Ocean on the cello. 'The Swan' had been his favourite. Forever harping on things watery, you see.

So here's a question. Which came first? Were we putting him back where he belonged? Or had his interest in water been nothing all along but a premonition of his fate?

He was blessed with a perfect day, however one understands it. Simultaneous showers and sunshine, the rain light and warm, and then a rainbow, especially vivid, as they always are in Western Australia, in the lilac section. Why not? As with farce, so with the pathetic fallacy. You get it in life, so there's no reason why you shouldn't get it in death.

I thought we were finished, ready to return to the living, when Eric suddenly began to speak in maritime tongues. Not an address, just a quiet, private blessing. He wished his old friend a fair wind. A billowing sail. A good landfall.

I felt shamed. Wasn't it incumbent on me, the English-literature person, to essay something similar? Surely I had some apposite quotation. But the only nautical line I could think of was ''Twas on the good ship Venus'. So much for a solid grounding in the classics.

What had happened to the John Masefield I'd read at school? What about all the Joseph Conrad I'd lectured on? What about *Moby-Dick?* What about the *Ancient Mariner?* 'Alone, alone, all, all alone / Alone on a wide wide sea!' Wouldn't that do?

Pathetic. Better with the good ship Venus. He'd liked a touch of rhymed ribaldry in his time, Allan Sadler. He could take a seasoning of profanity. He knew it wasn't all 'The Swan'. So I let him have it – man to man, me to him, but silently, for no one else's ears. 'By God, you should have seen us . . .'

CORRUGATION ROAD

Life is a perpetual margarita. You sip the tequila and the lime, you taste a little salt, you need to sip again, you taste more salt, and so it goes – you grow increasingly thirsty on what you drink. If you're not a drinker you could say life's a perpetual Cleopatra. She too made men hungry by what she let them feed on. If you're not into the flesh either then scrub the whole thing. I only write for the incontinent.

I *think* it was incontinent of me to have done what I have just done, though I guess to some people it would merit about as much remark as a picnic in a layby. It's all to do with the way you were brought up. I was taught to count every penny and never to travel further than a quarter of a mile for any pleasure. Had Cleopatra lived more than a shilling's bus ride away my parents would have suggested I find somebody cheaper. 'There's plenty more fish in t'sea, our 'Oward.' So to *me* it feels pretty reckless to have flown in from London to Perth (Perth Western Australia, not Perth Scotland – I'm not that much of a cheapskate), and then a day later to have flown out again to Broome, 2,500 kilometres up the coast, just to take in an Aboriginal musical.

I'd said no at first when a particular person suggested it. I was jet-lagged. I was middle-aged. I was skint. And I didn't like Aboriginal musicals.

'Name one.'

I couldn't. I thought perhaps *South Pacific*, or *Porgy and Bess*, but I wasn't prepared to risk ethnic approximateness.

'Why don't you let me sleep for a week then I'll take you to the pictures?' I said, and where I come from you can't say much fairer than that.

'Are you a man or a mouse?'

'I'm a man,' I said, 'who is just going through a mousy patch.'

Four hours later I am 2,500 kilometres up the coast, sitting in the gardens of the Mangrove Hotel under a scimitared moon, listening to the wind rattling the louvred palm fronds, waiting for the curtain to go up, and trying to make it right with myself. I add up the cost of the plane tickets (no discounts when you don't book two years in advance), the taxi fares, the accommodation in Broome (height-of-season prices), the stiff thirst-making margaritas, and calculate that Onassis would have shelled out this much in aeroplane fuel every time he jetted out from Santa Barbara to catch Callas doing *La Somnambula* at La Scala, which he must have had to do on a pretty regular basis. Don't you hear of people selling their houses to pay for one night of Pavarotti? Isn't there a woman, on a moderate income, who has been to the first night of *Phantom of the Opera* in every city in the world barring Kabul where it hasn't yet opened?

It's terrible to have been born in the north of England and brought up to be careful. Behind me there are dolphins leaping in Roebuck Bay; above me there are whistling kites and wedge-tailed eagles waiting motionless for the red tide to trickle back out through the mangroves and reveal the whereabouts of mudcrabs; the night is as quivering and velvety as a Balinese maiden's first embrace; stars are falling out of their appointed places in the heavens with giddiness, and I – I am doing my accounts.

And then the musical begins with a woman wailing for her pidgin lovers – 'I bin losin' three mans' – and her grief is so inordinate that the hairs above my collar prickle and money is suddenly the last thing on my mind. Remarkable, though, that Aborigines in the audience – in so far as one can be certain in a place as richly mixed as Broome who is Aboriginal and who isn't – find the inordinacy comic. Another way of putting it is that what they find comic is themselves. Remember comic? It used to be a quality of musicals prior to *The Phantom*. It also used to be a quality of Australian life prior to Pauline Hanson, the one-time fried-fish lady from Queensland who has recently risen from the stale chip oil of far north Australian discontent like some anti-Venus of un-love, and formed a minority-phobia party – One Nation – on the strength of a vocabulary of twelve words and a platform of a dozen ideas fewer.

The fact that the party is called One Nation tells you all you need to know about it. Why would anybody want only one anything?

To say that *Corrugation Road* was written as a musical rejoinder to One Nation would be unjust to its author, Jimmy Chi, who was making art when Pauline Hanson was battering saveloys. But in its celebration of variousness and plenty, in its magnanimity in the face of cultural schizophrenia even – and you have to see the blackfella in his Father Christmas hat with your own eyes to take the full measure of that magnanimity – it plays like a riposte. That's how we take it, anyway, sitting mixed and merry in the mongrel night. That's what makes us laugh and cheer and sing along.

It is, of course, especially pleasurable if you are an Aborigine, to see comedy made out of all those missionised Christmases in the course of which you had to dress up like little white-faced angels and hymn 'Silent Night'. But the laughter is good for all of us. It multiplies us. It makes the world a bigger place. You never see Pauline Hanson laugh. You only ever see her succumbing to a hot flush when some fellow monoglot pumps her fishy hand.

I, meanwhile, have worked out how to halve the cost of flying 2,500 kilometres to see a musical. By staying another night and seeing it again.

SUDDENLY I'M HOMESICK

It's beginning to get uncomfortable here. The wet's coming. Season of floods and murderous humidity. Already you walk out in the morning and there is a moat of moisture around your dwelling. Buildings are starting to weep. People who don't have to be here all year are looking for house-minders and drifting south. And yesterday a crocodile was sighted in the bay.

I don't know whether there's some psychological explanation for it, but crocodiles always make me homesick for Manchester. Could be that crocodiles were the only peril my mother never warned me against when I went out to play by the Ship Canal.

For the most part, people in the Kimberley are cool about crocs. Come the wet there's every chance you'll find one swimming down the high street, or waiting behind you in the queue for the automatic bank teller, but he'll be a freshie, and freshies aren't dangerous unless you surprise them. If a freshie locks his jaws on to you at least you'll have the consolation of knowing it's not malice. He's as unhappy about it as you are. Yesterday's croc, though, was a saltie – a twelve-foot adult male saltwater crocodile – and a saltie will have you for breakfast, no worries.

Hence my hankering to be home.

But it's not only a temperate climate and safe streets I'm missing. It's men. The consideration of men.

There are no men here. That's a preposterous thing to say, I know, since this is reputed to be man's country, and I do read of men piloting light planes over the Bungle Bungles, putting out fires, fishing for barramundi, driving camels, pearling. But they're not where I am. Where I am there are only women – women writers, artists, critics, gallerists, teachers, administrators, fortune-tellers, reflexologists, basket-weavers – and I'm at my wits' end with them.

On paper it doesn't look as though I have much to complain about. I am shipwrecked on the Fortunate Isles. The sirens sing, Penelope cooks, and the Hesperidean nymphs dance circles around me: Arethusa, the Ministering One; Erytheia, the Blushing One; Hirsutia, the Bristly One.

I was at a dinner party the other night in honour of Elizabeth Durack, a distinguished artist embroiled in unseemly controversy, late in life, with the gatekeepers of Australian culture, than whom few are more sanctimonious, even in these sanctimonious times. We sat at a table in the red sand behind her daughter Perpetua's gallery – 'My little gallery,' the nymph Perpetua calls it – washing down fiery chilli shepherd's pie with iced champagne and watching rare Siberian waterfowl leave town in their thousands, wave after wave of them, a translucent silver against the sky, like the guileless souls of angels.

After dinner it was photo time, Elizabeth attaching her camera to a tripod, composing, focusing, setting the delayed-action timer, then running to join us at the table before the flash went off. 'Us' being the Hesperides and me. 'Cluster around the man,' one of them said. And they did – they clustered around the man!

I know, I know, I should count my blessings. I'm in Lotus Land. But you can have too much of a good thing. Remember Ulysses.

The long day wanes, the slow moon climbs. A man's a sword and it's not right for him to rust unburnish'd in his scabbard.

Besides, the women can get rough when they have the place almost entirely to themselves. They tumble and scratch. They upbraid and abuse.

It's the soothing male companionableness of darts and pool and poker I'm feeling the want of. At the risk of sounding metropolitan, I'm missing the understanding a man finds at the Chelsea Arts Club and the Groucho. Those velveteen nights, sitting swapping troubles at the mirrored bar, or falling in from some party somewhere else, man wrapped around man in the old love-and-death embrace, Coriolanus and Aufidius, unable to remember when the clock strikes twelve whether this one's your friend or your enemy, but what the hell – you'll take him in your arms anyway and suffer the self-hatred and the beard rash in the morning.

Do you lose the trick of it? Afraid that I would no longer know what to say to a man should I ever again encounter one, I persuaded the only woman I've met in Broome who has a husband to lend me hers for half an hour. Just to practise on.

It was all right. Nothing to write home about, but not a disaster. I didn't put my hand on his knee or blow him kisses. I didn't call him sweetie-pie or lambkins. I wasn't completely at my ease, though. His fault, partly. He didn't know how to behave around a man either. 'So what do *you* do when you're up to here with women?' I asked him.

'I go into the desert for a couple of months,' he told me, 'and prospect for water.'

'On your own?'

'Oh, you're never on your own in the desert. There are snakes, birds, lizards . . .'

Too drastic for me.

And then I heard that a number of famous triathletes were flying in from all over Australia to contest an Iron Man competition on Cable Beach. Men in Broome – at last! I turned up in time to catch the final of the tug of war. Darwin Killers versus Premier Security. A man short, the Darwin Killers turned to me. Would I?

Would I! Ha!

We spat on our hands, dug our heels into the soft sand, and took the strain, all for one and one for all. 'Heave, men, heave!' And when we pulled Premier Security over the line, with what innocent selfless manly joy did we fall into one another's arms! 'Well pulled, men!'

I'm lying. Premier Security won. And Darwin Killers never asked me to join their team. I merely watched from the sidelines with my sandals in my hand.

But I'm allowed to dream. 'Heave, men! *Heave!*'

AUSTRALIAN HAIRDRESSERS

The girls at my hairdresser's in Melbourne call me Heoward. It's a nose-ring thing. 'Hi, Heoward! How *air* you?'

It's queerly comforting. They are like little talking marsupials. I gaze at them in amazement. They don't look big enough to have the wherewithal to produce words. The only time I see such creatures is when I come here to have my scalp massaged, my beard trimmed and my hair scrunched.

They're all scrunched themselves. And dyed. If you were dropped here from Mars with a knowledge only of Earthlings' colours and cuisine you'd say they were all wearing red chilli noodles on their heads.

I've stopped asking for a cut. If you ask an Australian woman hairdresser for a cut you come out bald. You know what marsupials are like: they nibble everything. So I just pop in for a scrunch. Then halfway through I suggest they take a bit off here and a bit off there.

We are in what is called the Flinders Quarter. *Le Quartier Flinders.* An acre of quaint bohemian village lanes in the middle of a straight city. You buy recycled Levi's here, designer trash, books about the environment, freshly squeezed carrot, lettuce and mango juice, and strong cappuccinos. It's a brave part of town, favoured by people in wheelchairs, sellers of the *Big Issue*, junkies and assorted crazies. One particular crazy has taken a set against my girls. He is diagonally scarred from his right eyebrow to his left cheek and has Michelangelo's *Last Judgement* tattooed on his neck. 'Get fucked!' he shouts whenever he happens to be passing. Maybe they took too much hair off him once. I blush for my marsupials, who aren't old enough to be subjected to such verbal violence.

I love them. They're so small. They have no breasts or buttocks. I can't imagine how you sit when you have so little flesh to sit on. But they manage it. They hover on invisible cushions of air, an inch or two above tiny upholstered toadstools, and ask me how my day's been.

They look Greek to me. They could be Nana Mouskouri's grandchildren. But my scalp masseuse comes from Colac in the west of Victoria and my scruncher from Walhalla in the east. So how have they got to look so Greek? It's partly environmental. Melbourne claims to have a bigger Greek population than any city outside Athens. Greek is in the air and communicates itself to everybody. Even the Chinese in Melbourne look a little Greek. It works the same way in Manchester. It doesn't matter from what exotic place you hail, live in Manchester for a generation and you end up looking like a clog dancer. But my girls have made them-selves look even more Greek by not eating. If you starve yourself your nose starts to stick out like Maria Callas's.

However, it's not Maria Callas on the CD player. It's Blondie. She seems to be singing *Denise Denise* – the name of a lesbian lover, for all I know – but they tell me it's *Denis Denis*, in French. Just the thing for *Le Quartier Flinders*. They're surprised I don't know it. 'You know Blondie, Heoward? Debbie Hairy?'

I nod and smile, reaching for a biscuit and sipping my tea from a stainless-steel teacup designed for fairies. The minute I lean forward to sip tea they have to stop working on my hair. So why do they force tea on me in the first place? They don't give you tea when you're having your tonsils out.

'Don't you think she's great, Heoward?' Kylie Stassinopoulos asks me.

I reserve judgement. 'Why do you like her?' I ask.

She scrunches up her teensy body. She is wearing jodhpurs today but takes up so little room inside them there is space for the horse. 'I dunno, Heoward, I just like her music, you know?'

Once an academic, always an academic: I give her C minus for critical vocabulary, E plus for effort and Z for intelligible inflection.

'So what's your favourite Debbie Hairy song, Heoward?' she asks me.

'I'm more a Maria Callas fan,' I say. Tight bastard.

'Who does she sing with?'

'Freddie and the Dreamers,' I say, but she hasn't heard of them either.

This isn't the best conversation in Melbourne, but I come here to escape conversation. It's worse if you go to a men's hairdresser. Worse for me, anyway. I have bad memories of men's hairdressers. They abused me as a child. They sat me on a narrow wooden plank, which was a humiliation in itself, and whispered stuff in my ears. Psst! – want a camera, binoculars, carton of Scotch, black-and-white television, three-piece suite? No? What about a jam jar then? What about an MG, resprayed, new plates, soft top, false reg, taxed for the year, the lot? I was six years old – what use did they think I might have for an MG?

But the more I refused the longer they kept me, and the longer they kept me the more hair I lost. I feared for my safety. It didn't seem wise saying no all the time to a man with a razor in his hand.

You don't have worries of that sort in *Le Salon Quartier Flinders*. It's safe here. I feel as though I am on retreat. It's like camping by a river and waking to discover that the tiniest birds know your name. 'Hi, Heoward. Hi Heoward.'

I am Romulus on the she-wolf's teat. I am baby Tarzan up a palm tree with the apes.

And now a wonderful thing happens. The foul-mouthed crazy with the *Last Judgement* tattooed on his neck pauses in the lane, pops his slashed head around the door, and treats the girls to a glorious smile. 'Love you,' he calls sweetly. 'Love you.'

I am not at the hairdresser's, I am in Disney heaven. Attar of Greek roses falls from the skies like happy tears while marsupials with angel wings gently blow until I'm dry.

O SOLE MIO

Years ago, when I was fancy-free and light of foot, I frequented a pub deep in the Oxford countryside where they served hare pie on medieval trestle tables and tested your general knowledge on an electronic IQ machine installed in the snug. If you pressed a button saying LITERATURE you were asked to name the two cities in which *A Tale of Two Cities* was set (anagram clue: Nodlon and Ripas), the author of *Pride and Prejudice* (anagram clue: Enja Staune), and the personal possession beginning with h which Desdemona lost (was it a: her honour; b: her handkerchief; c: her handbag?). Get these right first time, without any further clues, and the machine would go beserk, ringing bells and flashing the word GENIUS for everybody to see.

Until they changed the questions I found this a useful place to take company I was anxious to impress.

It wasn't only LITERATURE at which I excelled. I was a bit of a smash at CLASSICAL MUSIC as well. Who composed *Carmen* (anagram clue: Zibet)? How many Beethoven Symphonies are there (a: 9; b: 150; c: 0)? – I got them all.

So here's one for you. Which Neapolitan song – so popular

that even Elvis recorded it — celebrates its hundredth anniversary this year?

Your anagram clue is: *O, I'm loose!*

Another? *Me? Oslo? Oi!*

Still not got it? Not as easy as you think, eh? One more anagram clue only. *Ooo, slime!*

Then I'll have to tell you. 'O Sole Mio'.

I'll come clean and admit I didn't know 'O Sole Mio' was a hundred this year either until I saw an announcement of a party to be thrown in its honour by Melbourne's Italian community at the Crown Casino Showroom. As a lover of all things Neapolitan, I had no choice but to put on a striped fisherman's jersey and go along.

I enjoy being the only non-Italian at an Italian gathering. It's the one time I get the chance to be the tallest person in the room. And I like being given a wide berth, everyone stopping talking and scattering when I approach, for fear I might be Interpol.

Half an hour after the birthday concert was scheduled to start it started; a labially liquid lady in evening wear taking the stage and explaining that 'O Sole Mio' wasn't only a treasure of Neapolitan civilisation but 'formèd part of European cultural tradition that has all but disappear'. My Italian being non-existent and her English being only so-so, I didn't fully grasp what this cultural tradition was. Only that it had something to do with feeling homesick.

Eduardo di Capua was handed the words of 'O Sole Mio' just before he left Naples for a tour of the Ukraine in 1898, that much I did gather, and set it to music two or three years later while he was stuck in Odessa, looking out of the window of his hotel and wondering where the sun had gone. So, if you want to be pedantic, this isn't the hundredth anniversary of 'O Sole Mio' as we know it at all, only of the lyrics. And with respect to the lyricist, Giovanni Capurro, it isn't really for the words — 'What a wonderful thing is a sunny day / But who needs it? / My very own sun / Is on your forehead' (my translation) – that we love it. But I didn't stand up and point this out. Let's party now and then party again in another two or three years. Some songs you cannot celebrate too often. Especially when, to quote a programme left on my seat, they come 'straight from the heart in simple and direct words and notes like a hot pizza beaming out of a hot wood oven'.

Now you know why a pizza is red and round. It symbolises the sun.

What a wonderful thing is a sunny day / But who needs it? / My very own pizza / Is on your forehead.

Once they've sorted out the sound system, stopped the elderly violinist from clapping himself on his lapel where his microphone is pinned, and got to the bottom of how come a massed choir of eighty men and women with round rigatoni chests is coming over more muted than a bashful kindergarten duo, the concert starts to be wonderful. I have always loved this stuff – sobbing tenors dreaming of Sorrento in high fluting voices, bewailing ungrateful hearts, promising undying love. I used to be able to do it myself when I was young and had the lungs and the emotionalism for it. I'd seen a film in which talent scouts for the Metropolitan Opera spot Mario Lanza standing on a pair of stepladders in a field outside Naples, picking grapes and funiculi/funicula-ing, and I hoped that something similar might happen to me, light as we were on vineyards in 1950s Manchester.

I couldn't imagine a better life – eating huge breakfasts, wearing fishermen's knits, and knocking off top Cs before adoring audiences in the world's leading opera houses. And this was long before Pavarotti, Domingo and Carreras. Nowadays every kid wants to play for Manchester United and sing with the Three Tenors, but in my time only the very sensitive harboured such ambitions.

It never happened for me. Too tall, I suspect. But when night comes – *Quanno fa notte*, in Giovanni Capurro's words, and *me vene quase 'na malincunia* – and I get to feeling quasi-melancholic (my translation) . . . but I don't have to tell you the rest. We're all a long way from Sorrento.

The birthday bash for 'O Sole Mio' turns out to be the best I have ever been to. Domenico Cannizzaro sings it operatically; Toni Marchi less dramatically but with more subtle Neapolitan intonations, and we, we thousand exiled Italians sick for home, we sing it from the heart. *Ma n'atu sole* – but another sun, *another sun* – *sta 'nfronte a te* – is on your forehead!

And it is all I can do to stop myself from weeping.

DINING OUT SOLUS

For reasons that need not trouble your compassion I have been dining out solus this last week. As a result of which I now understand what women mean when they speak of the humiliations of hitting the town unaccompanied. Yes, people look at you strangely. Half in pity, half in fear. Be seen dining solus and it is assumed you are some sort of sexual outcast, a trollop, a molester, an onanist, at the very best a bottomlessly sad human being who is unable to find love.

The strange thing is that it is not only other people who think this, you think it yourself. I am eating alone – I must be a pervert.

But you would still prefer this fact to be kept a secret. So you search for premises in which you can eat unnoticed. Never mind the food, all that matters now is the size and configuration of the eating place. Too much space is no good, for you dare not dine alone in the middle of a barn. But a cosy intimacy won't do either. Find yourself without a companion at a tenebrous table on which a flickering candle burns and your heart will break with self-pity.

This search for a well-balanced inconspicuousness can take

up the whole evening. As the last of the late-night restaurants lower their shutters you catch sight of your reflection in the window of a taxicab which refuses to stop for you – a red-eyed, green-toothed, prowling beast with hair growing where it shouldn't. And now they know for sure you are an onanist.

I descend upon Lygon Street, Carlton, one of Melbourne's busiest eating boulevards. The night is almost as sticky as I am, so the restaurants spill out festively on to the pavements and roads. A small table in the gutter is what I am after. With the single proviso that I can get wine by the glass, for a man alone at a table in the gutter with a whole bottle of wine to himself is a sad sight indeed.

What I'd forgotten was that Carlton's Italian restaurants have men out the front touting for business, Roman-style. This is precisely what someone in my position does *not* want. 'Dining alone tonight, signore?' they call out as I scuttle past. My neck concertinas into my shoulders. 'Never mind,' one of them says, blocking my progress with his stomach. 'Eat with us anyway. I have just the table for you.'

He does, too. Not quite in the gutter but at the very edge of the heaving pavement, where I can see the life but the life cannot really see me. Perfect. Eating is a nightly carnival in Melbourne and positioned here I can at least feel I am not excluded from the procession.

I should eat fish, which is good here. But fish is for two, I always think. A bone thing. Just as pizza is too obviously for one. So I order a spaghetti marinara by way of compromise, and a glass of Chianti in memory of all the straw bottles I bought for girls to make table lamps with in the days when I never ate alone.

Minutes after my Chianti arrives a second solitary gentleman is seated at the table next to mine. It feels deliberate, as though the waiters have engineered this proximity as a sort of social experiment, much as they put recalcitrant pandas together in zoos.

The second gentleman is as sad as I am, but I am careful not to acknowledge him for fear he may be sad in a *different* way. I note his well-pressed short-sleeved shirt, his boyish blue-grey haircut, the beaten silver ring on his marriage finger, and the precise way he cuts up his *champignons*. Without any warning or preamble he turns to a woman at a nearby table and says, 'I love your diamonds. I love the way they catch the light.'

So I am right. He *is* sad in a different way.

We eat in silence, uncomfortably aware of each other. A very tall waiter with a very small head collects our plates. 'Yum, yum, yum, yum?' he asks my double. To me he says, 'How was *that*?'

Neither of us replies.

'In Sydney,' my double suddenly bursts out, 'they tout for sex. In Melbourne they spruik for food.'

'Well, in Melbourne food *is* sex,' I say.

He ponders that, then, inserting his ring finger into the fist which is his other hand, he says, 'I don't think I like it.'

He orders another glass of Shiraz from the unmannerly waiter. I ask for a second Chianti. He tells me that he is in Melbourne for a conference, that he is a mathematician and a lawyer, that his soft skin and brown eyes belie his age – 'Look at them!' he orders me – and that his brother always introduces him with the words, 'This is David, he's got five degrees and all he thinks about is sex.'

Solitary eaters, I think. Every word of what they say about us is true.

The waiter is back with our wine. 'Are you circumcised?' David asks him.

The waiter's sangfroid goes up in smoke. Serves you right for 'Yum, yum, yum, yum?' I think. He starts to blurt out something about the interesting people he meets in his job, but David isn't listening. 'I'm just a slut,' he says to no one in particular.

Once the waiter is gone again, David asks me, 'Do you want him?'

'I wouldn't know what to do with him,' I laugh, wondering

how I can bring mention of my wife into the conversation. I may look sad but I have a wife. *Wife*. You read me?

But by now he is bored anyway. I watch him totter off into the night (to find a prostitute, he tells me), his hands in his pockets, his little blue-grey bullet head bravely erect, a man not ashamed of being out on his own.

FREED FROM RAGE

In Bristol with an hour or so to kill the other day, I happened upon Queen Square, recently restored to some of its Georgian glory by the removal of the dual carriageway which, in coarser times, someone in transport had thought to run through it. Perhaps he knew that before it was Queen Square it had been a rubbish dump, and so was acting as a true conservationist. But all's well that ends well, as they say. Except that something, or someone, in Queen Square, isn't remotely well.

In the middle of the square sits an equestrian statue of William III, sculpted by Rysbrack. Widely regarded as Rysbrack's greatest work, and the finest statue of a king on a horse made by any sculptor working in eighteenth-century England, it is, as you would expect of Rysbrack, classical in conception, judicious in choice of materials and, as these things go, only marginally pompous. The King rides stirrupless and carries what looks to be a roll of wallpaper but is probably his plans either for a European settlement, put into practice after his death by the Treaty of Utrecht, or for granting independence to the judiciary, as ratified by the Act of Settlement. A serious-minded king, then, seriously mounted. Carved into the pediment of the statue is the artist's name, and above that, in graffito, is, or was the other day, a startlingly naked expression of unhappiness. 'My name is Maureer. I hate you and all you stand for.'

How long did I linger there, pondering the significance of this, measuring its hurt, fathoming its reasoning? Reader, how long is a ball of string?

The first thing I wanted to understand was why Maureer felt it to be important we knew his or her name. Does it help to get your name, as well as your hatred, off your chest? And was I reading Maureer for Maureen? Type Maureer into the Internet and it thinks the same, correcting you in that sniffy way the Internet does – 'Do you mean Maureen?' (One of modern life's great frustrations, that the Internet can talk to you as though you are a moron, but short of typing invective into your computer, or smashing it, you have no effective redress.)

Anyway, Maureer and not Maureen it definitely was, the hand chillingly steady, inscribing the second r identically to the first. Not a Christian name I recognise, Maureer, though I know it as a surname. There's a Monsieur Maureer, for example, working on Leonardo da Vinci and chaos theory in the Ecole Normale Superieure in Paris, and a Christian Maureer who plays jazz saxophone in Austria, and a J. M. Maureer who is co-author (with Pugh and Pringle) of 'The Impact of Wort Nitrogen Limitation on Yeast Fermentation Performance and Diacetyl', but none of these is associated with Bristol as far as I have been able to ascertain, nor would you think that any of them has reason to hate unseasonably, though it's always possible J. M. Maureer wished his work on worts sold better than it did.

But the more important question is not who Maureer is, but who Maureer hates. 'You and all you stand for.' Since these words deface a statue of William III, William III has to be prime suspect. Netherlandish by birth and temperament, and subsequently a victor in the Battle of the Boyne, William III must have made many enemies of a non-Protestant persuasion. So could Maureer be a Dutch-detesting Irish Catholic? And a homophobe to boot, since rumours have always abounded – none of them substantiated, but then hatred needs no substantiation – of William's having indulged a taste for foot soldiers no less than for mistresses of the more conventional sort. A xenophobic anti-militaristic Catholic homophobe who loathes all lowlander Protestants and opposes adultery – is this who we're looking for?

Or is the sculptor Rysbrack the problem? Rysbrack beat his rival Scheemakers to the commission and this might rankle still with Scheemakers' descendants of whom Maureer Scheemakers could easily be one. And then there are the relatives of Van Oost, the flower painter, who actually made the sculpture, though Rysbrack won all the plaudits for the design. Or failing that, Maureer's hatred could simply be aesthetical. 'I hate you and all you stand for.' That's to say classical sculpture, judicious choice of materials, pyramidal composition, and the whole lickspittle business of dressing royal personages up as Roman emperors.

So much to hate, once you start. Queen Square itself is no monument to human goodness, having housed the slave traders who made Bristol rich. Were your ancestors shackled and sold for two-and-sixpence, Maureer? And so it is us you hate – we post-colonialists who go on obscurely enjoying the fruits of a heinous trade, accepting our culpability in one quarter only to recidivate in another? Little museums and monuments all over Bristol, commemorating slavery, adding to the total of the town's attractions – here the river where the slavers sailed, there the mansions where the slavers lived it up, nice places to sit and have a heritage cappuccino now.

So much to hate, once you start. And no one telling you it's not a smart idea, not good for you, not good for your heart, let alone the peace of mind of those you hate, and everything they stand for. Not even *some* of what they stand for? Wouldn't that do, Maureer?

Freed From Rage

On an almshouse close to Queen Square, a returned seamen's poem. 'Freed from all storms, the tempest and the rage / Of billows, here we spend our age.' Freed from rage. It seems a novel thought today, that we should welcome quiet, and not rage against whatever dares to rage at us. A blessed thing, quiet. Wherein to read, compose the mind, listen to Schubert, maybe recall the words of those who once advised we learn to love our enemies. But Maureer's storms carry the day. Maybe he is a human bomb in waiting. Why not? He who is unhappy has no choice but to hate and kill – violence is ineluctable – isn't that what we now believe?

BLUBBER

While the world was protecting its eyes last Wednesday, staring into buckets to watch the reflected sky go dark, I was weeping buckets of my own. You could say the two events were not unconnected: there is nothing like interplanetary activity, after all, for reminding you of your own insignificance. But insignificance wasn't the reason I was blubbering. Quite the opposite. A sudden, piercing vision of human grandeur, the immensity of our appetite for sorrow – that's what set me off. And what more cause for shedding copious tears do you need, than that you have copious tears to shed?

Call this self-indulgence if you wish – I confess I was playing old records of Caruso and Mario Lanza at the time, both of whom I turn to when I want the tears to flow – but it was the spectacle of someone else's sorrow that had softened me up the day before, when I happened to walk past a man in anguish in a doorway in Leicester Square.

Why does one person's distress speak more eloquently than another's? If you live in London you walk past a fellow creature in anguish every five minutes. Here's one who sits with his dog at his side by the cash machines all day, pleading for small change.

Here's another who is in bed in his cardboard box at noon, whimpering like an abandoned baby in his sleep. And there's a third, raging the length of Shaftesbury Avenue in a filthy blanket, looking like Poor Tom from *King Lear*, houseless and unfed, biding the pelting of the pitiless storm. He must have a hundred silver studs in his face. 'Don't come near me,' my eyes warn him. I have rehearsed what I will say to him should he ignore that warning: 'If you're so needy,' I will hiss, 'why don't you pawn your jewellery?'

I know, I know. But you can't feel compassion for them all. George Eliot is the person to trust in this area. 'If we had a keen vision and feeling of all ordinary human life,' she says in *Middlemarch*, 'we should die of that roar which lies on the other side of silence.' I read *Middlemarch* the way others read the Bible – for enlightenment and forgiveness. 'As it is,' she goes on, 'the quickest of us walk about well wadded with stupidity.' Which I take to be her way of saying, 'I forgive you, Howard.'

So yes, you, go pawn your jewellery. And no, I have no small change.

And then, quite out of the blue, you see a person sitting in silent anguish in a doorway in Leicester Square – not slumped, simply emptied of resolution – who wants nothing from you, who does not notice you are there, who does not notice anyone is there, and you hear the roar which lies on the other side of silence and your heart breaks. He isn't a refugee from the elements. He isn't unaccommodated man. From the cut of him you would say he has a comfortable house in Islington or even Hampstead. A publisher, maybe. He is handsome, dark, well groomed and well appointed in a houndstooth suit and expensive shoes, sleek as an otter. But he is sitting on the pavement, his back against a doorway, careless of himself, his eyes as sad as any eyes I've ever seen.

There is a question I must ask myself. Is it only because his fall is temporary, because he is on the street, seeking the anonymity and succour of the street, without being a street person, that I feel for him? Am I a grief snob?

I fear I may be, though I would prefer to put it differently. Of course it makes it easier on my pity that his grief is not his profession. And I am hardly the first to feel the poignancy of a man's fall from high estate to low. However communistical we may be, Lear the king moves us more than Poor Tom the beggar. But there is a further consideration which explains my preference. Taking into account his apparent prosperity, and measuring the depth and fixity of his pain, I decide that what has poleaxed my man of sorrows is bad news from the front line of the heart. I think his hands are folded over a mobile phone. It would make sense, then, to suppose that his wife has just rung to say she is leaving. Or his mistress. I am not concerned for the morality of the situation. Let it be, for all I care, someone else's wife who rang, barely a minute earlier, while he was sauntering hound-stoothed up Charing Cross Road to his sun-filled offices in Bloomsbury, to announce, 'Enough, over, it's been wonderful, but something more wonderful has come my way. Goodbye, my darling. Pause to think of me sometimes, as I will never again pause to think of you . . .'

I am a schmaltz merchant, you see. Not all the poverty and suffering in the third or fourth or however many worlds can touch me as the story of tormented love touches me. That's why, when no one's watching, I sit listening to lyric tenors singing of their exile from romance. Even as the moon briefly cast its shadow on the sun, Caruso was *Pagliacci'*ing it on my turntable, mocking his clown–cuckold's reflection, his own light put out forever. Now it's not for me to explain the emotional motivations of others, but I do suspect that all our recent planet-watching was metaphorical. Why are we moved when one orb eclipses another? Ask Caruso. Ask the man in the doorway of the Leicester Square Hippodrome.

GISELLE

What is it about the phrase 'Austrian legend of Slavic origin' that makes one want to slit one's wrists? Maybe it doesn't make you want to slit yours, in which case I'm the one with the problem. I hope it's not that I'm anti-Austrian or Slavophobic. I think it's the word 'legend' that gets under my skin, and then the word 'origin'. Something to do with superstitions mouldering in rural antiquity, and my wanting them to stay there.

But let me contextualise. My wife had proposed going to see *Giselle* at Covent Garden. The deal is that she'll come with me to opera if I go with her to ballet. I'd agreed to *Giselle* on the safe assumption that as she didn't have tickets on the day, she wouldn't have them on the night. Maybe one ticket would materialise if she beat the returns queue, but not two. Whereupon I would do the noble husbandly thing, sacrifice my pleasure to hers, and let her go on her own. If that meant I had to stay home, drink a bottle of Barolo and watch Chelsea play Barcelona on television, well, such are the deprivations a man who loves his wife must occasionally accept. But blow me if she didn't come back with a pair of tickets, centre stalls, row J – best seats in the house for people our height. I could barely, as you might imagine, contain my joy.

Now you can go to the ballet not having a clue what's going on and stay that way until the final curtain call when you applaud like a man who's just been rescued by a helicopter after twenty days at sea, or you can mug up on the story. Something made me mug up on the story. Maybe if I grasped the plot, I thought, I would understand why my wife would be sitting with tears streaming down her face.

'In the quaint little villages snuggling amidst the romantic forests of the Rhineland,' I read, 'many strange, mystic legends of ghostly visitants . . .' And that was when I wanted to slit my wrists.

I have mugged up on ballet stories before but I had forgotten how much more plot there is in a ballet than you'd imagine there'd be need for. Girl in acres of white tulle meets boy in what my Yiddish-speaking grandparents used to call long *gatkes*, falls in love, gets jilted, turns into a swan and dies. That ought to cover it but never does. Even in synopsis, *Giselle* is more complicated than *Twin Peaks* and *Saved* run together. Giselle falls for Loys who is actually Count Albrecht; her previous lover Hilarion does a lot of spying on her behind trees; Berthe, Giselle's mother, warns her against Loys on grounds which I assumed would become clear in time – so far so good. But then comes the moment when you know you are lost and are going to be lost forever – 'Wilfrid, Albrecht's squire, secretly warns him that a hunting-party is approaching, led by the Duke of Courland and the Countess Bathilde, Albrecht's future wife.'

It's that unexpected arrival of a duke leading a hunting party that dashes me every time. Not just in ballet, in opera and in drama too. It's an invariable law of the performing arts: there's always one duke more than your comprehension can cope with.

Still, even to have got this far in my researches meant that I'd have some idea what was going on when I was sitting in row J. At least for the first twenty minutes. But no. No amount of preparation can prepare you for the miming if you have no instinct for it. And I am a dumb-show illiterate. Part of this is wilful. I don't want to watch lovers fall in love in silence. For me, the better part of love is language and if lovers are not talking I can't connect with them. How they manage to connect with each other without words is beyond me. No words, no jokes, and since when did a woman fall in love with a man who didn't make her laugh? All right, there's the sight of him leaping in his *gatkes*. And there's the sight of her with flowers in her hair, balancing on one toe. But after the leaping and the balancing, where does the relationship go? Which might be precisely what Giselle's mother was getting at.

Then again it might not. This is the other problem I have with miming: I am blind to its semiotics. As in ballet, so in life – I am unable to read the signs. In my susceptible years I could not approach a woman who had not signalled her unequivocal interest in me first. The sign I was waiting for was a crooked finger, the nail painted vermilion, beckoning me to the darkest corner of the room. To be certain I was reading the signal correctly I needed the owner of the finger to be wearing a concupiscent smile. And, ideally, little else. Only an undressed, lewdly grinning woman crooking a finger at me would do it. Any gesture less definite I read as cold indifference. Will you therefore be surprised, reader, to learn that I spent my susceptible years alone?

And now here I am trying to understand why Berthe makes a basket shape with her arms, holds it over her daughter's head, then spills it at her feet. In the interval I venture an interpretation to my wife. Loys, aka Albrecht, is too high and mighty for Giselle, who is just a country girl, and when push comes to shove, for all his attentive leaping he won't bring home the bacon. But this is wide of the mark. What Berthe is actually warning is that there's an Austrian legend of Slavic origin that tells of jilted brides turning into troubled spirits known as Wilis – a fate awaiting Giselle if she goes on crooking her finger at Loys. And this my wife intuits from a woman miming a basket.

And now guess what? I am spellbound. The Wilis materialise from their graves in a gauzy mist, their morbid ethereality, their frustrated vitality, somehow perfectly suited to the unnatural way ballet dancers move their limbs. That I am not slitting my wrists is due in part to a wonderful ballerina called Tamara Rojo, but it's also the power of the metaphor, the exquisite madness of erotic love, the everything and the nothing of our bodies, which I suppose ballet can speak of as nothing else can. Whatever the explanation, I too have tears streaming down my cheeks when the tormented spirit of Giselle, appeased at last, vanishes forever into her silent tomb. Ah, reader, reader, these Slavic legends.

HOLIDAY READING

Will somebody please explain to me what 'holiday reading' is? I'm not asking for recommendations. I want to know what's meant by it. Is it a specific genre, like the misery memoir, only presumably the very opposite to the misery memoir? Is it determined by congenial subject: a happy-ending romance cooled by summer breezes? Or by congenial place: a grown-up version – though not too much of a grown-up version – of *Five Go Doolally in Dorset?* Is holiday reading about holidays, or is it a promise that nothing will be demanded of the person reading it that will take his/her mind from a holiday which anyone would think, given the spirit in which lists of holiday reading are compiled, is invariably a thing of sunshine, lovingness and bliss.

But that's not a truth about most holidays, is it? Aren't holidays essentially opportunities to break up with the people we thought we loved? Don't we realise how much we hate our children on holidays or, if we're the children, how much we hate our parents? There are photographs in my mother's possession which attest to the living hell I made of every family holiday. In snap after snap, there are my mother and father making the best of the lousy weather and the appalling food

– we're talking the 1950s when the sun never shone and all we ate was peas – and there I am with the same long face, not wanting to be there but then again not wanting to have been left behind. That's me bawling in Blackpool; that's me moping in Morecambe; that one's taken the time I sulked myself into the measles, chickenpox, whooping cough and, very nearly, had I got my way, malaria in Anglesey.

And why? That's easy to answer. Sex. I needed sex. I might have been no more than seven or eight with not the slightest idea of what sex comprised but I needed it. Holidays do this. They heat your blood and turn your head. I saw men strolling down the promenade hand in hand with their girlfriends and I longed for a girlfriend of my own. To be honest, what I think I longed for even more than a girlfriend was a mistress. I'd heard the word, formed a dim conception of what it meant, imagined kissing had something to do with it, and hankered for one of my own. That's me at Middleton Towers Holiday Camp stamping my foot and shouting, 'I want a mistress.'

Nothing I've observed of other people on holiday leads me to believe they have a better time of it than I did. I used to help run a craft centre in a clapped-out water mill in Cornwall. The usual thing – a Delabole slate etcher specialising in hunchbacked blue tits, a reclusive woodturner who wouldn't turn if anyone was watching, two tattooed jewellers of indeterminate sex who squabbled in front of the public, a glass-blower who was the subject of predictable ribaldry, about which she could hardly complain as she would get pissed blind on hot days and take her top off regardless of the families streaming through. Awful glass she blew, but nice breasts, as I recall. Had I encountered her when I was seven or eight I'd have screamed the place down until my parents persuaded her to be my mistress for the afternoon.

Working here, whatever its attractions, taught me how horrible holidays for the majority of families are, even if they aren't cursed with a boy-pervert like me. Because it's on holiday that couples get to reacquaint themselves with one another and discover how little there is left to like or talk about. Parents who have been working hard all year and have barely seen their offspring now wish they didn't have to see them at all and can't wait for work to begin again. Through the craft centre these poor souls would troop in their dripping wet cagoules, pushing prams, squabbling, skint, each one's idea of a good time clashing with the other's — not that there was a good time on offer for any of them — like the damned in Dante's *Inferno*.

You take my point. Shouldn't that be what they're reading when they come on holiday – Dante's *Inferno*? There's powerful stuff on cruelty to children in *The Brothers Karamazov*. *Death in Venice* is good on art and fatal sexual obsession on the Lido, and you could always skip the art and get quickly to the fatal Lido bit. Wouldn't that make ideal beach reading, whatever beach reading is?

Help me here. What's a beach book? I assume it's similar to a holiday book but with the specific requirement of being sand-proof, water-repellent, and not so heavy in physical form or emotional content as to spill you out of your deckchair the minute you open it. Explain it to me: why would you want to read on something as uncomfortable as a deckchair on some-thing as unconducive to concentration as a beach? All those distractions, all those echoing shrieks, people jet-skiing and paragliding, babies crying, children drowning — unless it's a lonely beach, but then you'd want to walk along it, wouldn't you, hand in hand with your mistress with whom you might indeed want to share a book later on in your hotel room, when the moon's up, but it wouldn't be anything on the routine holi-day reading lists: it would be *Antony and Cleopatra*, *Les Liaisons Dangereuses*, *Lady Chatterley's Lover* or, if you're ready for a little intimate abstraction, *L'érotisme* by Georges Bataille.

Holiday reading, beach reading, summer reading – what next?

Winter equinox reading, midweek reading, Sunday reading, middle-aged reading, deathbed reading? Books to read when you're wearing a frock as opposed to books to read when you're wearing jeans. Books that go with your trainers. Books to read on clifftops, books to read while you're snowboarding, books to read while you're fighting in Afghanistan.

According to his wife, the critic F. R. Leavis took *Othello* and that other great work of sexual jealousy, *The Kreutzer Sonata*, away on their honeymoon. We laughed, we students of Leavis, when we heard that. But we laughed with a sneaking regard. It was an example to us all. Stay serious. Serious is more fun than not serious. And if you want a holiday from serious, try being more serious still. The dichotomy between great works of literature and the books we 'secretly' enjoy is a false one. Trashy novels are less enjoyable to read than good ones. The greater the book the more pleasure it gives. Holidays are hideous enough already: why make them even worse with dross?

PITY THE POOR PORKERS AND DAMN
THE SWINE THAT GAVE THEM FEVER

Nothing illustrates the sadness of mute creation more poign-
antly than the life and tragic death of sow number 847Y, on
whom the recent outbreak of swine fever has been blamed.
Even before the story unfolds, it is bleak. We know that pigs
are intelligent. There are allusions in Shakespeare to a pig at
whom the Elizabethans marvelled on account of its numeracy,
easy social graces and low opinion of the plays of Christopher
Marlowe. Is it not a cruelty, then, that a sentient being with
more skills and better taste than most graduates from our
universities should be deprived of the dignity of a name and
sent to meet its maker known only as 847Y?

Then there is the village where 847Y was raised and
perished. Quidenham, in Norfolk. I am not aware that I have
ever been to Quidenham, so what I am about to say is not
personal. Like everybody else, I love place names that have a Q
in them. The Quantocks, in Somerset. Qingcheng, in China.
Quetzaltenango, in Guatemala. Qs are cute. And exotic.
Exotique! But is there not something Latinately and legalisti-
cally indeterminate about Quidenham? It sounds as though it
means 'that which a thing just happens to be'. It seems to

imply blind chance, mere nameless accidentality, moral no less than geographic arbitrariness. In the village of That Which a Thing Just Happens to Be lived a pig called 847Y . . . Heartbreaking.

But it gets worse. 847Y was a free-range pig. That should have been an advantage. No doubt, to 756K and 934Z, confined to the stinking battery sty down the road, in the village of That's Just the Way It Is, 847Y was living in pig heaven.

But beside the farm on which she roamed ran a little foot-path. And you know what footpaths bring. Behold, then, striding our way, a sticked and knitted-hatted quidnunc in walking boots and thick red socks, a rambling map, sealed against the elements, around his neck, and a sufficiency of lunch kept fresh inside a ball of silver foil kept fresher still inside a plastic box kept fresher yet inside a backpack. Hey ho, let's stop and eat.

It may be lunchtime, or it may be the power of suggestion, for the lunch that the quidnunc carries wrapped like a Russian doll upon his back is a ham sandwich and a pork pie, and your thoughts are bound to turn to ham and pork when you espy 847Y grunting on the other side of the hedgerow. Pig, pig, snap!

I said this tale was sad, and there is more sadness yet to come. What would make a man feed a ham sandwich or a pork pie to a pig? What brutality, what horrible perversity of humour, what distortion of kindness (to take the charitable view) would lead you a) to think of such a thing and b) to go ahead and do it? Here, piggy, piggy, come and eat your own.

The prohibition against cannibalism acknowledges a prin-ciple of kinship that extends beyond humankind. You don't eat family. You don't encourage family to feed on family. You don't throw one cat to another. Soon we will breed cats who don't feel pain. At which point the earth will open and swallow us down. In the meantime, we try to act as though we understand the difference between good and evil. Which means we know better than to offer pork pies to a pig.

Yes, 847Y should have refused. It's no excuse that she didn't have the Book of Leviticus to help her to make the right decision. Uncleanness is uncleanness. You sense when you are transgressing dietary laws, because they are the laws of your nature. Besides, the smell tells you. Nonetheless, it remains true that, in the case of livestock, we are our brothers' keepers. The whole point of our stewardship being that we set a good example. And in this instance we did not.

One month later 847Y and all her piglets were dead. Some life! The cause – pork or ham imported from a country less nice about swine fever than we are. The rest is history; 60,000 pigs so far slaughtered, and plenty more to go.

That somebody knows the person who started all this goes without saying. The usual telltale signs. Depression. Nightmares. A compulsion to burn hiking gear. Plastic lunch boxes going missing. And a sudden and uncharacteristic aversion to pork pies. If that description fits your husband, hand him over. You owe that to the farmers and the pigs. Look on the bright side – since he wears thick red socks and carries his lunch in rucksacks, you'll have been wanting to get rid of him for a long time anyway.

But I'm more interested in the fate of sow number 847Y – the Typhoid Mary of the swine world – than that of just one more human clown. It's strange to me, and I cannot pretend I understand all it means, but I am noticing a growing fellow feeling with animals (if that's not a contradiction in terms), the more I age. I used to think it pathological of Gulliver to prefer the company of horses to humans on his return from the Houyhnhnms. Now, hunting for meaning and desperate to escape vanity, I'm not so sure. I haven't yet reached the stage of forbidding my wife and children to touch my bread or share my cup, but my pigs understand me tolerably well, I converse with them four hours every day, and they live in great amity with me and friendship to each other.

DEATH OF DUDLEY

Alas, poor Dudley. If his death pricks our tears more keenly than did Peter Cook's that is only because he was the cuddly one, and his dying was the more cruelly protracted. Now it is as though Peter Cook has died again. A double sorrow. Or maybe it amounts to more sorrows than that even. For I think we watched Peter Cook die several times in the course of his separation from Dudley Moore. And we certainly watched Dudley as good as give up the ghost when he succumbed to Hollywood, playing the jackass for Americans who can only take their Englishmen that way.

We don't as a rule do obsequies for the famous in this column. We are uncomfortable showing too much feeling for those we never knew personally. Maybe that's wrong of us. Maybe it is a sign of our humanity that we can accept celebrities – those walking shadows – into our hearts and miss them as our own. I remember watching a lady schoolteacher break down in front of the class when the news came through that George VI had died. I couldn't understand it. What's she to Hecuba? I wondered. Or words to that effect. When I went home I asked my mother if she thought Miss Venvell could have been related to the royal family. My mother explained that King George VI had been an important symbol to us throughout the war. And besides, she added, he was a lovely man.

How did my mother know that? I asked myself. For I was a sceptic early. I also doubted whether anyone with a public image could be lovely. I still have a streak of that puritanism in me. Succeed and you must have sold your soul to the devil, I think, fame being a harlot, money being the root of all evil, and a moving image being a contradiction of God's wishes and intentions.

Dudley, though, was an exception to all this. He was intelligent, for a start, in the Oxbridge way, and I make allowances for Oxbridge intelligence. One of the reasons I failed to get on with the alternative comedians of the eighties was that they came from red-brick universities. I don't doubt you can be funny if you have a degree from Manchester or Leeds, but you can't be philosophically funny, you can't make the heart itself laugh. You can do knockabout and you can do polemic but you can't do heart. Don't ask me why that is. Something in the water. Something sad about these university towns. Some excruciating anticlimax from which you never recover. Whatever the cause, Dudley Moore touched the heart effortlessly before he went to America – which is sad in another way – both as a musician and a comedian. Though no sooner do I say comedian than I feel I must retract the word. What he was best at was not raising mirth but being the cause that mirth was in others.

I know what it is that has long upset me about the break-up of Peter Cook and Dudley Moore, and I will resist saying that they are together again, now, in comedic Elysium, at last. Like all the best double acts, theirs was a love affair. Did you see that film footage of Jerry Lewis breaking down in a limousine, remembering his days with Dean Martin? Did you see Ernie Wise on television after the death of Eric Morecambe? Widows, both of them. Their grief unbearable to behold. But Peter Cook and Dudley Moore seemed to be entwined even tighter still. And that was because Dudley Moore appreciated Peter Cook's genius to the depth of his soul, got him as no one would ever get him again. And the sign of that appreciation was his laughter, his failure, no matter how hard he struggled, to keep his face straight, his divine incapacity, once his partner was in full flight, to hold himself together.

There, I think, you have the story of Peter Cook's life. He had the fortune (maybe the misfortune) to meet someone who broke up more spectacularly, more profoundly – I will even risk saying more erotically, for there is undeniably a sexual component to such disarrangement – than any other person on the planet. Thereafter, what else was there to live for but to go on cracking Dudley up, splitting him asunder, dissolving him, tearing his very heart out with laughter. You can hear it on that sublimely filthy record, *Derek and Clive (Live)* – Peter Cook scaling wilder and wilder heights of scatological absurdity and invention, in order to test what condition of hysteria he could reduce Dudley to next. Sex? Yes, but even better than sex.

And there was the tragedy of it – because finally Dudley left. Finally, no doubt, Dudley had to leave. Put yourself in his place. He wasn't the stooge. His role was always more active than that. But he was the convulsed sea to Peter Cook's controlling moon. There comes a time when you want to exert your own magnetic force.

For a while – and Peter Cook malevolently encouraged this view himself – it looked as though envy was the engine house of their estrangement. The contrast in their fortunes was too great: Dudley getting off with beautiful women twice his height in Hollywood, and Peter Cook getting pissed at *Private Eye* lunches in Soho, no disrespect meant to the latter. But I know in my bones it wasn't primarily envy, though envy will insist its way into everything. It was heartbreak. You can't enjoy such complete and cultivated admiration, then have it stolen from you. Not in the matter of your jokes, you can't. Alas, poor Peter.

CHERIE BABY AND THE BOMBERS

As a bald statement of consequences, free of all history and context, it is so unexceptionable and self-proving as to be without meaning. 'As long as young people feel they have got no hope but to blow themselves up, you are never going to make progress.' Step forward whoever believes that as long as young people have got no hope but to blow themselves up, we are making excellent progress.

Myself, I'd go further than Cherie Blair. Why stop at young people? Surely as long as any people – the middle-aged, the elderly, the geriatric – have got no hope but to blow themselves up, we are not making progress. Unless you would argue that in the case of the geriatric we *are* making progress, since their blowing themselves up in large numbers would be some sort of solution to the problem of an ageing population. That is as long as they are only blowing *themselves* up, and not indiscriminately blowing up other people along with them. It begs a question, you see, this phrase 'blowing themselves up'. Indeed, it doesn't only beg a question, it buries it.

Try the sentence again, then, paying more attention to the specifics. 'As long as young people feel they have got no hope but to blow up as many other people as they can, you are never going to make progress.' Put like that, progress becomes a rather pale word for what we are not making.

Now share the emotional adjective 'young' between the people who are doing the blowing and those who are being blown. If it is tragic for one young person to be without hope, surely it is still more tragic for another young person to be without life, especially as the decision to be without life is not one he has reached in the extremity of his own hopelessness, but is thrust upon him.

The English language is subtle enough to make all the necessary distinctions. A suicide kills himself. A murderer kills other people. A murderer who chooses to kill himself in the process is no less a murderer. Even-handedness of sympathy is not the issue here. We do not need to be told later, by way of redress, that Cherie Blair is a staunch supporter of the State of Israel. You fix the problem in the text itself – the text being an indicator of the mind, and the mind an indicator of the sympathies – by not omitting to mention that it was first and foremost murder to which the latest Palestinian depressive was driven.

Terrible to be so driven, terrible indeed, but let us properly name the deed he was driven to.

Which brings us to the assumption – almost an *idée fixe* now, in some quarters – that between hopelessness and murder there is no moral or behavioural transition worth talking about. 'As long as young people feel they have got no hope but to blow themselves up' etc., etc. *No hope but to* – how trippingly off the tongue that comes. How trippingly off the tongue it has been coming since September 11, when the world woke to many surprises, not the least of them being a whole new system of measuring longevity of suffering and patience. People were fed up. People had had enough. What do you expect? Of course they flew planes into the World Trade Center, what else were they meant to do? Not nice, of course not nice, but . . . The new 'but', hacking away at our every compunction. No hope but to.

What collusion in grievance, and what an elision of responsibility and culpability the idea of 'no hope but to' masks! Once upon a time we thought it unacceptable to deduce from our hopelessness the right to kill ourselves. (Had not God fixed his canon 'gainst self-slaughter?) Now it makes perfect sense to be hopeless and go kill someone else. How did we manage before? People have been hopeless for centuries without stuffing their pockets with explosives. Pushed from pillar to post, crushed, enslaved, demeaned. For how many millions of people over how many thousands of years has hopelessness been the fixed, unquestionable condition of life? There are even those, though I am not one, who would argue that it has been good for us to know such oppression, that religion and philosophy have grown out of it, that we are the better for our sorrows. Give mankind everything to hope for and it hopes to be on *Big Brother*. Well, *Big Brother* is a risk worth running, I say. Let everyone have hope, however they choose to squander it. But it is fanaticism of sympathy to grant the power of life and death to those who are dissatisfied, as though unhappiness were a sort of absolution that wiped out every other human obligation.

As for just how lacking in hope, in this instance, the actual bomber was, we have his own words to go on. Tricky, I know, to determine truth from bravado here. Of the mysteries of despair and elation, none of us can speak with certainty. A man who is down one day may well be up the next, especially if he has slaughter on his mind. But Mohammed al-Ghoul's murder note does not evince any of that lassitude of vocabulary or defeatedness of cadence we normally associate with having nothing much to hope for. 'How beautiful it is to make my bomb shrapnel kill the enemy,' he writes. 'How beautiful it is to kill and be killed . . .'

The politics of active hate, not inexpectancy, speak here. And not to know the difference is to be a fool.

The best one can say for Cherie Blair is that her folly, maybe like the bomber's, is not to have thought for herself. She opens her mouth and out pops one of the unthinking commonplaces of her time and milieu. To wit: it must follow, where people are unhappy, that they resort to murder. That there will be countries where this is taken to be an endorsement of murder, I do not doubt. Because semantically – 'no hope but' – that's exactly what it is.

HUMAN VALUES

I note that *The Truth About Vince* has just won a special prize at the Rose d'Or television festival in Montreux for displaying the strongest 'human values'. Interesting that you have to invent a category for that. If 'human values' mean anything, wouldn't you expect every programme ever made, with the exception, say, of *Skippy* and Rolf Harris's *Animal Hospital*, to display them? What other values do we have?

You can half see what the golden-rose cultivators of Montreux are getting at. With wall-to-wall tits on the box and the reinvention of the freak show by Jerry Springer et al. – turning emotional impoverishment into a spectator sport – it's no surprise that your average grossed-out viewer hankers every now and then for something with a touch more moral elevation and uplift. But is 'human values' really the right phrase for what we're groping for here? Doesn't *Getting 'Em Off In Ibiza* also display 'human values'? How much more human can we be, when all is said and done, than pissed and butt naked under a Spanish street sign at five o'clock in the morning after a night trying to make babies?

When we use the word human in an attempt to confer

dignity on ourselves, I suspect we are actually alluding to an idea of something not human at all. Something ethereal. Soaring up and away, as far as we can get from ourselves. God, as we used to say. Or spirituality, if God's coming it a bit thick. Some art critics, worn out by Tate triviality, have resurrected the word spirituality. What we're looking for, they say, are 'spiritual values' in art, and you know the game's up with them as soon as they say it. It's too futile a gesture towards gravitas in a feather-light universe. Maybe it's the 'values' part of the phrase, in both instances, that lets us down. You only use the word values when you don't have any.

As always, it's the feebleness of our language that shows the trouble we're in. We can't make a claim for substance without our words drifting away on the wind like the puffball of the dandelion – sugar-bobbies, as we used to call them in the north. Fine spores of sweet nothing.

I'm musing upon all this as I relocate my library. It is about the tenth time I have done this since I began collecting books a hundred years ago. Manchester to Cambridge to Sydney back to Manchester to London to Wolverhampton to Cornwall back to London . . . Sir Thomas Browne's *Religio Medici*, Bunyan's *Holy War*, Cobbett's *Advice to Young Men*, the *Letters* of Lady Mary Wortley Montagu, all in crumbling dirty green editions, their pages glued by time and neglect, back and forth, back and forth, a renewed reproach, with every move, to my lack of industry and resolution. Still unread, still unopened, so many of them.

Few things convince a man of the vanity of life more than relocating his library. What am I carrying all this lumber around with me for? Into boxes, out of boxes. Why am I breaking my back for them? Throwing away money on removalists, on shelves. Why am I repeating patterns of ownership that have served me only fitfully in the past?

Some of my friends have sold their libraries now. They have

that preternaturally fresh-faced look of people who divorce late in life, or on the spur of the moment give up a job they've toiled at for forty years. They look free suddenly, disencumbered, not quite themselves. It's terrific, they tell me, having got rid. It's a liberation. And I incline my ear to their lips, letting the poison drop, wondering if I am capable of such treacheries myself. Although I know I'm not.

'Not more books!' my father used to complain when I came back from the second-hand barrows of Shudehill, weighed down under another filthy cardboard box, excited by my finds. A complete Thackeray for five bob, for God's sake! The Caxton illustrated Balzac in a translation by Anonymous, incomplete but only sixpence a volume . . . !

'Bargains!' I cried.

'I believe you,' he said. 'And the bargains you got last time? How many of those have you read?'

How do you explain to somebody who doesn't understand that you don't build a library to *read*. A library is a resource. Something you go to, for reference, as and when. But also something you simply look at, because it gives you succour, answers to some idea of who you are or, more to the point, who you would like to be, who you *will* be once you own every book you need to own.

Sentimental, of course. That's what my friends who have parted with their libraries have finally rejected in themselves – the sentimental idea of being a man of letters, of being made good through books. 'Human values.' A pity I wasn't clearer about my motives for buying books in the days when my father twitted me. 'Not more books?' 'No, Dad. Not more books. More human values.' Me and Vince.

In fact, books worth owning speak to us of our humanity as vexedly as the drunk returning to his vomit in Ibiza. It's trouble, being human. It's bad for us. In the days when my first marriage was breaking up, my then father-in-law knew where the blame lay. 'It's all those books,' he said. I took offence at that at the time. My books? How could you lay a failed marriage at the door of literature? But he was right. Books had made a bastard out of me. As they're meant to.

GIRLS WILL BE GIRLS

Question of the week: 'An accomplished woman, who can find?'

Cadences sound a bit stereotypically . . . how shall we say . . . Old Testamentish? An accomplished woman – *oy gevalt!* – who can find already? You're right. An accomplished woman blah blah is the first line of a poetical reflection on womanhood recited by the female equivalent of the bar mitzvah boy – the bat chayil girl – on her coming-of-age day. In my time girls knew their place and left the whole rites-of-passage business to the boys. We were the ones suffering the sudden fluctuations in body temperature and voice range. Girls had always been women about to happen. We became men in a sudden rush. We needed a ritual to mark the change. Today there's a bit of a fad for female bar mitzvahs, on quasi-feministical grounds I suppose, though it's interesting that you don't see any equivalent rush for female circumcision. Can't have the one without the other has always been my position, and that position has hardened since the weekend when I watched a couple of sweet girls with plastic daisies in their hair make a dog's breakfast of a solemn ceremony.

You will understand if I don't say where exactly I attended

this double bat chayil, but I can tell you that the rabbi's name, as if he didn't have his hands full enough already, was Portnoy. Now in any altercation or difference between a rabbi and his congregation I am invariably on the side of the rabbi. I like rabbis. I am easily persuaded that a beard and a long jacket are earnests of moral seriousness, and I am a sucker for sophistical theology. 'Ah, but do the words actually say that?' they have only to ask, and I am theirs to do with as they please. In its essentials, being a rabbi is like being a literary critic: you pick at texts, affect a deracinated Central European accent and tell people how to live. I would be one if I could. Failing which I see everything entirely from their point of view, not least the uncontrollable giggling of two schoolgirls called up to address Hashem, the one and only, the dark and nameless warrior god of Israel.

So I'm the rabbi and I'm sitting behind the girls, stroking my beard, giving them time to come to their senses, reorganise their expressions, and remember the awfulness of the occasion. I am a man of wisdom so I know that giggling is something you do when you are nervous and self-conscious and need not mean you have a disrespectful nature. But the giggling won't stop – the girls even giggle over the name Hashem itself, an offence which brought a visit from the angel of destruction in the good old days – and the generosity with which the congregation at first greeted their girlish hysteria has turned to embarrassment, to shame, and in some hearts to anger.

In my heart, for example – mine, not the rabbi's – it has turned to boiling rage. Funny that, for as a rule I welcome a seasoning of blasphemy. Or maybe not so funny, since to be a blasphemer you must understand belief, whereas to be a giggler you need understand nothing.

I am surprised, too, by the weight of tears behind my eyes. I have been softened up by the cantor's exquisite sobbing to the God who never shows His face. But it's the indecorous girls who finally make me weep. For they are loosed from themselves, and to be loosed from oneself is a sort of madness, and the sight of madness is always desolating.

I am the rabbi again and I know what I think. I think an accomplished woman, who can find? I remember that I didn't giggle during my own bar mitzvah but suspect that I might if I were doing it today, because a contemporary child is given over to popular influences so disinheriting that he is neither the owner of his face nor the familiar of his nature. Are the girls unable to confront solemnity because they are, at this very moment, dreaming of David Beckham? Probably not. The links are less direct. But triviality will have its way. Here a trickle, there a droplet. Until the human soul is worn smooth by banality and nothing of consequence can ever find a sticking place.

We are as one on this, the rabbi, as I imagine him, and me. We wish woe to those who make slop buckets of the minds of children. But where I suspect we differ is over the accomplished woman-who-shall-find of the panegyric to ideal femininity. 'Strength and majesty are her raiment, she joyfully awaits the last day.' Between living only to die and living only to watch another Spice Girls documentary on Channel 4, is there nothing?

Rabbi Portnoy has now decided it is time to put an end to the fiasco. Enough is enough. He rises with imperious calm, addresses the girls in words of fire, opens his palms as though he can part the Red Sea with his fingers only, and chases the imps of inconsequence from their hearts. Thrilling. I am so excited by the spectacle I can hardly speak. Someone older castigating someone younger in our time! Isn't this what rabbis and literary critics are for? To impose authority on an uncultivated populace? To clear a channel for seriousness in the intelligences of the young?

The girls recover, do well, even manage to say 'her hands she stretches out to the distaff' without collapsing into mirth again. But they waver when the rabbi embarks on one of those interminable shtetl parables about two communities, one free to read Torah, one not, the moral of which – surprise, surprise – is that the one that's not tries harder than the one that is. This is what I hate about rabbis – no sooner have they got your attention than they treat you like a moron.

But it was fun being religious while it lasted.

ME OL' BAM-BOO

Of the sorrows that afflict the writer, none are less likely to win him sympathy than those that attend the publication of his latest book. Ill-positioned reviews, unflattering publicity photographs, being mistaken on the Underground for someone else who has a book out – who cares! He who would be a writer must take the kicks with the halfpence.

I accept this callousness myself as the price I pay for an easy and opinionated life. But just once in a while we writers have to go to such extremes to drum up notice – agreeing to read and review another writer's book, for example, in return for some fleeting mention of our own, or attending, on the same principle, a West End show we would ordinarily suck ratsbane rather than sit through – that it is only common humanity to feel for us.

Spare a passing thought for me, then, penned into a seat at the London Palladium, surrounded by a species of person – part grown-up, part child, part I cannot tell you what – for whom the appearance onstage of a toy motor car called Chitty Chitty Bang Bang is the occasion for such delirious ovation that I fear the balcony in which I am imprisoned will come crashing down, that the rubble of the London Palladium will be my final resting place, and that the words 'Oh you pretty Chitty Bang Bang / Chitty Chitty Bang Bang / We love you' will be the last I ever hear.

There is an upside to this. In the course of accepting that you must sing for your supper and be willing to discuss work other than your own, you are occasionally forced to reread something wonderful, such as, to take one example from last week's labours, George Orwell's *Nineteen Eighty-four*. And guess what? A remarkable coincidence, I grant you, but the subject of *Nineteen Eighty-four* turns out not to be dictatorship and the tyranny of orthodoxy as I'd remembered, but *Chitty Chitty Bang Bang*.

In fact, the film of *Chitty Chitty Bang Bang* first came out in 1968 not 1984, but all that proves was that Orwell underestimated the rapidity of our decline. Otherwise he foretells it with great accuracy, charging particular departments at the Ministry of Truth with the production of exactly that genre of proletarian musical entertainment to which *Chitty Chitty Bang Bang* belongs. We need not concern ourselves here with the ministry's other responsibilities – the 'rubbishy newspapers' stuffed with nothing but 'sport, crime and astrology', the sensational novelettes or the pornography for the masses put out by Pornosec; sufficient to our purposes are the 'sentimental songs which were composed entirely by mechanical means on a special kind of kaleidoscope known as a versificator'.

That the Sherman Brothers, Richard M. and Robert B., would not care to think of themselves as mechanical versificators I do not doubt. They did, however, write regularly for Walt Disney, who knew the sentimentality he wanted and kept repeating it, to the detriment of children's imaginations the world over. What I heard in the Shermans' contribution to *Chitty Chitty Bang Bang*, anyway, was a musical banality that made me want to vomit, and an emotional vapidity that made me want to vomit over them.

Take 'Me Ol' Bam-Boo', a knock 'em dead, slap it around, do it again and again song-and-dance number for men dressed in a loose-crotched ethnic olde worlde version of long johns. Quite what these ersatz morris men had to do with anything that one might call *Chitty Chitty Bang Bang*'s narrative or musical integrity, I have no idea. They just appeared, carrying their staves, with the sole intention, as far as I could tell, of cockneyfying the occasion. I don't think I need to remind readers of this column that cockneyfication in any of its manifestations is an abomination to us. We didn't like it when Tommy Steele or Max Bygraves did it, we like it still less when Young British Artists and Young British Telly Chefs do it, but when Americans who wouldn't know a cockney if he brained them with his ol' bam-boo do it, we are ready to go to war.

Of the host of unwarrantable cultural assumptions in this utter wasteland of a song, I draw just two to your attention. The first relates to punting on the Thames. Someone should have told the Sherman Brothers that punting on the Thames, with or without a bamboo, is the equivalent of riding your horse into a saloon on Fifth Avenue.

The second assumption is that morris dancing, as it is normally performed, is effete and needs energising. Now I happen to be a great admirer of morris dancing. Forget the real ale and the hairy polytechnical jesting; what can be marvellous about the morris dance is the fearful mockery of it, the joshing lightness of those burly men, hinting at other sorts of agility, and the rasping knowingness of the music.

As far from rural innocence as any activity could be, the morris dance teases you with its ambiguities, making your heart stop, sometimes, with its unexpected reversions to violence. Done well, the morris dance puts you in touch with the vital force of the English themselves; yet it is this, the power of their own lungs and intelligence, the depth and complexity of their own passions, that they are *prepared* to see diluted into the perky pap of 'Me Ol' Bam-Boo'. Prepared? Reader, they stomped and roared for the joy of it.

'What could possibly become of such a people,' Orwell asked, 'in whom the living intuitive faculty was dead as nails, and only queer mechanical yells remained?' Except it wasn't Orwell who asked it, it was Lawrence. Proving that once upon a time there was more than one man who took our aesthetical degradation seriously. Never mind whether *Chitty Chitty Bang Bang* inspires kids to dream, or teaches them the wrong attitudes to foreigners. The thing is 'prolefeed': an aesthetic offence. And as Orwell showed, whoever would ruin us, ruins us aesthetically first.

TRAVIS

If you are reading this in bed mid-morning it's unlikely you'll be making it over to Selfridges in Oxford Street in time to catch a glimpse of Travis in what Gaywired.com calls his 'tightie-whities'. Shame. I think you'd have enjoyed it. But if it's any consolation, I'll be there.

Hard to imagine there's anyone who does not know who Travis is. But should you be living out of town, for whatever reason, there's a chance you won't have seen the poster campaign. So, for you, allow me to explain that Travis is Calvin Klein's latest underwear model and that he's been pointing his package at the rest of us – 'package' being another term I've picked up from Gaywired.com – for weeks.

Funny old world, ours. We do what we can to rein in our appetites in public places, try not to bare our teeth when we are angry, or our behinds when we are aroused, putting distance between ourselves and the primeval forest where we originated. Civilisation, we call this: the finest tracery of etiquette and reticence, having regard to our own self-respect as upright beings, and the feelings of our fellow citizens whom we must regard as capable of embarrassments and compunctions as exquisite as our own. And yet we accept as normal a hundred thousand photographs, positioned where it is impossible to miss them, of a young man showing us his penis, or at least intimating the presence of his penis (its shape, weight, configuration) at a three-quarters diagonal slant, neither coming up nor going down, neither pendulous nor protrusive, in soft clinging cotton tightie-whities.

It could be argued that for a man of the slackie-blackie generation to have paid quite so much attention, something about the promotion must have worked. I don't doubt it. When you prick me, do I not bleed? When you hit me over the head with a club, do I not faint?

I recall visiting Perth, in Western Australia, for the first time and being unable to escape the magnetic influence of a billboard which dominated the town, partly by virtue of its size, partly by virtue of its subject – a woman unsuccessfully holding down her unruly skirts – but mainly because it said LOOK, NO KNICKERS. I am squeamish about this sort of thing. I do not care for the word knickers. Panties neither. Should some alien power wish to extract secrets out of me it would do well to forget thumbscrews or Chinese water torture, and simply order me to say knickers or panties a hundred times onstage at the London Palladium. Rather than say knickers twice, or panties once, I'd tell them everything they wanted to know and a little more besides.

My peculiar fastidiousness apart, it is impossible to take a city seriously when the only thing you see on raising your eyes to its skyline is LOOK, NO KNICKERS. Thereafter, in my estimation, Perth was forever in dishabille, a frisky, tarty little town with a bubbly personality, but only a fool would marry it.

And my fear is that Travis is doing the same to London. Forget the National Gallery, St Paul's, Westminster Abbey – welcome to Dick City. That Travis is himself an Australian only makes it worse. Not from Perth, as it happens, but from Melbourne, where civic solemnity is of no small account. It's because they won't have Travis flashing himself in Carlton or St Kilda that he's doing it here. I say 'he' but there is a girlish look to Travis, soft pleading eyes, easily bruised skin, a waifish twist of leather ('Find me a home, Daddy') round his swansdown neck. For reasons buried deep in its national psychology, Australia throws up this appearance of androgyny effortlessly. Take my word for it if you haven't been there, every third person in Australia is a girl with a penis.

The actress Nicole Kidman is not, to my knowledge, kitted out in this way. But she is possessed of a freckled, hoydenish demeanour which ill-suits her for half the parts she's given. Whatever else you ask an Australian woman to be, you don't ask her to be a femme fatale, not even in jest. Every time I nipped indoors to escape an eyeful of Travis last week I had the misfortune to catch snippets of Nicole Kidman on television, vamping it up for the BAFTAs in *Moulin Rouge*. Now, I have admitted to strange sensitivities in the matter of the naming of women's undergarments, but nomenclature has nothing to do with the pain I feel when I see Nicole Kidman in her Parisian stockings and suspenders. Few sights on this planet are sadder – not a wounded elephant, not a tiger cub separated from its mother – than a woman who does not fill or look seductive in a stocking. No time here to plumb the mysteries of it; whether it comes down to actual fleshliness, the voluptuous swell of thigh (or not), or simply to conscious-ness of sensuality (or not): the fact remains that some women can and some can't, and those who can't are desolating when they try.

I wish they'd ask me first. I wish that middle-aged lady novel-ist with a trampy name had asked me how she looked in fishnets before letting the newspapers snap her in them, extended on a chaise longue. 'Heart-breaking,' I'd have told her. But then fishnets become no one. In fishnets a woman only ever resembles a fish.

And tightie-whities are no better. Down to our drawers, we are all pathetic. If I'm killed in the crush to see Travis, I'll admit I'm mistaken.

LOVING THE INCHOATE

Lovely word, inchoate. Meaning incipient, barely begun, rudimentary, immature. Like Estelle Morris, who I'll come to anon. I
introduce the word – inchoate, not Morris – without ceremony
on the assumption that you've been reaching for it in recent
weeks, or maybe months, or maybe years, to describe the quality
our age values above all others. I was in an argument recently as
to whether we are acting the child or just acting dumb. Neither
of your examples has anything to do with the child *qua* child, my
interlocutors put in when I cited Channel 4 as the home of the
moral infant and BBC2 as the home of the intellectual infant.
What you're describing in both instances, they insisted, is simply
brute, opportunistic inanity. So here's what's so useful about the
word inchoate – it bridges the two positions. And maybe tempers
both with compassion, for that which is inchoate might be said to
be struggling towards something better, like BBC2 with its use of
words like 'book'. Look, Mummy, book!

All of it, of course, whether in politics or the media or art, is
just a variation of *nostalgie de la boue*, the yearning of civilised
man to return to the condition of being uncivilised. Which is
another reason I favour inchoate. You can hear the mud in it.

I take it as read myself that the glorification of the suicide bomber by normally peaceable people, people who are appalled by the yobs who throw peanuts at an illusionist, is actually glorification of the inchoate made active. That a suicide bomber might have a degree in sociology or racial hatred does not make her, or him, a jot less rudimentary. For it is a rudimentary response to events, however you interpret those events, to turn yourself into human explosive and once and for all close down argument in the act of blowing away as many other people as you can. It is psychologically retarded, an introjection of a grievance and a projection of your selfish will. It is not just the end of life, it is the end of the *idea* of life.

Whenever I voice this conviction, peaceably, I am bombarded by letters in little envelopes from, I suspect, widowed ladies usually living in Leicestershire. What they have to tell me is invariably the same. Suicide bombing is a legitimate defence against the new Nazis, the Israelis. Now I know, because I have been told enough times, that it is not anti-Semitic to be critical of Israel, but the gratuitous use of the word Nazi always does seem anti-Semitic to me (since there are many other less emotionally loaded but equally brutal and militaristic nouns we might use), as does the frequent recourse, in such little letters, to the subject of Hebraic genes. Might I be entitled to accuse of anti-Semitism those who put all our misfortunes down to some kink in the Jewish genome?

Anti-Semitism, too, it has always seemed to me, is yet another branch of devotion to the inchoate. Sartre said that the anti-Semite wanted to make himself as stone; I think the anti-Semite wants to make himself as mud. What the hater of the Jew fears above all else is articulacy, the Jewish project of giving voice to the reasons of belief, to codification of the law, to social justice – that latter articulateness so much despised by the democracy-despising Nietzsche – and, if you like, to the very basis on which we possess and refine our humanity. There are those who believe we can be too refined. I feel it myself, sometimes. All Jews do. It is a natural recoil of the bodily man against the mental man. Which is why Jews make better anti-Semites than anyone. But in the end you resist the suck of the inchoate or you go under. To hate is to drown; but to hate the mind for its powers of clarity, to hate lucidity of expression, to hate the strivings of language to know itself – none of which, let me make clear, do I think of as uniquely Jewish preoccupations – is to drown in mud.

But I am distracted, against my intentions. Observe the seduction of inchoateness. It maroons you in the incipient. In fact, the object of my attentions was meant to be Estelle Morris, Minister for whatever it is we call it now – Culture, Sport, Environment, Bingo, Popping Down to the Pub, Hymning Guns and Being Proud When Your Teenage Daughter Opes Her Maiden Treasure on the Telly. Estelle Morris spoke to the nation via the Cheltenham Literature Festival last week, demonstrating her bona fides as an arts and creativity person ('a consumer, not a connoisseur', in her own words) with such exercises in bathos as, 'Creativity is becoming acknowledged as a key driver for economic growth and public service improvement.' Which is just the sort of sentence you go to a literary festival to hear.

The burden of Estelle Morris's talk – and I choose the word carefully (burden, that is, not talk) – was the artificial distinction between excellence and access, a distinction which she would like to see 'our museums and our galleries', and no doubt our epics and our symphonies, remove. 'Is there an unwritten rule of life that says the more excellent a piece of art, the fewer people will be able to appreciate it?' she asked, before triumphantly refuting her own question with the closely reasoned answer, 'Of course there isn't.'

That's the spirit of the inchoate speaking. Because actually there is such a rule, and it is determined by the fact that appreciation of a 'piece' of art necessitates more often than not, unless it is itself inchoate, a sophistication of sensibility not to say an education of judgement which is not available to everybody. If we would have it otherwise, and I am one of those who would, then it is not for the art to stoop to the inchoate, but for the inchoate to rise to the art.

But it's warm in the mud. And the idea of rising has grown inimical to us.

BAD TIME OF THE YEAR

This is always a difficult time of the year for me – school broken up, summer climaxing in the arms of autumn, the trees heavy with whatever trees are heavy with. Maybe if I knew what trees were heavy with I'd be having it easier. Name a thing and you take away its mystery. Horticulturists don't look as though their knees knock in nature. They pause, sniff, label and walk on. But because I don't know what anything's called or why anything is the way it is, I'm destined to wander summer parks and gardens like some sorrowing Werther or Melmoth, forever outcast from the consolations of green.

Who can ever trace beginnings? What made me a boy whose thoughts invariably turned to desire the moment school broke up and the trees grew heavy with whatever? Clearly there are biblical precedents for finding gardens erotic, but other boys at my school were able to read the Old Testament without it making them soft in the head about lawns and shrubberies. The Ritz, that was where they headed to find romance the minute term was over. Or the Plaza. Everly Brothers on the turntable, spinning balls of splintered light above your head, Gladys from Accrington's head on the

shoulder of your school blazer, and love followed as sure as day
follows whatever day follows.

But not for me. School broke up and I was out haunting
municipal parks. What did I hope to find? Truth, if you really
want to know. But if truth eluded me, company. Someone sweet.
Someone who smelt like grass. Someone I could thread dandelions with, which meant someone who could show me what
dandelions looked like.

I was always between girlfriends in the summer holidays –
that's to say I was always between not having one and wanting
one. And if nothing showed up locally, by the bowling greens
and duck ponds of Cheetham Hill, then I travelled further afield.
One of my friends, Malcolm Meggitt, carried lists on his person
of towns that had the most girls in them: Leicester because of
the hosiery industry; Aldershot for the reason that all the men
were in the army; Dagenham on account of the all-girl pipe
bands. I have no idea where he obtained this information or
whether any of it was genuine, and we never got around to testing it – not in each other's company anyway – I suppose because
we didn't want to suffer the indignity of failing where sociology
showed it was impossible to fail. Besides, Dagenham and
Aldershot sounded altogether too inorganic for my taste. And
the people of Leicester were notorious floricides.

I had my own preferred list. Chester, where the Dee tinkled
like fairy bells and the riverbanks were grassed like carpets.
Harrogate, which threw year-long flower festivals and where
even the main roads were laid to lawn. Buxton, where the faint-
ing daughters of the northern aristocracy went to take the
waters, and where the earth was so rich in health-giving miner-
als you had only to suck on a stick of hay – or however hay
came – to be cured of every ailment. But Malcolm no more
fancied Buxton than I fancied Leicester. So he went where his
list took him, and I followed mine.

In order to compensate for the inherent ponciness of looking for love in orangeries and allotments, I wore dark glasses, a maroon hand-me-down smoking jacket, a yellow paisley cravat from Austin Reed and lovat-green suede shoes. Since I was wearing a smoking jacket I thought it behoved me to smoke. Stuyvesants in the squashable packet. Two a month in term time, but one every five minutes in parks. That my face blazed hotter than a blacksmith's furnace goes without saying. It's embarrassing to be an outcast in nature. Even the flowers know you've come to the wrong place. I must have been a fearful sight. It's a long time since I made a public apology in this column, but I make one today to all those women – they will be grandmothers now, if they've survived at all, inpatients of sanatoria all over the north of England – who were unlucky enough to be surprised in a parterre of geraniums by a creeping red-faced boy with a voice as husky as the Boston Strangler's and smoke coming out of his ears.

'Excuse me, I don't suppose you've seen a short fat man with ginger hair go by recently, have you?' That was my line. Don't ask me where it came from. It's possible I was making an unconscious connection with Cain, the other wanderer, whose hair was reputed to be red. But I have no idea what advantage I thought would accrue to me, however they answered. 'Yes, I have just seen a short fat person with red hair.' Then what? Would you care to lie down with me among the sphagnum and swallow my smoke rings?

Mainly, the unfortunates I approached didn't answer me at all. I suspect they were too shocked by my demented appearance to know what to say. That some suffered seizures I don't doubt. That others would have miscarried on the spot, succumbed to hysterical blindness or gone instantaneously mad, I am also prepared to believe.

Perhaps I exaggerate the dreadful spectacle I presented. I was only fourteen. How dreadful can *anyone* look at fourteen? But it was the unwontedness of my presence that was so shocking

– black desire suddenly showing up, like the carrier of plague, in the quiet of a late-July rose garden. The invisible worm that flies in the night, except that I was visible. The devil, stripped of all disguise, breathing Stuyvesants in Eden.

And maybe that's all evil is: alienation from nature. Had I only known what trees were heavy with, I might never have turned bad.

EVERY DAY IS FATHER'S DAY

I wonder if you can have too much jubilation. You go to bed to the sound of crowds hosanna'ing the monarch and you wake to English football fans partying outside your bedroom window. Hurrah to Her Majesty and another hurrah to the boy with the Mohican. Next day you're hurrahing again because the most fearsome boxer in the world has been flattened by a gentle giant with a British passport. Ropy accent and inane mannerism, acquired in some foreign place, of referring to himself in the third person, but a British passport's a British passport. Still got a hurrah left in you? Then let's hear it for the Irish, putting three past those footballing giants, Saudi Arabia. Huzza, huzza, huzza!

It's like spending too much time at sea and finding, when you hit dry land, that everything's still moving. Even when there's no one cheering, cheering is all I can hear. A couple of days ago I thought I was being cheered in my shower. Just the pipes, but for all the world it was as though I had a hundred fans in there with me, roaring every time I soaped. The idea is not entirely preposterous. Though no longer athletic in the Leni Riefenstahl sense, I suspect I am still a sight of some ruined magnificence – like the tomb of Ozymandias – when I lather. Worth a shout or two, all things considered. But I am not a fool: I know when my ears are playing tricks on me.

It will be good when we revert to losing and can enjoy some peace and quiet again.

In the meantime the festivities are making me melancholy. My father, methinks I see my father. Maybe jubilation enjoins memories of fathers on men whose fathers are no longer alive, causing us to remember them with peculiarly fervent longing. Memories of being hoisted aloft on strong shoulders to see a cup presented or a royal personage drive by. Lift me, Daddy. We hug our male friends every time a goal goes in, and maybe that's a substitute for our earliest same-sex embraces. Enfold me, Daddy. Mothers make the world safe for us, blinding us on the breast. A father's grip might be just as sure, but he holds us out towards the naked flame.

I have a friend my age who heaves his six-month-old son on to his chest and takes him into the shower with him. It would seem the baby loves it. How could he not? I love it for the baby. 'My mother groaned, my father wept / Into the dangerous world I leapt' – no weeping in this instance. Into the dangerous watery world they leap together. Infinitely touching, not to say biblical, I find this – the patriarch Abraham, full of years, making a great feast of the unexpected gift of fatherhood. Age apart – and my friend's not that old – it's stirring. An elemental bond, sealed elementally.

But then as I've explained, when it comes to fathers I am myself all water at the moment. On top of everything else it is the tenth anniversary of my father's death. Ten years, fled like a dream. Ten years in which much has happened for me, and nothing has happened for him. As always, my mother rings to make sure I know it's yahrzeit, the day to remember him by, as calculated by the Jewish calendar. The Jews commemorate the dead with candles. Man is a flame, the flame is extinguished. You can't fault the imagery. So we keep it simple, the yahrzeit candle a mere deposit of wax in a miserable Methodistical little glass, guaranteed to burn for twenty-four hours and then go out with a dead sizzle, like hot oil escaping down a sink. This at least you do not confuse with the sound of crowds cheering a penalty.

And would he have been a fatherly sort of father, my father, this last week or so? Hard to say. I doubt he'd have lifted me up to see the Queen, or bought me a flag to wave or had much to say about Rio Ferdinand. Lennox Lewis knocking out Mike Tyson, though, might have got him going. He'd have admired that final punch. 'Sheesh – you wouldn't have wanted to be on the end of that, eh, Howard?' he'd have said, by implication returning the question – not what sort of companionably male father he, but what sort of companionably male son I. And we'd both have known the answer to that.

His one true sporting passion was wrestling. 'For God's sake, Dad,' I used to jeer, catching him biting his knuckles in front of the box, 'they aren't touching each other.' 'That's how it looks to you,' he'd say, 'because you don't understand the science.'

The science wasn't all he was in it for. What he really loved was needle. In every wrestling bout, he reckoned, there was a moment when needle entered and the play-acting gave way to genuine anger. 'Now it really is needle,' he'd say, rubbing his hands, and had the house gone up in flames around him, he would not have noticed.

He had a weak heart, else he might have become a wrestler. He had the build for it. As it was, he settled for judo, buying himself what looked like hessian pyjamas and a square of coconut matting upon which, because he had no other opponent, he'd pin my mother. 'That's a waza-ari,' he'd say. 'Three points to me.' It was her idea that he join a club. But then came his heart operation. 'No more judo for you,' the doctor warned. Just to be on the safe side my mother confiscated his outfit. But after he died we found a new one under the mattress, together with a fourth degree black belt – a *yodan* – three higher than the *shodan* he had when he told us he'd quit.

Briefer than a candle, man's life. So you might as well burn yourself out as wait for the wind to do it. His philosopy. To which I'll raise a cheer on Father's Day.

IN DEFENCE OF MELANCHOLIA

Been brooding, in these toxic times, over the story of Manfred Gnädinger, the German-born hermit whose sculpture garden in Camelle, on the Galician coast, was damaged by the oil spill from the tanker *Prestige*, and who subsequently died, according to those who knew him, of melancholy.

Not enough of us die of melancholy. And when we do, the doctors call it something else. Depression, usually. But depression and melancholy are not synonymous. Depression is a condition you are meant to deal with. Take pills, get pissed, play with your genitals, leave your genitals alone, join a gym, find a partner, leave a partner, try liposuction, put your buttocks where your mouth is, go on *Big Brother*, get kicked off *Big Brother*, change your sexual orientation, get thee to a nunnery, expose yourself to light – fly to Galicia even.

Melancholy, on the other hand, though it was long thought by the ancients to be a morbid condition caused by excessive secretion of black bile, was also called by them 'the sacred disease'. Which might have meant that the gods had a hand in it, or that those it claimed enjoyed other privileges as a consequence. There is argument as to whether it was Aristotle or his pupil Theophrastus who made the famous connection in the *Problematica* – 'Why is it that all those who have become eminent in philosophy or politics, or poetry or the arts, are clearly melancholics?' – but it's a true observation, whoever it was.

True if you leave out politics that is, politics no longer being a calling with which eminence has anything to do.

Depression happens to you, melancholy is an option. 'I imagine that for one to enure himselfe to melancholy,' that distinguished melancholic Montaigne wrote in an essay on the variegations of our natures, 'there is some kinde of purpose of consent and mutuall delight.'

How much delight there was in Manfred Gnädinger's decision to die of melancholy I would not dare to guess. But we must assume, since he had been a hermit in Galicia for more than forty years, that he had consented to the sadness of that calling. The Galicians called him Man, short for Manfred, but suggestive of something pared down and elemental in him too. 'I was looking for a place to be alone,' he told a journalist just before his death. 'This is my world. I don't think I like other people.'

Misanthropy, we are inclined to call that. A judgemental term. We are not meant not to like other people. I prefer melancholy. It restores dignity and refuses the tyranny of normative behaviour, there being no reason on earth why we should like other people much, and every justification, even in the blue and green of Galicia I would imagine, for not liking them at all.

Photographs and descriptions of Man's sculpture garden, known locally as *el museo del alemán*, suggest one of those domestic eccentricities you sometimes drive past in remote areas, art and dereliction mixed, amorphous forms, piles of twisted stones, things thrown away as much as thrown together, but nothing wasted, the detritus of life somehow making a terrible sense. Normally you accelerate by such a place, for fear of who you'll find there, and because it calls into question the ordered nature of your own existence – nice things here, rubbish there, and no melancholy commingling of emptiness and meaning. But tourists visited Man's garden, for which privilege he charged them a dollar – chicken feed.

He could see the sea from his tiny hut. And presumably would have watched the oil approaching. Shortly before the end, the authorities gave him a pair of wellingtons to wear with his loincloth, so oil-drenched had his garden become. Wellingtons and a loincloth – I wish I had seen it. Not to smirk but weep. You try to keep it simple but the bastards always have to complicate it for you. Nobody has ever told me how wellingtons are made but I wouldn't be surprised if there is oil in them.

Man's final wish was that his 'museum' should be left untouched, as a permanent reminder of the spill.

Behold what I bequeath – ruination.

No doubt he wasn't a laugh a minute, Manfred. And would probably have shooed me off had I tried to talk Montaigne or Theophrastus to him. But I have grown attached to him as an idea. We don't do hermits any more, for the same reason we don't do melancholia. We do good works or Viagra instead, go clubbing, waylay the unwary with charity boxes. Refuse the body its needful hour of rest; refuse the mind the indifference to desire it craves. We grind away, making ourselves rich or famous or purposeful. Anything not to look unhappy.

'I have of late, but wherefore I know not, lost all my mirth,' Hamlet told his friends, and even then, when melancholy was all the rage, they had to set about searching for the cause. Women, ambition, madness. Leave the man alone. He simply didn't find the world funny any more. Russell Harty once asked Peter Cook if he had returned from America in order to recharge his batteries. I forget the exact wording of Cook's reply. Something to do with would have if he could have, but frankly did not know where his batteries were to be found. But I haven't forgotten the depths of distracted melancholy in his expression.

Misogyny, we charge Cook with. All the mises – misogyny,

misanthropy, misorder, with envy and drunkenness thrown in. We can't allow that he had forgone all his mirth, misplaced the batteries and consented to those losses, full stop.

The heroes of our time are too hectic. They don't mope enough. Young Werther's sorrows once had all of Europe by the ear, but he wouldn't do for us, he'd be too listless to solve a crime or fabricate a fantasy.

Ah! Sun-flower – I have always loved that most languorous of Blake's *Songs of Experience*, 'Where the Youth pined away with desire.' So I sorrow for Manfred, who pined away on my behalf, I being too busy.

JORDAN OR IRAQ

Which would you say is worse, what's unfolding in Iraq or what's happening with Jordan? Both were discussed with chilling incision in this newspaper last week. Iraq by the philosopher John Gray in an article entitled 'The Road to Hell'. Jordan by the *Independent* columnist Terence Blacker. In a piece full of foreboding, Blacker eyed the ongoing Jordan situation and concluded that there was reason to be scared, very scared, if the much-implanted celebrity in question – yes, I'm sorry, *that* Jordan – had indeed become a role model for women in their teens and twenties.

Myself, I'd seen it coming. Whether Baroness Warnock was among the 36,000 readers who bought *Being Jordan* in the first few days of its publication, I have no way of ascertaining. Nor whether she joined the queue several thousand strong outside a bookshop in Brent Cross to get the authoress to autograph her memoirs. It is likely that Baroness Warnock has not read a single word more of Jordan's prose than Jordan has read of hers. But the Baroness was vocal on Jordan's behalf several months ago, when the latter was firming up her readership in a clearing in the Australian jungle. Not wishing to appear stuffy – though I would have thought that stuffiness, as a professor of ethics, is what she's for – Baroness Warnock joined other women of intellectual distinction in praising Jordan for independent-mindedness vis-à-vis the size and constituent materials of her breasts, candour vis-à-vis her sexual relations with men, womanly ingenuity vis-à-vis her quest to win *I'm a Celebrity . . . Get Me Out of Here*, and exemplary resolution vis-à-vis making herself more rich and famous than she already was. Thus ethics in our time: if it earns, it must be good.

The manner in which celebrity demeans all that comes within its ambit (including, it would seem, feminism and the academy) is deserving of a socio-psychological study of its own, always assuming there's a socio-psychologist out there who is familiar with the verb 'demean'. In the meantime I reckon we could do worse than purloin the language of indignation employed by philosophers when they survey the wreckage of American policy on Iraq. No dread of appearing old-fashioned, out of it or confined within an ivory tower, inhibits Professor Gray. He calls an inhumanity an inhumanity, and a debasement a debasement. He is not alone in saying it but he says it well: that the Americans have come to see the people of Iraq as 'virtually subhuman', in proof whereof he cites the parading of Iraqi prisoners naked in front of American women soldiers, on dog leads, with women's underwear on their heads, and understands this as not just any old humiliation but a systematic assault on their 'identity and values'. You locate the prisoner's locus of shame – in this instance very different from your own – and you outrage it.

In war, it seems, we can say what we cannot say in peace. In war we become moralists again. We acknowledge the existence of depravity. We allow that men can demean and be demeaned, and we recognise the powerful part that sex plays in that process. We take it as axiomatic that of all the ways open to us to render another person inhuman, affronting his sexual dignity is one of the most effective. Which in itself presupposes what celebrity-driven television denies – that sexual dignity exists.

There was a dramatic passage in ITV's excellent *William and Mary* the other week, in which William's older daughter embarked on an erotic adventure which was both necessary to her and demeaning of her. The way such a thing can take you in those contrary directions was wonderfully written and acted. But what struck me about it particularly was the sadness it released. The girl's younger sister wept for she knew not what – her being marooned by her sister's actions, her being left alone at the end of her own childhood, the fracturing of the idyll of the family, and in some way, too, the loss not simply of her sibling's innocence but of innocence in general. Sex in the age of Jordan and the thousands who will waste their lives trying to emulate her is ignorant of itself. To be reminded that it has the power to capsize us, that it shares a home with our deepest emotions, and is as soon the cause for regret and sorrow as it is the occasion for greed and gossip, was like being locked away for an afternoon with your granny's photo album. Sadness – God, yes, I remember that. Innocence . . . innocence . . . wasn't that something to do with embroidery?

There is, of course, in pantomime and other forms of clowning a place for actions which invigorate by demeaning. When I first caught sight of Jordan's disfigurements I wondered if she intended herself to be a species of clown, an embodiment of the grotesque, a carnival figure who turns everything upside down for a brief fly-sprung hour, making us long for excesses we know we can't afford, before the clock strikes and brings us back to normality. And if liberation through the hyperbolic-grotesque body of a clown was what those girls were queuing for in Brent Cross, I beg their pardons. But clowns aren't role models. Clowns are role-reversal warnings. They do low that we might glimpse high. And something tells me that that wasn't quite where Jordan's readers were going.

As for my opening question – which is worse, Jordan (to borrow her name for a tendency) or Iraq – I am unable to decide. Both attest to our limitless capacity for low behaviour. Why it is that we are shy of moral judgements in relation to the one, when our outrage knows no bounds in relation to the other, I don't know. But human beings cannot function except critically, and it is possible we have chosen to attack our culture through its foreign policy because we have grown inured to its domestic grossness.

THE GREAT CHAIN OF BEING

I saw God in Selfridges the other day. To those on more familiar terms with the deity than I am there is probably nothing surprising about that. They see Him everywhere. But as a non-believer I have always been more picky. If I am going to encounter God I want it to be somewhere special. On a mountain top at sunset, or after a particularly good paella on the Ramblas, or where the Ganges spills into wherever the Ganges spills. Not in the basement in Selfridges. Not in a demonstration of domino toppling.

To be fair, this was not just any domino toppling. Empty your mind of two old men losing their temper with each other in a pub in Pocklington, and imagine, instead, tens of thousands of dominoes arranged, narrow ends up, on snaking tracks, now level, now precipitous, now rotating on a merry-go-round of their own making, now setting off the most unexpected reaction, not only in themselves but in other hairspring devices which agitate more dominoes to fall in sequence, the whole thing culminating in two great walls of dominoes collapsing in a shower of tiles that would gladden any vandal's heart. Except that this isn't vandalism we're watching but order. Myself, I'd go further: to see the topple of a single tiny tile in one corner of a room effect such mayhem in another is to be witness to meaning. That providence which is in the fall of a sparrow.

What Selfridges was doing staging this exhibition I am not sure, but I understand that what they originally wanted was a live version of the 'Cog' commercial for Honda in which components of a motor car set off an ingenious chain reaction that seems to know no end. But 'Cog' is cinematic and requires countless takes, whereas the dominoes topple before our very eyes.

So wherein lies the satisfaction of these chain-reaction installations? In the wit, partly. In the elegant comedy of pitting small cause against large effect. It is possible we are back to chaos theory, the butterfly beating its wings in Shanghai as a consequence of which (maybe) an earthquake shakes downtown Los Angeles. Not that that's particularly witty, least of all if you happen to live in downtown Los Angeles. But then chaos theory originates in speculation about the weather, and weather is never witty. Whereas the car components performing their functions in a new way, creating unexpected dependencies and consequences, are.

In fact, the ad's conclusion, 'Isn't it nice when things just work?', doesn't adequately render our pleasure, although we do of course enjoy the precision functioning. What it should say is 'Isn't it nice when things display a codependency, when small and large cooperate, even exchanging roles, in their ineluctable progress towards a greater good?' But that might only persuade you that I was right not to go into copywriting.

The last I heard, a couple of conceptual artists were threatening to sue Honda for ripping off a film they'd made years earlier, showing everyday objects affecting one another similarly. *Der Lauf Der Dinge*, it was called – *The Way Things Go*. But then plagiarism, whether the charge is true or false, is only another word for influence, and what is influence but the motivating force of a chain reaction. Which goes to show that all might not be well if you happen to be at the wrong end of the chain: the ball bearing envying the silencer, the silencer the steering wheel, and the steering wheel the car.

A couple of days earlier, out of vulgar curiosity, I had gone along to see David Blaine swinging comatose in his glass box. Or rather I had gone along to see people behaving loutishly, hurling insults and chipolatas, and with a bit of luck baring their breasts. I wanted to test the theory that the medieval mob was still alive in us. There was the BBC thinking that the only way they could get us to appreciate Chaucer was to update him, set him in a world of karaoke and soap operas, as though such things define our modernity, while all along it was still the Middle Ages in our hearts. But in fact a couple of hours of Blaine-watching yielded nothing rumbustious whatsoever, a couple of cries of 'Wake up, David, you lazy bastard!' and that was it. Maybe you need to see the eyes of your victim before you can bait him in earnest. Maybe prone he excited more pity than resentment. Or maybe we were just baited out.

Nonetheless, my head was still sufficiently full of stories of irrational hatred to fear for the safety of the dominoes before the toppling began. What was to stop one of these mindless louts I had read about knocking them over for the sheer spite of it? Well, the fact that he was unlikely to shop in Selfridges for a start. But even in the blameless, ten thousand poised dominoes can excite instincts of wanton destructiveness.

In the event no one did anything to spoil the show. We watched quietly, delighted, as every domino performed its task, and then stood around with broad smiles on our faces when the walls came down. It was not like staring up at David Blaine in his ugly box with its white sheet flapping in the night. It was more pleasing aesthetically for a start. And it demonstrated some law, or some fallacy that looks like law, in nature. The great chain of being, that discredited system of social theology which declared that all was ordered for the best, the rich man in his castle, the poor man at his gate. An intolerable concept to us now, though it is hard to believe we have put anything more calming in its place. But at least where Blaine established distance between himself and us, by that means instigating animosity, the dominoes reminded us of harmony, that great illusory chain of human interdependence ensuring that things work out as they are meant to. In other words, God.

In domino dominus.

AUSCHWITZ

The philosopher Theodor Adorno's famous assertion – that 'To write poetry after Auschwitz is barbaric' – was not his final thought on the subject. 'Perennial suffering has as much right to expression as a tortured man has to scream,' he later wrote, 'hence it may have been wrong to say that after Auschwitz you could no longer write poems. But it is not wrong to raise the less cultural question whether after Auschwitz you can go on living – especially whether one who escaped by accident, one who by rights should have been killed, may go on living.'

So that's all right then. We can write our poems as we can scream our screams, it's just living to which, after Auschwitz, we have lost our entitlement.

Adorno's logic would seem to lock us in a terrible circularity: the very act of survival calling for 'the coldness, the basic principle of bourgeois subjectivity, without which there could have been no Auschwitz'. In other words, if we are human we die, if we live we do so at the cost of our humanity. But it is by no means intended punitively. Far from precluding survivors from what remains of the human family, Adorno asks us to imagine how, by virtue of their survival, they might feel they have precluded themselves. So his argument is an expression, if this isn't too bourgeois and banal a word, of pity.

That survivors will be plagued, as Adorno further imagines, by dreams that they are not living at all, that their whole existence since has been imaginary, would seem to be borne out in many cases by their long silences, as though words have lost their sufficiency, and then later, as though the walls containing silence have suddenly collapsed, by the terrible urgency with which they deliver their testimonies at last. Like so many Ancient Mariners, they tell their tale wherever they can find a listener, and having told it they must find another listener to tell it to again. It is without doubt a crucial calling – to keep alive the memory of what happened; to memorialise the names and maybe even the faces of those it happened to; and yes, yes, to ensure there will be no repetition, though repetition peeps at us every day wherever one person is granted sovereignty over another. But the Ancient Mariner's compulsion is like a death in life, no matter how necessary his horror story is to us – the now sadder, wiser recipients of it.

Unless we are insensate, to be modern almost requires that we aspire to the condition of survivor ourselves. At its most innocuous the ambition resembles a sort of fellow feeling, an entering too vividly into other people's anguish. At its most offensive it is spiritual ghoulishness. In between, it reflects a proper conviction that Auschwitz represents, in Adorno's words again, a 'caesura or irredeemable break in the history of civilisation'. And after such a caesura only a fool would suppose he can live a life no different to the one he might have lived before.

(Half the country's kids have never heard of Auschwitz – there being no band of that name – but they exist in the darkened knowledge of it, their nihilism a direct consequence, the oblivion they seek in artificial stupefactions a confirmation of Adorno's expectation of non-living.)

Laurence Rees's series about Auschwitz, currently being

shown on BBC2, refuses to indulge any of the vicariousness which often mars Holocaust documentaries. It moves meticulously, at a sort of moral snail's pace, resisting melodrama or hyperbole, and resisting metaphysics too – so far, at least, not seeking to explain 'evil' – allowing the evolution of the most ambitious act of diabolism ever to have been brewed in the mind of man to unfold matter-of-factly, as it must have done for many of those who little by little became its active agents. If it's understanding we want – and I sometimes wonder why we want it, or imagine it is somewhere other than under our noses – then this is the painstaking course it should take: one brick laid upon another.

'The compelling objectivity of these photos,' Günter Grass wrote, 'the shoes, the spectacles, the hair, the corpses – spurns any dealing in abstractions; it will never be possible to comprehend Auschwitz, even if it is surrounded with explanatory words.' This series allows the shoes and the spectacles to do the explaining.

None of which, of course, will stop the revisionists and deniers taking the edifice apart again. If evil is gradual literalmindedness, the final triumph of the bureaucrat, then the mind of the revisionist historian is its consummation. He is in perfect harmony with the very event he denies, proving its slow accretion of malignities in the slow accretion of his own. Scales and tape measures are his tools, architects' plans and memoranda his elements, pedantry his mindset. You will see him on a roof, looking for the hole through which Zyklon B could have been deposited; you will find him in a gas chamber, calculating the number of people it could have held, then multiplying the answer by how many chambers in how many camps, by how many days in the week, by how many weeks in the year.

There is a philosophical desperation of nitpickery in revisionist historians which would make them fascinating to study if one could bear the proximity. For theirs is the greatest flight from existence imaginable – the ultimate proof of Adorno's contention that life after Auschwitz is untenable: measuring away the truth, seeking a mitigation now by an inch, now by a yard, imagining that they can weigh what was into something that it wasn't if they can lose a hundred here, a thousand there, chip chip chipping away at the millions until they can show that not a hair on a single head was harmed.

Where is the man who with his own eyes saw or with his own lungs breathed a gas chamber? they ask. To which the answer is, gassed.

'No one will believe you,' the Nazis said.

That's the sole lesson of Auschwitz. Believe.

GAY IN THE JUDY GARLAND SENSE

I too went through an anti-gay phase once. I must have been in my late twenties – somewhat younger than the Anglican Church, but then we each age at our own speed. My problem was that all my friends had suddenly decided to come out, come clean, cross over, whatever you call it, and I was afraid of being left to stew in solitary heterosexuality. I saw my future stretching out before me: companionless in Straightsville. And loneliness can make you say terrible things.

Not that I went as far as the primates we've been hearing from in recent days. I never, for example, said, 'Homosexuality is just filthy,' like the Most Reverend Remi Rabenirina (no doubt known to his fellow primates as Irene) of the Indian Ocean. I've always been more careful, for a start, about the way I use the word 'just'. If homosexuality is 'just' filthy then what's the fuss about? My accusation was more temperate. I just thought homosexuality – and I blush now to recall it – was unnatural.

A woman friend – because women friends were all I had left – took me to task. 'So who are you to be a champion of nature and naturalness all of the sudden?' she asked. 'You don't have a natural bone in your body. You have never wanted to propagate.

You have never wanted a family life. When you were presented with a child by your first wife – and you marry the way other people get on and off a bus – you ran screaming from the house the minute you saw a nappy. You will not go on a date with anyone who has less than three inches of make-up on her face, you invite the women you love to whisper depravities in your ear, you dress them like street prostitutes, you beg them to perform lesbian acts in your presence, you suggest sexual variations that would make a strumpet blush, to my certain knowledge you have never been against buggery between the sexes, you refuse to go to Denmark or Sweden on the grounds that Danes and Swedes consider copulation a healthy activity – natural, you? Don't make me laugh! If you're so in favour of nature, tell me why you never leave the house. Tell me why you're so frightened of weather. Tell me why you fumigate the lavatory every time another person has been in it. Tell me why you fumigate the lavatory every time YOU have been in it. Name me a park you've ever visited, Mr Nature Man, name me a tree, name me a fucking flower!'

What can you do when a woman talks to you like that, short of asking her to perform a lesbian act in your presence? You think, that's what you do. You ponder. You consider. And then you accept the justice of her every word. Thereafter I did not allow a single reference to nature to pass my lips again.

I would humbly urge the Anglican Church – if urge is not too inflammatory a word in this context – to do likewise. Forget hetero or homo – any appeal to nature, using scripture as a guide, is hypocritical. Strip away the refinements of theology and what does religion exist to do but subdue the natural man? 2 Peter 2:12 (the only way to talk to Anglicans is in numbers) – 'But these, as natural brute beasts . . . shall utterly perish in their own corruption.' Nature equals brute equals beast equals unregenerate. And the unregenerate cannot receive the Spirit of God. 1 Corinthians 2:14 – 'But the natural man receiveth not the things of the Spirit of God: for they are foolishness unto him: neither can he know them, because they are spiritually discerned.' That from the mouth of Paul the Apostle himself, Paul the prime source of loathing of those who 'abuse themselves with mankind'. Count the ways in which homosexuality is unnatural and Paul, were he consistent, ought to have seen each of them as a positive recommendation.

But at least Paul is even-handed in his abhorrences. No one is spared, not the adulterers, not the fornicators, not the incontinent of either sex, not even the marriers. Better to marry than to burn, but best not to marry at all, for it is 'good for a man not to touch a woman'. In other words, Most Reverend Remi Rabenirina, it is all filth, man on woman, man on man, woman on woman, beast on beast, you name it.

This is my position: whoever has looked into the deep dark abyss which is heterosexuality cannot be bothered or surprised by what the homos do. Since it is all filth, it makes no sense to discriminate. And please don't shy from the filth word, remembering the beauty of love, the exaltation of the feelings you have sometimes experienced in your bed of lust. Of course you have. We are an extraordinarily idealistic species and find poetry everywhere. Good for us, until the poetry fails, whereupon there follows disappointment, infidelity, heartache, violence, separation and every other sort of calamity until we can restart the engines of idealism and find poetry in lust again. Whether sex is even natural in the unregenerate beast sense I am not sure. Observe dogs locked in passion and you will see that they look abashed, look away, have an air of creatures doing something else altogether, as though they neither understand why they are occupied as they are, nor ever wish to repeat it. Shame and confusion, even in the animal kingdom. Shame to be driven to such filth. And dogs don't have to reconcile their actions with God.

Filth without exception, bodies entering bodies through the

unlikeliest corridors and porches, putting this here and that there, unless you happen to be numbered among the subtle who put this there and that here. Poor Dr Jeffrey John, or Jennifer as I believe he's called, having to assure us he's stopped all that and is now gay only in the caring, Judy Garland sense.

Pity: a little less care and campery and a little more unapologetic sodomy would do wonders for believers and doubters alike.

WHEREFORE ART THOU CHARLIE?

Three cheers for mature love, I say. If we are to have marriages then let them be between mature peoples only. Marriage, like love, is wasted on the young. If we were sensible we would make it illegal to marry, or indeed to fall in love, the baby side of fifty.

Seeing the famous newsreels again of Charles and Diana answering the question of whether they are in love – of course we are, says Diana; whatever in love means, says the Prince – it is hard not to shake one's head in sorrow over both of them. Since then, and with hindsight, we have come to see a terrible duplicity in Charles's prevarication; and it may well be that he was thinking of someone else even as Diana was flushing and starting by his side. But the truth is, they were so unevolved when they underwent the ordeal of declaring their love on television – mere embryos of people they look now, not a wrinkle of knowledge or understanding between them – that neither could have had an inkling of what love meant.

Whether Diana ever did get a better handle on the word or the thing it denotes is open to debate. She certainly enjoyed deploying the language of love for everyone to hear, and no less willingly unpacked her heart for everyone to see. That was a hot night for most men when she looked out of our televisions with fire in each cheek and said 'Oh yes, I adored him' about somebody the world has since forgot. But it always looked like an emotion in search of an object, which is the way of it when you're young, before experience yields or, in some lucky cases, confirms a choice.

It's for this reason that I have never been able to read or watch *Romeo and Juliet* to the finish. I cannot attach sufficient value to their protestations of devotion to care how things turn out. Badly – how else were they ever going to turn out? Now act me a play about grown-ups.

This is not to say I doubt the young experience intensity. I loved like a tornado when I was a boy – if you can imagine a tornado that bites its pillows and sobs into handkerchiefs. For a girl whose hand I held for five minutes in a field in Chester, but who insisted on wearing a woolly mitten while I was holding it, I was prepared to sacrifice my education. For a girl with her leg in plaster who asked my name on Oswestry market, then laughed when I gave it to her, I would have cut my mother's heart out. I can see neither of their faces now, for all that I was not able at the time to imagine a life worth living without them. Write a tragic drama about that if you will, but do not call it a tragedy of love, however much like love it felt to the soppier of the parties.

That we can feel so powerfully when we are young, and feel it almost without a cause – without what T. S. Eliot with leaden infelicity called an 'objective correlative' – is shocking for what it presages. A child with a seeming broken heart is among the saddest of sights. But it is sad not least for telling us how the seasoned heart will crack when the hour for making practice runs has passed.

The young of course will put their fingers down their throats at the spectacle of middle-aged lovers gazing into each other's eyes. Yuk! Myself, I put my finger down my throat at the spectacle of anybody younger doing it. Those creamy little unmarked moon-calf faces, those uncertain coagulations of puppy fat, that exchange of entirely second-hand sentiment and inarticulacy wrapped in baby fluids – yuk, yuk! Three cheers for mature love, I say. Give me Antony, long out of boyhood, and Cleopatra, no longer green in judgement, any time. It's not just because Shakespeare himself was older when he wrote it that *Antony and Cleopatra* is a greater play than *Romeo and Juliet*. It's because in the wisdom of his years he chose to write of wiser lovers.

Yes, Antony and Cleopatra are still as irresponsible as children when it comes to prosecuting their ardour, but the foundations of that ardour are deeply planted. They have knocked about the world, separately and together. They know what else is or is not on offer. And they are not embarrassed by their own sexual maturity. Very bold of Cleopatra to speak of herself as one who is 'with Phoebus' amorous pinches black, / And wrinkled deep in time'. No Botox, for a start. No concern about her complexion. And rather witty, wouldn't you say, to imagine the ravages of time as ravishments, the bites and bruises given her by the sun god in the diurnal course of their embraces?

I don't know how much of Cleopatra Camilla Parker Bowles has in her nature. It's hard to imagine her making the winds love-sick in a burnished barge in Clarence House, I grant you. But hopping forty paces through a public street might not be beyond her, would protocol allow. She is, after all, reputed to be a sporty woman. The mistake – a mistake commonly made with regard to English countrywomen – is to suppose that horsiness must be at odds with sensuality. I have seen photographs of Charles laughing with Camilla at the opera, where he unmistakably sees her as a morsel for a monarch. Conversation is the key to it. Enjoy the conversation and there is no extremity of love you might not reach.

I have always thought it, among other things, heroic, that in the days when he had for wife a woman thought to be the most beautiful in the world – the nonpareil of women in a ball gown – Charles would rather be tramping through the mud with Camilla in her scarf and jodhpurs.

And if you don't understand why that should be, you are definitely not old enough to marry.

NATES

Beware the curse of the acronym, I say. An auntie, gifted with the needle, sewed my initials in flowery embrace on to everything I wore when I was eleven – HEJ, which no sooner became Hedge than it became Hedgehog. And no boy wants to go through school with a hog in his name. The National Association of Teachers of English, all of whose members must have been to school themselves, should have been mindful of the Commonness of Acronym Contumely and Abuse (CACA), and found an alternative way of describing itself. NATE is hardly a dignified title for so distinguished a body as the National Association of Teachers of English, bearing in mind that the nates are the buttocks.

Inexplicably, I recall looking nates up in our school library's *Oxford English Dictionary*, round about the time that my nickname Hedgehog was catching on. Equally inexplicably, I still remember one of the illustrative quotations. It was taken from a book on diseases of the bladder by the nineteenth-century American surgeon Samuel David Gross, and read, 'A piece of oil cloth, placed under the nates, will more effectually secure this object.' Perhaps I was baffled, as I still am baffled, by what, precisely, 'this object' was. And by how a piece of oil cloth, placed under the nates, could possibly secure it.

The reason the National Association of Teachers of English – NATE – is on my mind is the report it has just issued recommending the scrapping of English literature as a discrete A-level exam. Sounded exciting at first. Not because I want A-level English literature scrapped – in my view everybody should be made to study A-level English literature – but because the proposal bore the promise of free and frank discussion of what A-level English literature comprised, and how it was being taught.

Out of that frank and free discussion, I dared to hope, would come a demand for the study of literature to be a trifle more exacting, not to say a trifle more precise, in that by literature we should mean literature, and not simply any old book or poem whose sole recommendation is that the ink is not yet dry upon its title page and that it appears, by virtue of its subject and expression, to be 'relevant' to the students' own experience, as though our inner 'experience' is quantifiable in relation to where we live and how we pass the time. Even supposing you could show (which you can't) that a pupil is closed to *Macbeth* because the play is about an eleventh-century Scottish king and he's a twenty-first-century commoner from Bethnal Green, you would not be justified in giving him a play about commoners from Bethnal Green to study for A-level English literature, unless it happened to be a work of uncommon distinction. And even then you might argue that it would serve him better to take his mind to somewhere else.

Would be good, too, I thought, to scrutinise the curriculum's submissiveness to the fads of critical theory. When we did A-level English literature, back in the Hedgehog days, it was all 'Discuss the use of dramatic irony in *Tess of the D'Urbervilles*', dramatic irony being what happens when a character says she couldn't be more happy at the very moment the President of the Immortals is preparing to fell her with a thunderbolt. Then theory came along with such equally mimsey concepts as it all depends who's reading (which it doesn't), and 'cultural context', as though you need to check Shakespeare against what others say about Elizabethan England to be certain he'd got it right. Tosh! The cultural context of a Shakespeare play is a Shakespeare play. And while you might have to look up a word or allusion here and there, you won't learn how either resonated for Shakespeare from anyone but Shakespeare. This, my dears, being what we mean by reading.

Three cheers for NATE, then, if their proposal is that all the pandering should stop. Only trouble is, it isn't. More pandering, not less, is what they're after. At the heart of the report, a suggestion that A-level English literature should merge with A-level English language, in order – though I don't see how this follows – that students be given a broader understanding of current culture, by which NATE has in mind 'the thriller, the romance, the crime novel' and, of course, the media. In other words – and still in line with the pious infractions of theory – the crap but who are you to say it's crap.

Why we want to give students a broader understanding of current culture when half of them are already dying of the stuff I cannot imagine. You might as well propose taking schoolchildren choking on the fumes of Wolverhampton for a holiday to Walsall. As for the media – well, my own view is that whoever employs the word 'media' forgetful that it is the plural of 'medium', which is an intermediate agency and therefore a possible conduit for literature, not some alternative to it, needs to take an exam in A-level English literature.

Besides which, no good ever came the media's way by people who studied it. You want to know when telly went down the tube? Take a look at the first influx of media graduates.

As for 'current culture', only its slaves assume its value. One of the supreme justifications for the study of literature is that it enables us to know a culture when we see one, and not to think of it as merely the value-free agglomeration of all we do. Out of the study of those alternative modes of thinking and feeling we call literature evolve the dreamers, naysayers, visionaries, revolutionaries, idlers, necessary for our freedom of mind. Far from liberating us from some imagined elitist tyranny, NATE's proposals would make cultural consumers of us all, enslaved to whatever pap happens to be pumped out to us.

I think I know now what that piece of oil cloth, placed under the nates, was for.

THE FULL MONTY

Sitting in a tapas bar in mixed company the other evening, minding my own business, I suddenly came to one of those understandings of life which the religious call a revelation. What was revealed to me was nothing less than the anguish of being a man; and what followed from it, though not a conversion exactly, was a profound conviction that no woman is worth the love we give them.

We had reached that tetchy stage of dinner in a tapas bar when you realise you've had nothing but half a cocktail sardine and a chickpea to eat, and dark suspicions are beginning to gather as to who it was who hogged the squid. It is always about now that the floor show starts. Don't misunderstand me – I yield to no one in my enthusiasm for flamenco. But all that yelling and stomping on an empty stomach! And then the fear – if you are a man – that the flamenco dancer is going to brush up against you with her skirt, fall laughing hoarsely into your lap, place the Carmen flower of gypsy allurement behind your ear, or click those ivory Andalusian knackers of hers suggestively in your face. There is cultural confusion here, I grant you: flamenco is not cabaret, and a malagueña is no Las Vegas torch singer. But that's part of the anguish of being a man – you know the rules but you can never be dead certain that they do.

While we men exchanged apprehensive glances with one another (will it be you or will it be me?), the women at our table yelled and stomped along with the musicians. No empty stomach problems there, notice. (If you're a woman you wolf the octopus first and stick your finger down your throat later.) But no shame either – that's my point. No embarrassment. No modesty. None of that excruciating anticipation of humiliation to which the delicate tissue of male self-consciousness is forever subject.

Hard to believe that bashfulness and pudeur were once held to be attributes of women. Show me a bashful woman today. When did you last open a newspaper and *not* read about some sad sack of a Sunday-school teacher reduced by the concupiscence of women to taking his pants off in the local church hall every Friday night to earn the necessary extra shilling? Ask yourself why he needs that extra shilling. So that he can pay for the mother of his children to go out on a Friday night and watch some other sad sack of a Sunday-school teacher take his pants off to fund *his* children's mother's weekly snatch at the posing pouch, that's why.

Sounds innocuous, doesn't it, the full monty? Sounds almost decorous. Just off to cop a full monty, my sweet. Sounds no more unbecoming than an evening of bingo or a George Formby singalong. You can even tell the kids. 'Mummy won't be able to read you *Thomas the Tank Engine* tonight, my little sugar plum. She's running an itsy bit late for the full monty.'

'That's all right, Mummy, have a lovely night. And blow Monty a kiss from Teddy.'

But who's to tell them the real reason they're going to bed storyless and cuddleless for yet another Friday night – that Mummy is out screaming herself hoarse in the hope of getting a total stranger to poke his dick in her eye?

Yes, yes, I know that men have been frequenting lap-dancing etablishments for as long as they have had laps to dance on. When I was twelve I spent an entire year's pocket money on strip joints. My friends the same. By the time we were thirteen we were on first-name terms with every stripper in the country. Some of us collected their autographs. Or their tassels. I myself had the best collection of sequinned nipple pasties in north Manchester. But that was different. We behaved ourselves. We didn't grab. We didn't exhort to lewdness. We sat red-faced and silent in the darkness, our mouths full of burning rocks, our shirts stuck with all the flaming secretions of shame to our chests, appalled by our own neediness, disgusted by our natures.

Take a look at any man coming out into the light from a house of sexual extortion. He is always blanched, furtive, guilty. A creature who would make himself invisible if he could, for he knows he is not worthy to be looked upon, least of all by himself. Nothing is more plain to him than that having traded in his virtue he has forgone his immortal soul.

And how do women disport themselves when they leave the scene of their disgrace? With mirth. Always with mirth. Unable quite to decide which was the more risible, their own temerity or the sight of the genitals of a man.

Women! They steal your tapas, they uncover your nakedness, and they laugh. Only apes and sparrows have so little sense of sin.

TOMORROW AND TOMORROW
AND TOMORROW

So now we know what 'minded' Jack Straw to give Mr Pinochet back to Mrs Thatcher. The general is reported to be deficient in memory of both distant and recent events, has a limited ability to understand complex sentences or questions, has lost the wherewithal to express himself succinctly, and suffers long periods of fatigue. In other words he is middle-aged. Case dismissed. Pack the old fart off to Spain tomorrow. Else we'll never again be able to hold a person over forty guilty of anything.

My own inability to understand the most simple, never mind complex, sentences was brought home to me forcibly in the toilet of a London club last night when someone offered me a line and I didn't know what he was talking about.

Context is important here. I had been to a charity premiere of an undistinguished film about death. I think it was about death. It died, anyway. But only after suffering long periods of fatigue, losing the ability to express itself succinctly, and forgetting what it had said five minutes earlier. Extraordinary this, considering that very young people had made the film. So maybe the Pinochet condition has nothing to do with age after all, but is caused by something in the water. Be that as it may, to a premiere I'd been, wearing the dinner jacket I now reserve for literary dinners (all weddings and bar mitzvahs having dried up in my age group), recognising and being recognised by no one. Don't get me wrong: I don't expect flashlights to pop the minute I slide a leg out of a taxi. It is not the job of a writer to excite the public. But it can be nice to exchange the odd smile of acknowledgement with a Scorsese or a Mamet across a crowded foyer, auteur to auteur. Besides, I spend long enough getting into a tux to hate the thought that it's all been for nothing. Hence my ending up at a club more suitable to people of my generation and profession.

Context. Context is everything. Had I not passed the earlier part of the evening anonymous in a velvet bow and patent dancing shoes, would I have been quite so flattered by the attentions of the person in the cardigan who accosted me in the club toilets? Who can unravel history? Had Napoleon not slept well on the night before Austerlitz . . . (Not that Austerlitz rings any more bells with me than Santiago does with Pinochet.) Idle to ask. However you account for it, flattered I was.

I was looking for paper towels when he appeared. But he was so urgent about shaking my hand that I gave it him wet. He was taller than me, a quality I value in a fan. And I could tell from the way he regarded me that I satisfied his expectation of an author – namely, that I wrote in evening dress. Once he'd paid me a sufficient number of compliments I began to back towards the exit. Experience. Sometimes, if you let them use up all their compliments, they start on the insults. He for his part was backing into a cubicle. Just before either of us could close our respective doors, he said, 'Would you like a line?'

'A line?'

Though last night is a long time ago to be remembering, I am convinced my mouth actually fell open. Truly, I was at a loss. From where I stood I raked his cubicle to see if he meant to read me a line someone had written on the walls. Or had I misheard? Had he asked me, as a literary personage he admired, to furnish *him* a line? I cannot tell you how close I came to saying, 'Tomorrow, and tomorrow, and tomorrow, creeps in this petty pace from day to day' – unless that's two lines.

It was also possible, though I am always loath to leap to this conclusion, that he was inviting me to join him in his cubicle. A line, if I was not mistaken, was what fishermen employed. Could it, while retaining all its angling associations, have taken on a secondary homoerotic meaning? Was a line something you throw an inexperienced 'swimmer', in order first to save him from drowning, and then gradually to reel him in?

He saw my confusion, though I doubt, in the time available, he was able to read its anguished constituent parts. 'I could let you have a line,' he repeated. Very sweetly this time, stressing the 'let', as though to rule out any idea of gross transaction.

I shook my head. Some faint light, such as intermittently comes on when you open a very old refrigerator, was breaking in the recesses of what Pinochet's doctors would say is no longer my brain. 'No thank you,' I said. And fled, I fear blushing, into the more public spaces of the club.

Maybe I should have been more careful who I went to with my story. In an establishment of this sort you don't plonk yourself down next to absolutely anybody and ask him to help you in the matter of 'a line'. Within seconds I was being offered another.

Now that more and more of us are staying alive after eighty, but are too *tsemisht*, to borrow a Yiddish word meaning confused, too bewildered to remember whether it was three, four or five million people we tortured in our younger days, oughtn't we to insist that a spade be called a spade? If someone wants me to sit on his knee in a toilet cubicle, snorting cocaine with him, why doesn't he just *ask*?

THE GREATNESS OF PHILIP GUSTON

Seen any good art lately? I have. Philip Guston, at the Royal Academy. Piccadilly. London. Opposite Fortnum & Mason. I recommend that you approach it at a leisurely pace, say via the Burlington Arcade where you can have your shoes polished by a flunkey in livery and maybe pick up a cashmere cardigan for the man or woman in your life, then pop across to Fortnum's tea rooms for a Welsh rarebit and English cordial. Make a treat of it. A truly great retrospective of an artist few of us know very well doesn't come along that often. A painter, to boot. A painter who isn't Picasso or Titian, or Andy Warhol or Jackson Pollock. A painter who isn't either abstract or figurative, but neither and both. A painter in whom every important twentieth-century argument about art seems to have been enacted. Reader, go. And if you don't skip through the Royal Academy's fountains on your way in to see Philip Guston, I guarantee you will skip through them on your way out.

I have an axe to grind, I don't deny that. Nothing personal. I never met the man. Nor do I have Guston canvases in my cellar whose value I suddenly see the opportunity to augment. No, if you're looking for a motive look to age. As I grow full with years, so do I grow to love the years in others. Give me an aged genius before a young one any time. And let's keep raising the bar. If I live to be a hundred it will only be hundred-year-old artists I admire. A wonderful provision of nature this, to forestall the cultural equivalent of paedophilia, that is taking an inappropriate interest in the doings of people younger than yourself. I'd enshrine it in law myself, and have the police maintain a register of offenders. Such-and-such a one has been seen hovering around young persons' art. Keep an eye on him.

Not that Guston made it to a grand old age. He was a mere sixty-seven when he died in 1980. And not that he wasn't brilliant when he was a boy. Aged seventeen, he could knock you off a Picasso-cum-de Chirico-cum-Piero della Francesca worthy of a knowledgeable and accomplished artist twice his age, and this while doing a cartoonist's course in his spare time. Six or seven years before, his father hanged himself in frustration and disappointment, a fugitive from Odessa whose life had not turned out as he would have liked it. Not every migrant's story is a happy one. Not even if you're Jewish in America. The young Philip Guston found the body. Such an event can speed up artistic development. Whatever the reason for his precocity, or its impressiveness, it's the evidence in Guston of its opposite – a quality for which words like culmination or ripeness or consummation seem to close more than they open – that is really exhilarating: prolificity in your pensionable years, creative abundance when you are meant to be getting feebler, not so much late as persistent, unabating florescence, and let death go take a jump.

All credit to the Royal Academy for hanging this show so that you follow the painter's evolution, stage by stage, room by room, anticipating development and change all right, but nothing on the scale of what's waiting for you – boom! – when you suddenly enter the grand scala showing Guston in the full bloom of his sixties, one spectacular canvas after another, grotesque creations, now depicting the painter as a potato head, one eye forever open like a camera shutter, unblinking whatever the horrors; now depicting him bound in a terrifying spider's web, bleeding crimson paint, while the giant insects advance on him as though he's good for nothing but their dinner; and now depicting him buried in his bed, grown into his wife, a huddle against the black immensity which engulfs this heartbreaking little everywhere, the painter's insect hands outside the coverlet, still grasping the brushes.

Always the brushes. This is art at its most serious, made by someone for whom it was impossible not to paint or to go on thinking and talking about painting. Talk. One of the best paintings in the show is called simply *Talking*, and shows the painter's hand holding a smoking cigarette – always a cigarette – and maybe a smoking brush – always a brush – nothing more, just the hand painted like a gun, with a hint of rolled-up sleeve, and a one-fingered cartoon wristwatch, but never have you seen such garrulousness evoked, as though the hand is the most voluble organ we have.

It was in Guston's case, most certainly. Though he was a great reader and talker, a devourer of ideas against which he was forever testing himself, unforgivingly most of the time, as though in despair that as an artist he was not more of a match for them, it is nonetheless the paint, applied intimately, three inches from the canvas, which does his talking for him. He'd tried silence. For a while, in the bloodless fifties, he'd been the all-American abstract expressionist, shimmering away in seas of luminous quiet, a hero of pure feeling, until he gave all that away in a fit of noisiness. 'I got sick and tired of all that purity,' he said. 'I wanted to tell stories.' Not everyone forgave him that. Some saw it as a betrayal. In fact he'd been the noisiest, most figuratively fraught abstract expressionist there ever was; it was just that the quiet ones hadn't noticed.

What came next, his famous hooded clansmen, candy pink

and puffing Groucho Marks cigars, sometimes murderous in their anonymity, sometimes just perplexed and sad, like baffled Jewish migrants from Odessa, and sometimes brandishing Guston's own smoking paintbrushes, are masterpieces of the grotesque. Wonderfully gluttonous works follow, in which seeing, talking, thinking, eating, smoking, suffering, joking do not so much compete for the artist's attention as entirely constitute it. This is what it is to be alive.

Reader, go. Before the forces of quiet finally claim you too.

DARTS AND THE MAN

You know you're in a bad way emotionally when you start crying over World Darts on television. Not just sniffles, either; not just a lump in the throat when one of the throwbacks from the old beer-and-instinct era succumbs to one of the game's new gin-and-tonic automatons – no, I'm talking real tears, big wet baby droplets the size of a bull's eye.

I've been lachrymose for weeks. All right, I've been blubbering for weeks. Hasn't everyone? There's been reason enough, God knows. The cruel pinch of winter. An old century dying in the indifferent arms of a new. Jesus on the cross – 'Erbarm' dich mein', pity me, pity me, my father. *David Copperfield* on the box. And now darts.

It was *David Copperfield* that set me off. Dickens on the cross. Was there ever a more naked book of needs and fears? Cruel supplanting stepdads. Lovely mothers dead. Childhood sweethearts ravished. The impecunious making it in Melbourne. The evil ones all routed. The good all filled with love for one another. The hero forever devoted to a stained-glass window. Who needs Freud? Sometimes art works best without subtlety. Tear the heart out, that's the way to do it. An injunction telly faithfully obeyed, ignoring, for once, the siren calls of reinterpretation and relevance (as though the torn heart can ever need reinterpreting). What, no flash of period buttocks? No Peggotty with her stays undone? Barkis stays willin', notwithstanding. And we must make what we will of the man-rejected, man-rejecting Betsey Trotwood keeping company with a kindly piece of eunuchry going by the name of Mr Dick.

But the real coup of the production, coming when it did, was this: by doing Dickens plain and faithful, the BBC reminded us of what it was like to encounter Dickens the first time, recalling to our minds ourselves when we were young, suggestible and tearful. No small matter, this. To reacquaint yourself with yourself in a familiar book is up there with flying balloons with Mr Dick, as one of the sweets of existence. And tears remembered . . . but you don't need me to tell you that.

Tears remembered must have something to do with my emotionalism around darts. I was a handy player once; even carried my own arrows about my person in a sort of spectacle case made of Bakelite. Nowadays, darts are so slender you can keep a set behind your ear. But they were more like feathered javelins in my day, boohoo. Scrub what I've just said about being handy. I was a master. Sometimes I thought it was possible I had a natural genius for the game. Which made me feel bad on other people's behalf – those who did not have a natural genius for the game – for it seemed to me I was gifted in too many other areas to be gifted at darts as well. I recall an occasion in a pub in Stoke Newington when the weight of my giftedness troubled me as it must sometimes have troubled Albert Schweitzer or Eric Bristow. First of all I couldn't stop making witty remarks which drew every woman at the bar to my side; then I was unable to lose to anyone at pool, even playing with my wrong arm; then I won a chicken in a raffle. When the darts were brought out, I felt a shudder of anticipation run through the women, a frisson of fear through the men. 'Time to fail,' decency whispered in my ear.

An Australian woman I knew had become famous in our circle for losing her darts bottle after exchanging a lover who was a thrower for a lover who was not. As a matter of unconscious psychic solidarity, or maybe just guilt, she was now unable to get a dart to reach the board. No matter how vigorously she tried to launch it, the dart dropped from her fingers like Desdemona's handkerchief and landed flightless as my chicken at her feet. I would throw limp-wristedly, like her. But here's a wonderful thing: the less you try to hit the dartboard, the more you find the trebles. The long and short of it being that I couldn't miss. Every three darts, however faint-heartedly flung, however precariously they hung – *One hundred and eigh . . . ty!*

Not a pretty sound, I know. *One hundred and eigh . . . ty!* Not exactly 'Erbarm' dich mein, o Herre gott', which is what normally gets me blubbering at Christmas. But there is a music of the associations, as well as the other sort. I am only flesh and blood. You can't expect me to hear *one hundred and eigh . . . ty!* on Sky Sports and not go at the knees remembering when I was as indestructible as a god.

And that's not all either. For the truth is, associations apart, that while darts is not normally held to be an affective sport, affecting is precisely what it is. Affecting in itself, I mean, not on account of any circumambient Cardiff Arms Park emotionalism, or because previous darts players once perished in an air crash. It's the fact that fat men with bruised faces play it. It's the sight of all that bulk concentrated on a needle point, refined into the most fastidious artistry of the fingertips: dainty, discriminating, immaculate. Which is upsetting in the way that elephants contradicting their own natures, performing tricks of weightlessness in the circus ring, are upsetting.

Whatever It Is, I Don't Like It

Anything where it shouldn't be – a fat man squeezed into a double twenty, a Dick on Betsey Trotwood's lawn, a deity weeping on a cross, someone my age slumped in front of the telly – that's what's sad.

EVERYONE'S GONE TO THE MOON

Much disappointment in my house when Channel 4 pulled its scheduled documentary about Jonathan King last Monday. Much disappointment from me, anyway. I had a nicely themed week planned. The hidden menace of shyness. With articles appearing in the press telling us what a retiring lad Mohamed Atta had been, and how becomingly, as a teenager, Osama bin Laden had blushed, Jonathan King's reputed adolescent bashfulness was icing on the cake. Neat, huh? One destroys New York. One destroys the world. And one puts his hand down the pants of pop-crazed teenage boys. Never mind registers of paedophiles, what we need to be told is where every shy kid hangs out, so that we can stone him to death in good time.

Let's not beat about the bush. I consider the treatment of Jonathan King a scandal. Not just his sentence but our universal approval of it. I do not say he is innocent of the charges brought against him, nor do I say those charges have been trumped up: I say that the crimes of which he has been found guilty do not amount to a hill of beans. I'll remind you what they are – playing with the penises of fifteen-year-old boys and as a consequence, in the victims' subsequent accounts (subsequent sometimes meaning after an interval of thirty years), causing them to suffer emotional distress. Just pause a moment and think of the fifteen-year-old boys you know. Those who try to steal your car, and if they can't get that, your mobile phone; those who throw petrol bombs at one another on the streets of Northern Ireland, or heroise Lee Bowyer, or routinely pack a Stanley knife in their satchels and don't hesitate to use it; or simply those who lie about in their rooms with their trousers down round their ankles, snorting coke, staring at posters of Kylie and going blind. And now tell me what possible sexual or emotional damage you can do to any of them that hasn't already been done.

I have inhabited the mind of a fifteen-year-old. I remember its configuration well. (And I was one of the shy ones, not the brutes.) The mind of a fifteen-year-old boy is a sewer.

One sewer is not another. Had Jonathan King stopped me in a record shop, invited me into his Rolls-Royce and asked me my top ten he wouldn't have got very far. First of all I wouldn't have been in a record shop. Secondly I wouldn't have had a top ten. Thirdly I was on principle unimpressed by cars. A bit of a prig, I grant you, but that was my prerogative. Most important of all, I would have known that I didn't want him to put his hands down my pants. Another prerogative. I just happened to be born pathologically heterosexual. So if a woman the same age as King, let us say of comparable standing and let us even say of comparable looks, had shown comparable interest . . . ? Exactly – I'd have reeled off my top ten and had my hand down her pants long before she'd opened the door of the Roller.

And the emotional damage? She'd have got over it.

It's a problem, emotional damage. The robust, common-sensical part of our natures laughs the very idea to scorn. 'Bollocks!' we shout – or at least we do in my house – when the latest soldier or policeman puts in his claim for having been emotionally scarred ·in the course of soldiering or policing. But we secretly acknowledge, at the same time, that this might be a somewhat insensitive response. We can locate a bit of emotional distress suffered by ourselves, once we decide to put our minds to it. All's not well about any of our hearts.

In the end, the two positions are not incompatible. Life is trauma, let's admit that. Experience is hard, and we are soft, and everything knocks us about. That being the case, let's go back to a black eye as a measure of prosecutable harm, and chalk the rest down to reasonable wear and tear. Distress, too, is a part of life.

Do not, however, suppose that I am minimising the crime of paedophilia. I am a hanging man when it comes to sexual assault on small children. Hanging, drawing, quartering. Touch a child, and you should expect mankind to turn medieval on you. Tar, feathers, Stanley knives, the lot. But a fifteen-year-old boy – especially a fifteen-year-old boy who keeps coming back for more – is no small child. On that shaky continuum which joins the perversion we call paedophilia to the consensual bliss we call partnership, fiddling with the penises of fifteen-year-old boys is far advanced. It's not marriage, but it's heading that way.

Which is not to say I remotely understand why anyone should want to do it. Having shared gym changing rooms with thirty naked sewer-brained teenage boys at a time, I will go to the grave not seeing the appeal. If that were the charge – inexplicable bad taste in sexual matters – then I'd happily see Jonathan King in jail for life. Ditto inexplicable bad taste in music. Not that I hold 'Jump Up and Down and Wave Your Knickers in the Air' against him specifically. I'd see him banged up for having anything to do with the inanity which is pop, full stop.

But by having indulged boys only too willing to be indulged

in the folderols of fame and rhythmic simplicity, often with the connivance of celebrity-crazed parents, he has done nothing more culpable than contribute to the cultural lowness of the times.

GOOD FOR YOU, BAD FOR YOU

Remember moral certainty? My generation grew up with it. Onanism makes you blind, red wine makes you pissed, and a nicely knotted tie makes a good impression. Thereafter there wasn't an awful lot you needed to know. Look smart, stay sober and keep your hands off yourself and you'd live to a ripe old age with all your faculties intact and all your grandchildren around you.

I even wrote an essay on the subject for inclusion in the school magazine. 'The Clean Life' it was entitled and ran to three thousand words, which was one thousand words longer than the school magazine. But length wasn't the only reason they refused to run it. They didn't like the tone of my opposition to such socio-sexual reformers as Alice Bunker Stockham. More than that, they didn't know who Alice Bunker Stockham was.

'She advocated karezza,' I told the editor, who was also our English master.

'Don't be smart with me, Jacobson,' he said. 'A Japanese invented karezza.'

'That's karate,' I explained. 'A martial art. Whereas karezza is the practice of withholding ejaculation.'

For which he put me in detention.

On the face of it, a clean-living boy like me should have approved of Alice Bunker Stockham. A doctor and reformer, born in Chicago in the nineteenth century, she numbered Tolstoy among her friends, was instrumental in the spread of the teaching of home economics in American schools, crusaded for the sanctity of marriage and fidelity therein, was active in the saving of fallen women, and otherwise shared my views on alcohol, tobacco and promiscuity. But in this one regard were we divided: she encouraged masturbation, with the proviso that you stopped before you finished – a declined orgasm, in her view, being a step to higher spirituality, and a sort of rehearsal for the *coitus reservatus* you were going to practise when you took a wife. Though I had no views on the benefits of karezza within marriage – for marriage was the last thing on my mind in the third year – I did oppose it in its solitary form, believing that without ejaculation a man would not feel as disgusted with himself as he ought, and therefore would come at last to see masturbation in a rosy light, with no downside in depression and disgrace. You can't have a waste of spirit and an expense of shame – this was my point – unless you've spent or wasted something. In a word, I objected to her because at the final hurdle she was an enemy of moral certainty – onanism makes you blind, red wine makes you pissed, a nicely knotted tie makes a good impression, and all the rest of it.

Turns out now that it was all a lie anyway. Research published in the last month alone has reversed everything we were taught. It isn't masturbation that makes you blind, it's wearing a tie. Masturbation, it turns out, is good for you. Pleasure yourself two or three times an afternoon until you're fifty and there's a fair chance you won't get prostate cancer. There's also a fair chance you'll have lost the power of speech, broken both your wrists and developed a pendulous lip, but that's another matter. We're just talking prostates for the moment.

If it's any consolation, Alice Bunker Stockham was no less wrong than I was. Because it isn't the stroking that helps keeps you healthy, it isn't the self-love or the daydreaming or the broad-mindedness, no, it's the release of semen. Leave it in there and there's risk of carcinogenic effect on the prostatic ducts; flush it through and you're cooking with gas. So much for karezza. Ha!

But elsewhere in her philosophy Alice Bunker Stockham was definitely on to something. When she wasn't persuading men to keep their powder dry, and thus leading them on to an early death, she was lecturing against the corset, which she believed to be more culpable in the matter of 'deterioration of health and moral principle' than 'intoxicating drinks'. Forget the drinks. We now know that unless you're blotto every other evening your heart won't work. But her argument against corseteering matches the most recent findings on the tie. Overlacing is bad for us.

Researchers in New York have discovered that knotting your tie too tightly can lead to an increase in internal eye blood pressure in just a couple of minutes. And increases in internal eye blood pressure play a significant part in the development of glaucoma. Ergo, look too sharp and you might end up blind.

Who's to say where it will end? There is always something threatening to make us blind, and there is no guarantee that this time next year we won't be learning it's taking a summer holiday or going to the pub. Nor can we be sure, just because of what the latest researchers have been saying, that the old certainties won't have their day again. Can we really be so scientifically definite, for example, that it's the tie? What if we were to discover that men who have just masturbated are so concerned to appear clean the minute after, so want to make a good impression and remove all evidence and association of filth, and so need to punish themselves for their weakness, that they find their tightest tie and symbolically hang themselves in it? What if the rise in internal blood pressure is a red herring, a mere coincidence, and it was the *post factum* horror of ejaculation that caused the blindness after all?

And what if it isn't the ejaculation that helps the prostate, but the sense of outrage? Not semen that cleans out the cells lining the prostatic duct, but shame. Whoosh! That's self-disgusted of Tunbridge Wells with his channels clear for another month.

You win some and you lose some. There is no other intelligent position. In the meantime, when you next see someone in the gutter with his shirt torn to his navel, a bottle of red wine in one hand and his dick in the other, don't waste your sympathy on him. He's the healthy one.

ANYONE SPEAK ENGLISH?

Did I recently read, or did I just dream, of a surgeon halting an operation on the grounds that the theatre nurses lacked adequate English to understand his instructions? A fine thing, multiculturalism in action; necessary, too, when you have hospitals to staff and all your nationals are immobilised by dreams of being on *Big Brother*; but a scalpel is still a scalpel and not a box of matches. Did I also read that the surgeon in question was reprimanded for his action? No surprise there. Language is the last taboo. By decree of right thinking we have brought down the Tower of Babel, come to understand one another perfectly – and anybody who says otherwise is an alarm clock.

Xenophobic of me, I admit, to assume that the nurses in question must have come from foreign parts. And unpatriotic at the same time. Are we not capable of producing our own unintelligibility?

That I am not able to understand half the things that are said to me, particularly when I am on the phone to a helpline, or getting software assistance from somewhere in the Orkneys, or being handed from 'agent' to 'agent' at a call centre in Romsey, I have now come to accept as normal. It's my fault, I tell myself, for asking questions and then not bothering to listen to the answers. I am grown incurious. I am losing my hearing. It's my age. But recently the malfunction has started to kick in the other way as well; increasingly, people are not understanding a word I say to them.

Seasickness, for example. Is that too difficult? Seasickness pills. The chemist's assistant looks at me as I though I am a madman. She leans towards me, making a hearing trumpet of her face. Not a syllable does she speak. Maybe she guesses, correctly, that if she did form a word I'd be none the wiser. I make a little boat of my hand and send it bobbing on the ocean waves. 'Seasickness pills.'

'Ah, pill,' she says at last. Not in an entirely confident spirit. This might be a pharmacy but only a pedant would take that to mean that they sell pharmaceuticals.

'Yes,' I say, encouraging her. I was a teacher once and know how to leap on the back of dawning intelligence and make it gallop. 'Pill, yes, good, but specifically pill for seasickness.'

She's in trouble again, looking around for help. Soon shops are going to have to employ translators to mediate between people born after 1980 and people born before it. 'Scenic pill?' she tries. And for a moment I wonder whether there are such things and whether I should be buying them. A pill for improving your appreciation of scenery, would that be, or a pill for calming you down after you've been too moved by scenery – a sort of Stendhal syndrome prophylactic? Which reminds me that pills can be for or against and that all this might be my fault for not being sufficiently precise in the matter of which I want. What if the poor girl has been wondering why I want to *induce* seasickness?

'Sorry,' I say. 'It's *anti*-seasickness pills I'm after.' And to help her I make the little boat with my hands again, this time puffing up my cheeks and blowing a gale, then pressing my fingers to my temples and turning green.

'Oh, headache,' she says.

'No, seasick,' I shout, though of course by now it's something for a headache that I need.

Whereupon she gives up on me and goes to fetch the pharmacist. 'Seizing pills,' I hear her asking him. Which strike me as another good idea. Along with pulverising powders.

Since you will have deduced that I was going to sea you won't be surprised to learn I needed shoes to go to sea in. 'Does G mean broad-fitting?' I ask the boy in the shoe shop.

He turns a quarter of his face towards me. 'G?' he repeats. 'What's G?'

He has a faraway look, dreaming of being in the final of *Pop Idol*.

I show him the shoe and point out the letter G next to the shoe size. 'What does this mean?' I ask him.

He shrugs, puzzled by how it got there. 'Dunno,' he says.

'A letter with the size normally denotes the fitting,' I persist. 'I want to know if this is a broad fitting.'

He repeats the phrase as though he has never heard it before. 'Broad fi'in'?'

I point to my feet. 'Big feet,' I say, giving away more than I want to. 'Long, but also wide.'

He looks down at my feet and then back up at the shoes, struggling to make the connection. Then he starts to walk away.

'Is there a manager in this shop?' I call out.

The boy stops and gives me another of his quarter-turns. 'Yeah,' he says. 'Me.'

I've been out for two hours and this is the first word I've uttered that anybody has recognised. Manager. I make a mental note to try it more often.

After which I decide to console myself with a steak in a French restaurant in Charlotte Street. 'A T-bone,' I say.

The waitress stares at me. 'A T-bone,' I repeat. I could help her out by making a T with my fingers, but why should I? This is a steakhouse. T-bone is on the menu. And I am still in England, home of English, whatever nationality the restaurant. 'T-bone,' I say a third time, showing my teeth.

'Ah, you want D-bone!'

And then there's the problem with camomile tea. She has never heard of it. 'Camomeeel,' I say. Bingo. Ah, camo*meeel*! But if I can work out that my camomile is her camomeeel, why can't she work out that her camomeeel is my camomile? No quid pro quo, you see. That's why I am become a stranger in my own land, no one's trying. Scalpel, nurse.

FRIENDLY BANKING

I am being attacked by my own phone. Correction: I'm being attacked by my bank, but they're doing it through my phone. They ring me up and then ask me to identify myself.

'I'm who you rang,' I tell them.

'Yes, but how do we know that?'

'Because you rang me.'

'But what if it's not you? What if you're your son? Or your father?'

'It's a chance you take,' I tell them. 'How do I know, for example, that *you're* who you say *you* are?'

They want to know my date of birth and my mother's maiden name. At my age I am likely to have forgotten both. And anyway, since they ring me every day to ask me, there's a better chance that they'll know than that I will.

'Dostoevsky,' I say. 'I think my mother's maiden name was Dostoevsky. What's yours?'

The bank won't tell me its mother's maiden name. I have to trust the bank. Given that they've been taking my money for forty years, know my phone number, know my voice, know my credit details, know how pissed off I always am when they ring, you'd think that by now they'd trust me. The trouble is they don't know it is me. It might be my father or my son who's pissed off. I might be impersonating myself. I might even be my own burglar.

Actually, that's not right. It isn't me they say they don't know, they say it's my address. Yes, they write to me and ring me here, but that apparently isn't enough. They need further proof.

'Why do you need further proof?' I ask them. 'Further proof against what?'

'Terrorism.' Government regulations, post Osama bin Laden, say that banks must ascertain for absolutely certain that people live where they say they live, otherwise they could be terrorists laundering money. If Osama bin Laden is himself having trouble managing his funds at present, that's the reason – they aren't sure where he resides. And when they ring him to ask his mother's maiden name, he puts the phone down. Which, I suppose they'd argue, is proof the system's working.

Recently I suggested to the bank that if they wanted to be sure I lived where I said I live they should send someone round to check. Let him even interest me, if he wished, in the bank's latest offers and inducements. New cards, new borrowing arrangements, carpets, whatever. Good idea. John, he was called. Hi, John, welcome to my home. But it appeared that finding me here still wasn't conclusive proof. What if I was my son, sleeping over? What if I had just let myself in through a window? I showed him my photograph. 'Me,' I said. He wasn't convinced. If it was me, how come I was smiling?

What it turned out he needed was documentation. Paper not flesh. A bank statement, say, dated in the last three months. 'Hang on,' I said, 'are you telling me that if I show you a statement from your bank, addressed to me here where you don't believe I live and to which address you therefore have no business sending statements, all will be well? You will believe your own mail, even though you ring me every day because you're not convinced it's me you're sending it to?'

Yes, he said. That should be fine.

Figure that. Figure why I didn't tell him he was a moron and let him out through the window.

Even though it should be fine, he took a photocopy of the statement just in case. But then must have forgotten to show it to the relevant personages, because the new business he got me to agree to cannot be initiated on account of there being no proof I live where I say I live.

Yesterday I rang them before they could ring me. 'I was born on X,' I told them, 'my mother's maiden name is Y, and now I want the card you refuse to send me.'

Hilary. 'Hello, the adviser you are dealing with today is Hilary, how can I help you?'

'By sending me the card.'

She asked me not to be abusive.

'Just send me the fucking card, Hilary.'

Can't. Won't. No trace of me at my address.

Then how come John knew where to find me, Hilary?

She is barely comprehensible. Which might be because the call centre is in Manchester and not Calcutta. She seems to be using the word experience. 'I rely on it,' she tells me. By which I take her to mean that she is well versed in terrorists and money launderers and knows one when she talks to one. 'If you are relying on your experience,' I reply, 'it should tell you that I would never have been offered this card you won't send me unless someone had known where to find me to offer it me in the first place. Experience, Hilary – if you've got it, use it.'

She told me I misunderstood her. I laughed at that. Ha! In fact I laughed twice. Ha, ha! 'I think I understand you only too well, Hilary. You say you are experienced but you won't call on that experience to make a common-sense decision. The card, Hilary. The card!'

But I *had* misunderstood her. She hadn't said she was relying on her experience, she'd said she was relying on Experian – *an, an* – a credit-rating firm, evidently popular with banks. It was the spooks working for Experian who couldn't find me.

Imagine that, my own bank – with whom I've been dealing for forty years or more, which knows the details of my life more intimately than I do myself, my outgoings and my incomings, my birthdays, the entire history of my financial perturbations, my mother's maiden name, everything – my own bank is check- ing up on me with a credit-rating firm!

Kafka was right. They will come to our lodgings in frock coats and top hats and they will cut our throats. Though since they don't know who lives where there is always a chance they will cut the wrong person's.

O THE OPAL AND THE SAPPHIRE OF
THAT WANDERING WESTERN SEA

I have Cornish longings on me. Maybe something to do with those poor Greek flower-pickers reported rescued last week from the horticultural hell of Hayle. Or BBC2's *A Seaside Parish*, transmitted concurrently with its series about the National Trust. The Seaside Parish in question is Boscastle in north Cornwall, itself a National Trust village, in which, on and off, I spent twelve years of my life. What if still in chasmal beauty looms that wild weird western shore? Not my question, but Thomas Hardy's, Boscastle's presiding ghost, and part of the reason I stayed so long.

Funny the difference words make to a place. Though it has to be said that his were not just any words. Boscastle was where Hardy met his first wife, and it was to Boscastle he returned, long after she was dead, to mourn her, find her, discover whether the bitterness that overtook their marriage was written in it all along, or could be undone in memory. The greatest poems of regret ever written. And impossible to imagine the place without him once you've read them – an old man faltering forward, leaves around him falling, 'Wind oozing thin through the thorn from norward / And the woman calling.'

Whatever It Is, I Don't Like It

A local Hardy scholar called Kenneth Phelps wrote an affectionate book about Hardy's Boscastle connection – *The Wormwood Cup*. We sold it in a shop I helped to run, not a big seller, nothing like witches' brooms or badgers etched on Delabole slate, but there was a steady interest. Two or three times a week Kenneth Phelps would come into the shop to see how his book was doing. He kept a small supply in his backpack so that if stocks were low he could replenish them. I was setting out to be an author myself at the time and hoped I would never be reduced to carrying my books on my back. But there is no knowing what will befall an author. I am sorry now that I felt scornful of him. It is a wonderful thing to put your life into a single book, to think about its progress every day, and to be absorbed in its subject matter to the exclusion of all else. Years later I wrote to a distinguished biographer of Hardy, querying something in his book. He wrote back saying he would have loved to help, but frankly could barely remember anything about Hardy now. He had moved on to someone else's life. Kenneth Phelps was not like that. Day after day he retraced Hardy's steps, the scenes of those heartbreaking poems, up the cliff, down, till he was lonely, lost. The idea of forgetting Hardy or moving on to someone else was inconceivable to him.

I seem to remember we fell out over the National Trust. The trouble with people who love poetry is that they are liable to confuse it with the mawkishness of heritage. Myself, I found no contradiction in loving Hardy and hating the National Trust. The latter made life hell for those of us who hadn't come to Boscastle to retire. They ran the place like an army of occupation, and if any of us stood up to them they sued. Just how many membership fees paid over by peaceable, unlitigious, nature-loving ramblers and mug-buyers got spent on fees for QCs I dread to calculate.

We went to law with them ourselves once. Against the wishes

of the village, certainly against the wishes of the business community who kept the village alive, they wanted to close the harbour
approaches to traffic, so that they could prettify the walk outside
their own shop. That was how we read it anyway. In response to
which we organised a sit-in, preventing their vehicles from entering the contested area. DON'T TRUST THE TRUST, we
shouted. My slogan, I fancy. The novelist in embryo.

They won. They always win. They have all those membership
fees and profits from rare-species butterfly tea towels to win
with. But in the course of our quarrel I was vouchsafed a brief
but terrifying glimpse into their unexamined assumptions. 'If
you think we're going to allow the place to be trampled all
over,' the head of the whole shebang told me in a moment of
temper, 'just so that you people can sell brass candlesticks to –'
He didn't finish. 'To whom?' I asked him, ignoring the 'you
people'. I knew who the 'you people' were. 'To whom?'

He was a man of distinguished not to say military bearing, as
befits a senior officer of an occupying power. He was not afraid
to look me in the eye. 'The wrong people,' he spat out. And
perhaps I only imagine the horsewhip.

The wrong people. There it was in a nutshell. The wrong people
were coming to Cornwall in general, and to Boscastle in particular, buying brass candlesticks and wearing away the cliffs, and
he intended to stop them.

Well, the wrong people get everywhere. I can't pretend I
never felt that myself in the course of being elbowed into the
sea by the contents of a tenement block from Walsall, a many-
headed monster in jesters' hats and comedy Valkyrie pigtails,
which had blundered into a part of the world that did not have
slot machines and was unable to find its way out. But I was not
a charity. I was not in trust to the nation. I sold books about
Thomas Hardy – a wrong person if ever there was one – not
know-your-hedgerow serviettes. So remember that the next
time you're seduced into joining. It's not the National Trust

you'll be a member of, but the Trust for People of High Income, Supercilious Class and Maudlin Pastoral Aesthetic.

Hardy hated such idealisation of the countryside by those to whom it was a mere plaything. Real places indurate, and wound the heart. (Ask the traumatised Greek flower-pickers.) Hence Hardy's own fraught pilgrimage to Boscastle in remorseful old age. But the village would not yield him what he wanted, would not be in actuality what it had become in fantasy. Real places never do.

UNCONDITIONALITY AND MURDER

The letter killeth. I can see why there is urgency within the Muslim community to disown terrorism as a perversion of Islam as strictly understood. But therein lies a contradiction. For it is not difficult to show that adherence to the strictness of Islam, as indeed to the strictness of any religion, is the first step on a ladder which will take some to sanctity, but just as many, in the name of sanctity, to violence. Onward march the Christian soldiers, despite Christ's refusal of militarism. Though the Bible teaches Jews to love the stranger, there are some Jews who find justification in the Bible not only for despising strangers but for making strangers of them where they live. And in the name of Islam, such crimes have been committed as would make the angels weep.

Never mind that this is not what any of the great faiths have meant to teach. Belief itself is where the problem starts. Laced with the usual humanising laxities and compromises, belief can be an innocent affair. And a little of it, in a naughty world, can go a long way and do a fair amount of good. But once belief hardens into a dogma which allows no deviation – call it ortho-doxy or call it fundamentalism – the believer enters the terrain of derangement. Purity has its attractions, but only madmen live by it.

'Objection, evasion, cheerful mistrust, delight in mockery are signs of health,' said Nietzsche. 'Everything unconditional belongs to pathology.'

Freud intended a service to the Jewish people when he argued that Moses was an Egyptian. In one stroke he reminded us that neither our most significant prophet, nor the Judaism he taught, was pure. This is not against the spirit of what the Old Testament itself says of Moses – concealed in a crib of bulrushes and found by one of the Pharoah's daughters who brings him up lovingly as her own. A little bit of somewhere else, we are to understand, was necessary to make Moses who he was. The requisite genealogy, this, for all the great men of mythology who give their names to new civilisations or beliefs. They are abandoned to shepherds, they are raised by wolves, they are discovered by alien princesses with compassion in their hearts. It is as though the founding hero, in order to be worthy to lead his people, must first be mongrelised. Thus does the mythical history of mankind give the lie to all theories of national greatness based on racial homogeneity, and to all religions insisting theirs is the one and only truth.

Everything unconditional belongs to pathology. But we would be fools to suppose that the only pathology into which our home-grown terrorists were abducted was that of the mosque. Where were they educated into this? we beat our breasts and ask. From whom did ordinary and apparently amicable Muslim boys from Yorkshire acquire this ideology of hate?

Forgive the brutality of the answer. From us! No doubt it took an induction into unconditional theology to ignite them ultimately into violence. And no doubt men more experienced in the ways of terror primed their final resolution. But what we call their disaffection – that miasma of rage and bewilderment and misinformation without which this death cult could never have taken hold of them – is the staple diet of our own left-leaning news media, no more virulent than anything the educated middle classes have been expressing for years, the received wisdom of teachers, students and academics from one end of the country to the other. Iraq, Afghanistan, Israel, Kashmir, the Balkans – you name them – all proof of the corrupt Western world's greed, degeneracy and Islamophobia. No sooner did the bombs detonate than we were chanting the litany of our sins again. We had it coming. On the letter pages of every newspaper, the same. Our fault. Our fault. And if we think it is our fault, why shouldn't they?

Basic laws of human decency, Law One: you do not say we had it coming when it is someone else who dies. If you want to say we had it coming, say it when *you* die. You can accept guilt for yourself; you cannot accept it for another person.

Decency aside, the we-had-it-coming lobby are those who, like the pure religionists of hate, subscribe to a purist interpretation of events. It should be no surprise to us to learn that the suicide bombers were not from among the unlettered poor. These days we must worry a) when our children fall quiet and take to reading Holy Scripture, and b) when they go to university. Neither can now be recommended to the impressionable. Both inculcate the unconditional. Witness the historical illiteracy of those academics who nearly pulled off a boycott of Israeli universities a few months ago – determined to see only one side of a cruelly complex conflict – and remember those marches which academics and their charges could not wait to join, associating one cause about which there is to be no discussion with another, and where the faithful have been so catechised into conformity that to demur from a single atom of the rationale would be apostasy.

Afghanistan and Iraq are comparable only if you think every move the West makes is *ipso facto* satanical. And even the invasion of Iraq, however impetuous, brutal and misguided, was not inspired by wanton wickedness alone. As for Zionism, that mantra of universal loathing, it is an aspiration to a homeland not an ideology of hatred directed at Muslims. And if it doesn't look that way to Muslims, that's all the more reason why it shouldn't be depicted irresponsibly by us. We don't help Muslims by flattering them in their conviction of oppression. Muslim paranoia, about which as a Jew I must admit I know something, is not only brewed up on Muslim streets. We feed it with the theology of our self-disgust. Unconditional in our hatred of our own culture, we strengthen unconditionality in others. And when that many pathologies collide, it's no wonder there's a bang.

WHAT THINGS ARE FOR

We forget what things are for. A lifetime ago, it now seems, we woke to the first Labour government in what might as well have been a thousand years. Old rusted ideas, together with the men that bore them, were at a stroke removed. The sun shone and the very pavements gleamed like El Dorado. Bliss was it in that dawn to be alive. This morning I don't care a fig who we have elected. Disillusioned.

Shaming, that a man my age should still be subject to illusions in the first place. But I'd forgotten what things are for. Governments are for the management of public finances. Idealism, seriousness, magnanimity, civilised discourse, the intellectual wherewithal to tell a hawk from a handsaw – nothing to do with government, not any of it.

Last week, writing in the Sunday *Independent*, Janet Street-Porter made a similar mistake with Gilbert and George. She forgot what they are for. The occasion for her article was Tom Stoppard's speech to the Royal Academy in which he said most of the things we all know to be true about conceptual art but feel too weary or too uncertain – in some cases, too browbeaten and too frightened – to say ourselves. Janet Street-Porter wheeled Gilbert and George into the debate in order to discredit Stoppard. Had they ever met the playwright? she asked them. To which their joint answer – for they don't do anything by halves – was 'Well, years ago we did go to one of his plays, but we didn't last long – there were too many words. So we left.' The value of which testimony is zero, for the very reason that Gilbert and George don't exist to say intelligent things. Gilbert and George exist to bend over and show us their ageing scrotums and whatever else they've got down there in order that we shouldn't entertain too grand an idea of the meaning of life or the function of art.

They are, of course, entitled to their position.

Why Janet Street-Porter thinks Stoppard isn't entitled to his – as a playwright, having views on contemporary life is exactly what he's for – I am at a loss to understand. As a newspaper editor, aren't words what she is for? It is one thing to argue that Stoppard is wrong – which he isn't – it is quite another to attribute his attack to professional jealousy, in Janet Street-Porter's words, to 'a big fit of the sulks'. Hard to imagine what, in the way of genius or success, Tom Stoppard might have to sulk about. That apart, it is a sad state of affairs when a person cannot demur to a fad without his motives coming under suspicion. There is such a thing as intellectual disinterestedness, which is what we all are for.

Myself, I view Stoppard's intervention – to use an art word – as an important event. A little in advance of Stoppard's speech, Sir Nicholas Serota had made his usual prickly defence of the latest Turner shortlist – 'I don't feel any pressure to make it easier for ordinary people to understand.' Had any one of us innocently enquired what extraordinary powers were needed to understand a blob of Blu-tack, we would only have demonstrated our ignorance and proved Serota's point. Conceptual art is not the thing you see, it is the strategic placing of a reference in the history of a philosophical idea. Not for you to bother your little uneducated head about, sonny Jim. Enter Stoppard, bristling with philosophical credentials – too many of them, anyway, for Gilbert and George to penetrate. If ever there were a man who did not need to have difficult concepts explained to him, it is Stoppard. O joy, O bliss! Things will no doubt go on as before, but the argument that we don't like it only because we can't understand it is much weaker than it was.

Implied in Stoppard's criticism is a conviction of what art is for. 'The term artist isn't intelligible to me,' he said, 'if it doesn't entail making.' An extremely bold assertion, given how indurated, in the visual arts, the arguments against making are, and what a ninny you are thought to be if making is your bag. Janet Street-Porter questions 'the "craft" factor', but in fact craft has got nothing to do with it. Nor, when we speak of making, are we thinking of William Morris and the honest labour of the hands. A work not made is a work not under-gone, a process of discovery and change not submitted to, revelations not revealed. Every good writer and artist will tell you that the most productive days are those which begin in ignorance and confusion, the tunnel ahead black, and not an idea in your head. Strictly speaking, ideas are your enemy. Ideas are what you had before. Ideas are where you stand, not where you might end up. 'Never trust the artist, trust the tale,' D. H. Lawrence famously wrote, meaning that an achieved work is another thing entirely from anything the artist merely wanted it to be.

The conceptual artist reverses Lawrence's dictum, in effect saying, 'Never trust the art, trust the artist's intention.'

In art we get beyond ourselves; here is part of the reason we value it. Marooned in the sterility of his will – decree-ing this idea, giving orders for that – the conceptual artist fears the process of change and contradiction which is art's justification. Hence the inertness of his work when we stand before it – no trace anywhere of what else it might have been or any argument it might be having with itself. Mere insistence. Which isn't, as Stoppard reminded us, what art is for.

HOW TO UPSET A MILLIONAIRE

There is a programme on BBC2 which I watch out of the side of my face while I am doing other things – the way you observe bad behaviour in someone else's children, disapproving and yet gripped – whose premise is that we would all like to make a lot of money, but only a few of us know how. Making money in business, that is, not making money by being a celebrity or writing columns for national newspapers. As the child of small business people who never made a penny, but never thought it dishonourable to try, I have a soft spot for business. I have sold leather goods on a market stall in Cambridge, and helped a friend in Wales manufacture crimplene dresses for little girls to wear in religious processions – a foolproof enterprise had the Welsh not been Nonconformists who don't believe in religious processions – and managed a craft centre where none of the craftspeople wanted to demonstrate their craft, and assisted in the running of a tea garden in Cornwall, my assistance consisting of ferrying hot pasties each morning from Liskeard where they were baked to Boscastle where they were consumed, stopping on Bodmin Moor when the sun shone to admire the scenery, pat the wild ponies and consume a few myself. A few pasties, that is, not ponies. Much as I like to think of mine as a life of letters, it has been no less a life of trade. So that when all my friends became Marxists in the 1970s it fell to me to make the case for capital.

Funny thing, though – no matter how fervently I argue for business, I only really approve of businesses that fail. The minute I meet a businessman who has made money, the milk of kindness in me curdles, my heart contracts, and I turn into a 1970s Marxist. Hence the problem I have with this programme on BBC2, in which a bunch of self-pleased millionaires decide whether or not to invest in the projects of a bunch of would-be millionaires, most of whom, it's true, are verdant shmucks who couldn't sell a pasty to a Cornishman, but who are, nonetheless, entitled to be treated with civility. Yes, they're tongue-tied – but then they are meant to be tongue-tied – their no-brain business plan (except that they usually no more have a plan than they have a business) subjected to the heartless inquisition of capitalists who might own half the world's resources between them, but between them don't possess a pinch of politesse.

Why can't they just say no? No, thank you. We would like to oblige you and invest, but we cannot. We wish you every success with your scheme to manufacture kitchen appliances with broadband access built in, so that you can surf the Net while you are juicing carrots, but it's not for us, sorry. '*Sorry*', not 'I'm out, you moron!'

I know, I know. Good television. We must have good television. And what makes good television is people being objectionable. But the millionaires could always refuse to play along. Since they are already millionaires it is a question what they are doing on television, anyway. They don't exactly need the fee. Why, while we are on the subject, did Alan Sugar waste precious business time on *The Apprentice*, a money-or-your-life game show in which aspirants to his title of Least Charming Business Personality of the Millennium were encouraged to talk about themselves in clichés – 'I am the kind of person who won't take no for an answer' – only to be put into situations where they had to take no for an answer? We don't believe that it was only through a telly programme that Alan Sugar could find himself a new assistant. So why did he bother? Fame, was it? Not famous enough? Or did he feel it was of benefit to an already greedy society to demonstrate the efficacy of ruthlessness?

The millionaires I've been watching through the side of my face are similarly wedded to the fancy that there is something winning about brusqueness when it's built on cash. Come the revolution, of course, the money-braggarts will be the first to go. But there ain't gonna be no revolution – that's the confidence that explains their complacency. This is the system we unquestioningly live by; love us or lump it. Except – and here's the reason I keep half watching – that they are not in fact anything like as complacent as they would wish us to believe. No, there ain't gonna be no revolution; but the world does still contain people who weigh and judge things differently, for whom the amassing of wealth, whether they approve ethically of it or not, is a matter of supreme indifference. And just as a clove of garlic will emasculate a vampire, so does indifference upset the entire edifice of material achievement on which the *amour propre* of any millionaire gross enough to advertise his millions on television is perched.

There was an interesting example of this the other week, when a man who had invented a way of economising on water when you flush the lavatory irked all the millionaires, reducing one of them to near apoplexy. Sure, he was self-engrossed – inventors are supposed to be – though nothing like as self-engrossed as those questioning him. But that wasn't his offence. His offence was to admit he cared more about saving the planet than he cared about making his fortune. You could smell the garlic.

Whatever It Is, I Don't Like It

Remember those self-made johnnies you would encounter when you were young, who used to tell you they could buy you with their loose change, and who, if you really got up their noses, would say they valued their shit more than they valued you? It's possible I remember them so well because I was a stuck-up little bastard who went everywhere with a copy of *Women in Love* under my arm and an expression of disdain on my face, and so found them wherever I went. It was the otherwise-engagedness that did it. The assumption of interior superiority – just me and D. H. Lawrence, and you can keep your self-made millions. Such, anyway, was the effect the lavatory-cistern man had on our millionaires. How dared he look down on them! They could buy him with their loose change. Did he not know that it was they who made things possible, gave people work, and in the end, when they had eviscerated the planet (they didn't quite say that), would save it. Who did he think he was?

Good to know about the filthy rich, that their skin is as thin as beaten gold and money cannot buy them any thicker.

DYING LIKE A GENTLEMAN

Took in a stirring *Messiah* last week, the more solemn for being in a church and not the Albert Hall, and the more affecting for being intimate – a chamber choir of about forty rather than the massed thousands which impresarios believe the Hallelujah Chorus necessitates. The church was Christ Church, Spitalfields, newly restored to its original austere handsomeness – the sort of church in which you converse with God rather than prostrate yourself before Him, but in which you converse, nonetheless, with a proper regard for what is sacred. The choir was Concordia – amateur singers under professional direction, which is just the way you want it. Nobody looking bored with having to turn out and sing it for the hundredth time this Christmas, but none of that veins-in-the-neck parochial eagerness you get with the Nether Piddleton Philharmonia either.

It helps with an oratorio, I now realise, to sit near the front. Where you would otherwise doze off briefly, you are, if you can eyeball the soprano or the bass and be eyeballed back, not only duty-bound to stay alert, but too engaged to do otherwise, fascinated by the relation the voice bears to the person. Intimate's the thing. Find a small church, find a small choir, sit on the front row, and see if you can match the individual note to the individual choir member. I am not saying Handel has longueurs, but no work of art was ever fashioned that doesn't allow the mind to stray occasionally. And anyway, the singers – not to mention, in this instance, the solo trumpeter whose 'The trumpet shall sound' had us all clamouring to get into heaven – *are* the art.

I was so taken with Concordia, so grateful to them for keeping me musically on the edge of my seat and giving me a *Messiah* which didn't come alive only in the best bits, that I looked up their website when I got home, still humming 'All we like sheep have gone astray'. Go to Concordia's members' information and you want to join. All those directions mixing bus times with must-have music lists, the *Oxford Book of Tudor Anthems* and why it's a good idea to leave valuables at home or in the hotel safe; all those suggestions as to what, in the matter of clothing and jewellery, scarves, belts, etc., is or is not considered discreet; the surprising, not to say thrilling, exclamation mark that follows the instruction to the ladies to wear a 'Long black skirt or trousers (or short with black tights/stockings!)'. Black stockings, exclamation mark, ah, why was I never in a choir when I was young and looking to go astray?

Here is an injunction we might consider adding to the British Citizenship Test – join a choir! Failing which, turn up to a minimum of one performance of Handel's *Messiah* every Christmas. Vehemently refuse, as a matter of respect to yourself and to your new country, any adaptation of English culture to your susceptibilities. Wherever there is a 'more inclusive' or 'inoffensive' version of anything English on offer, turn your back on it, for whoever would suppose you will not at the very least be curious to see how the English pray, sing, worship, marry or remember the dead, insults you to your soul.

Increasingly, as the censors and maulers and butchers of our culture assume more power, it will be to art – if we can save it – that we turn in order to remember who we once were and what we once believed. I don't know whether there's a *Messiah* presently going the rounds which has been de-*Messiah*'d out of respect to people of 'all faiths and none' (as though any atheist would alter his atheism out of respect to a believer), but Concordia sang it Christian-Englishly intact. God knows, there's matter in the libretto to offend some of us if we choose to be offended. 'The people that walked in darkness,' for example – who would they be, then, as though we didn't know. True, the line originates in Isaiah, but the people that walked in darkness in this context are those who chose not to see the light of Christ. And you could fairly argue that once you've consigned a people to darkness you have begun a process which ends in not thinking of them as people at all.

But there you are: one faith, like one culture, like one nation, like one neighbourhood or one *banlieue* even, inevitably defines itself against another. Non-believers do the same. We have to be grown up about it. We none of us think anyone else can see what we can see. All we can do by way of escaping this circle of mutual disdain and fear is to note with interest how various are the ways others find of saying that we are as blind as we say they are. But let no one in his heart believe that he is free of the prejudice.

Art enacts the history of the culture that makes it. In the *Messiah*, written by a German with a taste for Italian melody, we hear something of how Christianity spiritualised the English and in turn how the English societised Christianity. A swapping of refinements without doubt, but sometimes a swapping of brutalities as well, for they too constitute a culture.

Handel is not the equal of Bach. The *St Matthew Passion* sounds profounder notes than the *Messiah*, the suffering is more inexplicable and desolate, the relation of man to God more mystical. In Bach, however grand the composition of the orchestra and choir, you hear the individual at prayer. By comparison, Handel's great work is ceremonial, a celebration of English fields and English public life. 'I did think I did see all Heaven before me, and the great God himself,' Handel said of the writing of the Hallelujah Chorus, but the God he saw was entirely eighteenth century, well mannered, decorous and amenable to reason. The English eighteenth-century way of belief, like the English eighteenth-century way of death, was nothing if not worldly. 'He died much like a gentleman,' my old teacher F. R. Leavis used to recite in illustration of the spirit in which a polite Augustan prepared to meet his maker, 'and went to heaven with a very good mien.' Though he was not recommending a return to Augustan decorum, I always had the feeling that that was how he hoped he would die himself – though I'm told he didn't – with a very good mien.

We celebrate something of this, anyway, whenever we perform Handel's *Messiah*, especially if we can find a Hawksmoor church to perform it in. As for the stockings exclamation mark, they too minister to that greater glory we call Englishness.

DEATH OF ALMA

And so Alma finally passed away, sweetly confused and listening to Perry Como. Nothing in her life became her like the leaving it. And flights of angels sing her to her rest.

I am not, on principle – though while I'm in mourning I'm damned if I can remember what that principle is – a watcher of *Coronation Street*, but there are those around me who are, so I somehow know what's happening. You can follow a good soap from another room. Like rich cooking, its ingredients stay in the air a long time, getting into curtains and penetrating walls. Out of respect to Alma, though, I sat and watched. I have always liked Alma. A fragility thing. She has the face of a woman doomed to die betimes, and thus she touches on a profound male dread. In the catalogue of women a man is bound to hurt, Alma is the one you know you will feel worst about. She seems to have no defences against all you are going to throw at her. And now she's gone forever. Dead as earth.

The actual moment of her passing I missed. Couldn't take it. But I held myself together tolerably well for the funeral. A humanist affair, mourners in T-shirts, overseen by a secular offi-ciant with a plain manner, much like someone selling you a mortgage, though with less gravitas. Ken, of course, delivered the address, and Audrey read the nation's best-loved poem, the one exhorting us not to stand at the dead man's grave and weep because he isn't there and doesn't sleep, but has become the thousand winds that blow and something or other on the snow.

In fact, since Alma was cremated, there was no grave to stand and weep at anyway. It's time someone did an ashes version.

I can't say I care for humanist funerals. Or for cremations, come to that. The two often go together, presumably because it's not so easy to be irreligiously matter-of-fact with the earth's forgetful jaw yawning black and empty at your feet. No discreet curtain. No electronic organ music. Just the disgrace of dirt and decay.

The last humanist cremation I attended in the flesh was my aunt's, a woman I had been close to and loved dearly as a boy but had not seen for many years. The not seeing was probably my fault, so you can add a pinch of guilt to whatever I say next. But what grieved me most about her funeral was how little provision it made for grief. We wept individually, of course, but the service itself, if you could call it a service, was sorrowless. Tasteful, that was the word for it; the extracts from humanist works well chosen, the music sweet, the demeanour of all participants impeccable. But it was hard to believe that anything much of animal moment was happening. Maybe it wasn't. Just one more dead person. Yes, she was someone to me and to her sister and to her husband, but who were any of us in the great scheme of things?

I know what I want from a funeral. I want desolation. Howl, howl. If it truly doesn't matter whom we burn or bury next – for we are but a mote in Creation's eye – then that is all the more terrible for the dead and all the more desolating for those of us left standing. The end of a life, if we believe a life has meaning, is a dreadful event. The end of a life, if we believe a life has no meaning, is a more dreadful event still. Twist it how you like, death is neither decorous nor rational nor humane.

Then, after the desolation, should come that something else we feel for in the dark. Not comfort, not consolation, not even the peace that passeth all understanding. Something more like grandeur. At last, if we have been allowed to feel the enormity of a single lost life, there may follow a conviction of the grandeur of all lives. But nothing follows if we don't first find words for the magnitude of our despair.

And for this you need the psalms and liturgies of the great religions. Never mind what you think of religion the rest of the time – to hell with consistency – if you're going to die big, you have to die rocked in a religious vocabulary. I don't want 'Ode to a Skylark' read over me, together with a snatch from Brahms's Clarinet Quintet and Humphrey Bogart saying play it again, Sam. I don't want to be lowered into the ground like a reluctant guest on *Desert Island Discs*, with my favourite book (other than Shakespeare) coming down after me. Leave me and my tastes out of it, I want the words of God.

There's a wonderful description, in Dickens's *Hard Times*, of the death of one who in life had barely been alive. 'The light that had always been feeble and dim behind the weak transparency, went out; and even Mrs Gradgrind, emerged from the shadow in which man walketh and disquieteth himself in vain, took upon her the dread solemnity of the sages and patriarchs.'

Faultless, that invocation of the King James Bible. For the language of the Authorised Version – before we ironed what was epic out of it to make it 'relevant' to a cloth-eared age – aggrandises every life at the moment of its extinction.

And now I remember what my objection to soap operas is. They shrink the space around us in life, deny us our dread solemnity in death, and send us to eternity in the arms of Perry Como.

SOME OF HIS BEST FRIENDS

Are some of your best friends Jewish? Tam Dalyell's are. He told us so last week. Defending himself against the 'preposterous' charge of anti-Semitism, he also informed us that he and his children had worked on a kibbutz, that he had holidayed in Israel – but then so had Asif Mohammed Hanif of Hounslow, albeit with explosives in his belt – and that on occasions he writes affectionate obituaries of Jews, though whether the Jews are dead before he writes them he doesn't tell us. Thus the Father of the House, knight of the mournful countenance, and champion of causes so lost they do not even know they are causes until he rides in to champion them – the man whom history not so much forgot as never noticed.

So why take umbrage? Why break a butterfly on a wheel? Well, a) because I feel like it, and b) because there is no folly so particular that it doesn't shed light on folly in general. Besides, by parading his prejudices as unwittingly as he has, by express-ing such genuine surprise that anyone should find his words exceptionable, Tam Dalyell exposes the unexamined assump-tions of his time and place.

What he has been saying, for those of you with your minds

elsewhere, is that Jews punch politically above their weight, exercise an undue and disproportionate influence. As an off-the-cuff remark, dropped from the lips of a foolish fond old man, we would probably let it pass, but Mr Dalyell has been trying this on for size, to whoever will listen, for some time now. Last year, for example, in an address to the Zayed Centre, an organisation 'established in fulfilment of the vision of his highness Sheikh Zayed bin Sultan Al Nahyan' – that vision having included one symposium denying the Holocaust and another validating the *Protocols of the Elders of Zion* – Dalyell told the assembled Arab delegates pretty much everything they wanted to hear about the criminality of Ariel Sharon, which is standard practice if you're going to accept that sort of an invitation, but didn't scruple either to let them into his pet theory on Jews and their overinfluence. Whether or not the following were his exact words it is hard to tell, but he undoubtedly allowed the assembly to deduce from what he did say that 'there were 400,000 Jews in Britain who enjoyed a very strong and stunning influence'.

As I wasn't there in person, but have only the Zayed Centre's own report to go on, I am not sure whether that was 'stunning' in the sense of Marilyn Monroe, or 'stunning' as in what you do to a mullet. But I guess the latter.

Moving on from that, as in his recent interview with *Vanity Fair*, Tam Dalyell identifies a 'cabal' of Jews, both in this country and in America, which is exercising undue influence over our Prime Minister. In the context of Jews and the power they are said to exert, we have, I think, wherever Mr Daylell holidays, to take the word 'cabal' as incendiary. It means to bring to mind a tradition of Jewish mysticism mistrusted by those who have always feared the hermetics of the Jews, at the same time evoking a suspiciousness of Jewish intrigue rooted in medieval ignorance and hatred. The Jew in cahoots with the devil to secure world domination blah blah. Now showing on Egyptian television.

I don't much care whether any of this makes Tam Dalyell an anti-Semite. There are already too many charges of racism flying about between the peoples of the world. Let's just agree the man has a problem with Jews.

Why else would advisers who happen to be Jewish (or look Jewish, or sound Jewish, or simply make Tam Dalyell 'think' Jewish) become, in his imagination, a 'cabal'? Why else would their influence, supposing it to exist, be a matter of such grave concern to him? And why else is he so watchful of the stain of Jewishness that he can detect its spread in ministers and advisers who, to the naked eye as it were, are barely Jewish at all? Peter Mandelson, for example, who lacks a Jewish mother and therefore cannot marry in an Orthodox synagogue, supposing he should want to; Jack Straw whose single Jewish grandparent makes him but a quadroon. Such genealogical curiosity has its antecedents in Nazi Germany, though I wouldn't dream of labelling Mr Dalyell, who holidays by the Dead Sea and writes obituaries of Jews, a Nazi. But the question has to be asked, why Jewish bloodlines compel his interest the way they do. And why he thinks that a distant Jewish relative leads ineluctably not only to undue influence, but undue influence in a sinister cause.

Enough Jews are prominent in their opposition to the policies of the present Israeli administration, let alone to the manner of their implementation, for Mr Dalyell to rest assured that wherever two or more of them are gathered there will not be an identity of pro-Israeli interest. They protest, they march, they offer themselves, some of them, as human shields against the Israeli army. But even were this not the case, even if it could be shown that every Jew in Creation backed Israel to the hilt, where would be the wrong? Must a Jew empty his pockets of all traces of his Jewishness before the influence police deem him to be clean?

Interesting how seamlessly Dalyell moves between Israel and

the Jews. It is not anti-Semitic to be critical of Israel, we are forever being told. Nor is it. Nor should it be. But if the two are not identical, why is Tam Dalyell so quick to make them so? To what end of peace and understanding did he, in the same breath, and to an Arab audience, conflate the wrongs of Ariel Sharon and the 400,000 'stunningly influential' Jews of Britain? Does he see Jew whenever he sees Israel? Does he see Israel whenever he sees Jew? More to the point, does he see criminality and then see Jew, or does he see a Jew and then see a criminality?

THE GRAVE QUESTION OF THE BICYCLE

Ever had your thunder stolen? An interesting expression, whether you have or not. I have always taken it to be an allusion to some event in Norse mythology, Thor furious with Loki for purloining his elemental powers. But the authorities say not, tracing it back to a remark made by the unsuccessful eighteenth-century dramatist John Dennis. Dennis, apparently, had invented a new way of simulating the sound of thunder for his latest unsuccessful play, *Appius and Virginia*, though what was wrong with the traditional sheet of aluminium I can't imagine. Soon after *Appius and Virginia* was taken off – the usual: bad reviews, no Americans in town, everybody only wanting to go to musicals – Dennis was watching a performance of *Macbeth* when he heard his thunder machine in operation. 'That is my thunder, by God,' he cried to whoever was sitting next to him. 'The villains will play my thunder, but not my play.'

'Shush!' said a person – probably Alexander Pope – in the row behind.

Believe that if you like. Myself, I'm always suspicious of anecdotes which rely on eighteenth-century writers saying 'By God'. And since they were all wits in those days, isn't it likely that the whole point of Dennis's explosion of displeasure was its witty, mock-heroic allusion to Loki's having purloined Thor's powers?

Anyway, all this by way of preface to the villains having stolen my thunder, by God, in the matter of cyclists. Everywhere you looked last week, commentators and critics fulminating against bicycles, the people who ride them, the odious expressions of self-righteousness on their faces, the even more odious clothes they wear to mow down the innocent, and their all-round humanitarian and aesthetical offence. The justification for this explosion of bile was the publication, or the leaked publication, of a European Commission document arguing that motorists were *ipso facto* responsible for whatever befell the cyclist. You ride a bike, you go up to a motorist, you punch him on the nose, he pays you damages. That's the gist of it. So it's not altogether surprising that every crypto-cyclophobe in the country should suddenly come roaring out of the closet. But some of us, regardless of any EU document, have been steadily and tirelessly arguing against the bicycle for years, with little expectation of agreement or reward. Is not a cyclist responsible for the barrel-load of grief in my novel *Who's Sorry Now?* And will I not still be here, gentle reader, a foot soldier in an unfashionable cause, quietly pushing for the death penalty for cyclists, when all these sensationalist johnny-come-latelys – or should that be johnnies-come-lately? – have moved on to excoriating mothers with pushchairs or toddlers on three-wheelers?

Whatever comes of the EU document – and much of the speculation is no doubt fantastical (higher insurance premiums, the death of the car, the closure of our highways, civil war, etc., etc.) – it only enunciates a principle which is already tacitly accepted by the high-minded everywhere, to wit the blamelessness, whatever the circumstances, of whichever person is currently perceived by liberal society to be the underdog. 'Whoever is responsible,' the document says, 'cyclists usually suffer more.'

Here, in a nutshell, the ethos of our times – the more shocking for the flagrancy with which it owns up to itself. 'Whoever is responsible . . .' Like a rocker switch of blame, or worse, a shrug of jurisprudential incuriosity. He who suffers more is the innocent party by simple virtue of his suffering. Slight is right. As for any causal connections between the sufferer's sufferings and his actions, forget them. The question of responsibility is now off the table.

It is by this logic that a person who fills his face with hamburgers feels entitled to sue the hamburger. Just as it is through fear of this logic that the playing of conkers in school playgrounds is now under threat, unless all parties sign a legal disclaimer before any conkering gets under way, indemnifying the headmaster, the school, the local education authority and the horse-chestnut tree.

To more deadly effect, it is by this logic that we read half the conflicts in our world, exonerating the suffering however much the suffering are at fault, thereby fetishising victimhood and contributing to its murderous cult.

But, to return to the graver question of bicycles, if it is the case that suffering outweighs responsibility, and that the weaker form of transport can never be deemed to be a danger to the stronger, must that not put the pedestrian, to mix the metaphor, in the box seat? Cyclist punches motorist, motorist to blame. Ergo, pedestrian punches cyclist, cyclist to blame. Do you not see what possibilities have thus opened up for us, the strollers, the loiterers, the idlers, we children of Baudelaire, lovers of city clouds and crowds, wallowers in the universal ecstasy of everything except cyclists? Nothing now to stop us striking back. Here he comes, in his colours of hateful complacency, shouting 'Ding, ding!' as he shoots the lights, or 'Out of my way!', or more often something far more foul. So now here we come, too, with our umbrella handles out or our mugs of piping coffee or our Uzi semi-automatic mini sub-machine guns at the ready, and if we are lucky enough to unseat the brute, can we not plead our deeper level of suffering, 'whoever was responsible'?

Such violence of emotion may surprise cyclists who think their only enemy is the motorist. But just as they feel threatened by the car, so do we feel hectored by the bike. See the car as venomously racist and the cyclist as sanctimoniously anti-racist, if that will help. One doesn't want to die under the wheels of either if one can avoid it. But for most people, living in unexceptional circumstances, the sanctimonious present the greater nuisance. Get hit by a car and you probably won't live to tell the tale. Get hit by a bike and there's a fair chance you'll make it to your feet. The trouble is, it's the bike which keeps stealing the motor car's thunder.

BLUNKETT IN LOVE

The burning question is why it takes a year or a cheque to get a visa when you are not lucky enough to know someone who knows someone who knows a Home Secretary. Why doesn't it take nineteen days, whoever you are? Why must everything that proceeds from the dark heart of officialdom demoralise us? Are we not of the same human family? There's a backlog, they say. Try that on with your tax or VAT return. 'Sorry, no can do for a year, I have a backlog.'

Myself, I won't give a monkey's if it does turn out that Blunkett assisted his lover's nanny. Indeed, I'll be disappointed in him if it turns out that he didn't. Isn't this what we are supposed to do if we can – lend a hand? Isn't it something the great religions of the world enjoin upon us? Help a friend in need? It would be better if he helped us all, gave the birch and then the boot to every spitefully slumberous official at the Home Office, I agree, but a start's a start. In the meantime, of those preparing to take a stand on principle, is there one who's never done a favour for a chum, never dropped a word into an ear, never shared a chauffeur for an hour, never put a lover on a spouse's ticket? God help him, in that case.

They occur in Shakespeare from time to time, the whited ones, the Angelos for whom the letter of the law is sacrosanct, and they are always revealed to be morally despicable at the last. We like a man who has a little give in him ethically. In fact we more than like him, we know that his is the only true path to virtue.

But these, anyway, are trifles light as air in a drama which grows more tragic by the day. Love is love. I know the expectation: men in high office are meant to keep their heads, however much in love they are; but as in principle so in passion, it's flexibility that makes a man fit to govern, whether what he's governing is his country or himself. Flexibility, not laxity. *Blunkett in Love* would be a good title for a light comedy of indiscretion, but what's been striking about this amour as the details of it have unfolded, and in so far as we are possessed (and entitled to be possessed) of the truth, is how little of lightness or laxity there has been in it. Forget that romping boy Boris who is cursed with looking like someone out of the *Beano* even though, for all we know to the contrary, his heart is breaking. Blunkett weighs in much heavier. For good and ill, he has always been a forbidding and astringent politician, strict in his pronouncements, rugged and even rough in battle. Not a man you would tangle with lightly. And clearly not a man you would fall in love with lightly either.

Reports in the sewer press suggest that Kimberly Quinn grew frightened of him towards the end of their relationship, pulled back from the intensity of his attentions. Cruel if correct, since there could never have been a moment when intensity was not what was on offer. By all accounts she was a vivacious socialite – Kimberly Fortier when Blunkett met her – and you can hear in the contrasting poetry of their names something of what must originally have drawn them to each other: the international effervescence of a Kimberly Fortier, the northern asperity of a David Blunkett. Think *Wuthering Heights* – 'My

love for Blunkett resembles the eternal rocks beneath . . .' Think
Blunkett hammering in the Yorkshire night at Kimberly's closed
window.

And then there was, there is, the blindness. The moment this
story broke I found myself reaching for a sentence I half remembered from Nabokov's sadistic fable *Laughter in the Dark*. Going
looking for it, even as Blunkett himself was talking about 'dark'
forces being out to get him, felt like a grim descent into an
unaccustomed seriousness. The sentence itself, describing the
effects of a sudden blindness, tells of precisely this descent. 'The
impenetrable black shroud in which Albinus now lived infused
an element of austerity and even of nobility into his thoughts
and feelings.' Though that offers to delineate the blind man's
inner world, it gestures the more at the effect of blindness on
those outside it. Our sense – the sense of the seeing – that there
attaches to unseeing a dignity we do not customarily possess.
Blindness solemnises the air around, and commands, whatever
the dangers of special pleading, our reverence. It recalls us to the
gravity of things. Not for nothing does mythology give the
blind unusual powers of prophecy and wisdom.

That Blunkett would not thank us for our exceptional attention, I have not the slightest doubt. But we must own to what
we feel. I recall hearing a radio programme some years ago
about a blind woman, Judy Taylor, recapturing her sight. It is of
no relevance that the producer of that programme is the person
with whom I now live, except for the fact that when she
recounts the making of it an austerity attaches to her too, as
though it is an effect that can be passed on by association. Judy
Taylor was at pains to deny any specialness, but everything she
said about sight – how previously she felt that people were
'looking in on her', how now she felt that she could take the
husband she had never seen 'captive' with her eyes – brought to
mind ideas of invasiveness and power, of sensual trepidation and
exchange, that we do not normally consider. By virtue of what

she knew of blindness, and now of sight, she restored a sense of tremulous gravity to activities – to love especially – about which we otherwise galumph.

David Blunkett no more lost his heart for our edification than for our entertainment, but in an age of triviality it is good for us, however terrible it is for them, to regain a glimpse of something epic in our emotions.

PORN FOR ROYALS

So am I the only man in London whose baby Princess Diana did not want to have? Like one of Bateman's misfits I cower before the finger of derision – The Man Who Didn't Get The Call. A shame. I think I could have interested her in the criticism of F. R. Leavis. It might have been the saving of her. For myself, at any rate, I swallow the indignity and try looking on the bright side. At least she would not have been sending her butler off to buy my son pornography.

Ignore that last remark. I am pretending to a pudeur I do not feel. In fact my first response, on reading that one of Paul Burrell's duties was bringing home *Men Only* and the like for William, had more of surprise in it than horror. I'd always imagined that royals had their own pornography. Well-bred girls in unzipped jodhpurs falling off polo ponies. Debs curtsying in rubber wellingtons and tiaras and nothing else. And the Palace was surely full to bursting with photographs of bare-breasted Tongans and Tanganyikans, snapped by Philip on royal tours.

The point about pornography is that even at its most fantastical it must approximate to what's familiar. Readers' wives must look like readers' wives. So where would be the point in our future king getting off on commoners disporting themselves commonly? All that inelegance of limb. All that bad skin.

Unless that was Diana's plan, the people's princess peddling the people's filth to democratise the monarchy and bring it down.

No wonder they had to get rid of her.

As for the morality of it, parent to child, I am not sure. At one level it showed great emotional maturity. Not every mother is able to accept the sink of iniquity which is her son. Great consideration, too, since she understood that William couldn't be popping into WH Smith himself every time the fires of his young manhood needed stoking. And tact. She didn't involve herself, but got the butler to do it, man to man.

She seemed to learn from what she saw, Diana. And she was better placed than most women to observe how sexual reticence in the boy breeds catatonia in the man. In a trance, they seemed, those guardsmen of hers. Unawakened, like so many sleeping beauties. So in her own way she was a pioneer of mental health among the aristocracy.

But there was one aspect of the mental life of boys and men she didn't understand. The imperative to be furtive. Only think of what William missed out on by having Burrell deliver him his daily fix on the crested breakfast tray, along with the boiled eggs and soldiers, the Coco Pops, and the malted milk. No listening to the libido as it shapes its promptings, no mustering of the forces of resistance, no argument between the Jekyll and the Hyde of one's sexual nature, which argument Jekyll will always lose, but only after the libido has flooded the whole system with those chemicals to which we give the simple name of desire, but which in fact also encompass self-loathing and self-destruction and insanity. Merely to accede mentally, merely to acknowledge that you will shortly do what you know you should not do, and scarf your face, and flee the house, and scour the streets for familiar faces to avoid, and push open the door of the newsagent whose bell rings louder than the plague bell

– Bring out your dead! Bring out your dead! – merely to be thus embarked, reader, on the ethical maybe-I-will, maybe-I-won't of porno purchase, all this Diana denied her boys.

And then the scrutiny. The newsagent eyeballing you, you eyeballing the newsagent. And the other customers, fellow ethical maybe-I-willers perhaps, people of weak character like yourself, who therefore know your secret (and it is no consolation whatsoever that you in turn know theirs, for your shame is unique and indivisible) and who therefore resent you because they know how long you are going to take before you actually approach the shelf you're blocking, how long you'll be pretending it's *Yachting News* or *Macworld* you're interested in, until your hand accidentally knocks *Bestiality for Boys* off the top shelf and you think, oh well, in that case, since it's found me, and I won't be yachting this weekend anyway and I don't own a Mac, oh well, all right, why not – always provided the newsagent has a padded bag with steel locks to pop it into, though not so unobtrusively as to be obtrusive, just casually, like burying a dead body, but without a priest, while looking at you and yet not looking at you, and having regard to your complete indifference to change, although it's true that the expenditure is part of the illogicality, part of the reason you do it, because it's all to prove you are somehow engaged in hostilities against your own best interests.

As for getting the stuff home, it's the identical procedure only in reverse, though you must add the fact of your parents being awake now – for the above was of course a dawn raid, while ordinary humanity slept – which immediate logistical difficulty is nothing compared to the long-term problems associated with storage. Do not ever, reader, discount storage. Once porno enters a boy's bedroom we are in Edgar Allan Poe territory, where the bloody truth will always out, where dismembered corpses announce their whereabouts to the suspicious, and lewd material beats louder, no matter where you conceal it, than a torn-out heart.

And it is degradation on such a scale that I would wish Diana to have gifted her sons? Yes, absolutely. For it is in this forge of demoralisation that our characters are hammered out. What tolerance of the weakness of others we finally possess, we owe to this. What sense of our own ridiculousness, and what affection we bear to women, in pursuit of whose distorted image we have shamed ourselves so contemptibly. Thus does mortification make a man of us at last.

Poor William, missing out on that.

LIKE-MINDEDNESS

There's a moment of stillness that follows every triumph, when the history and meaning of the conflict are weighed in the balance and victory is felt to be no less bitter, no less futile even, than defeat. There is, perhaps, a reason in nature for this philosophic disappointment. Pity may be born of it. Or it may commemorate the hour when barbaric man learned finally to desist from savagery, heaven peeping through the blanket of the dark to cry 'Hold, hold!' For it could be that that's all that ever stops us, our own dissatisfaction with bloodlust and revenge. 'My rage is gone,' observes Aufidius, having delivered Coriolanus to the mob, 'And I am struck with sorrow.'

A bit late for that, old sport; but then again, without the futility which accompanies remorse, how could nature ever clean the slate? I have always thought this to be the only adequate explanation of post-coital tristesse, that sudden and profound disillusionment with the means of production without which there'd be no end to the pounding of the male machine. Though I accept that that might just be masculinist wishful-thinking.

Such a moment of muted regret followed, for me at least, the final public demolition last week of David Irving's murderous scaffold of denial. Down it crashed, every beam and board and girder of it. Not a rack left behind. And I'm with those who think there aren't enough cheers in Christendom to celebrate its annihilation. But after annihilation, that cold wind of wondering. Not remorse – don't misconceive me: never has a remorseless dismantling of one man's reputation been more justified. And not pity: it is hard to imagine an instance in which pity could be more wasted, however true it is that any broken piece of humanity is a broken piece of us. In the completeness with which he has been refuted, though, in the comprehensiveness of his defeat and the comprehensive vindication of his conquerors, is there not the sort of too-muchness that makes all go cold about our hearts, because we know that meaning is forever eluding us and only in equilibrium do we find our part in the harmony of things?

The still, sad music of humanity and all that. Don't knock it in a harsh and grating world. What Wordsworth was angling for in that famous phrase was the 'sense sublime of something far more deeply interfused'. A pregnant verb, in this context, 'interfused'. Something mixed or permeated with something else. And while we may want to argue, in the heat of battle, that truth is never more itself than when it is not interfused with David Irving, isn't it just as important to remember that truth is not truth unless it is permeated with everything, including that which on the face of it may seem to be truth's deadliest foe.

A decisive no to all neo-Nazi revisionism, but no as well to letting the Holocaust set as incontestable as stone. How will we adequately understand what it was, how it came about, what it goes on being in men's minds, unless we are forever asking questions of it? Irving cannot by any perversion of meaning be turned into a champion of the enquiring intelligence because his historical methodology, vis-à-vis the Holocaust at least, terminates enquiry, because his interpretation of what constitutes proof is ignorant and slanted, because he is insensitive to testimony, and because his mind has closed. Good riddance to him in the particular, but in the general we are the poorer for every disagreement not voiced, every dispute not pursued. It is not only history that will seal over if we let it; all around us, every day, we see the triumph of like-mindedness, and like-mindedness is scarcely to be distinguished from closed-mindedness, even among those who would be astonished to hear themselves called bigots.

Take, for example, if you don't mind stepping down from ill will to bad taste, the capitulation of British film judges to that pleasant but unexceptional film, *American Beauty*. Nowhere can you have a better illustration of the truism – and if it wasn't a truism before, it should be now – that just because a lot of people agree about something, it doesn't mean they're right.

Of course *American Beauty* carried everything before it in America. The self-flattering title alone was worth half an Oscar. And the other half was in the bag by virtue of the film's cunning cantilevered uplift. All for the best, give or take, in the best of all possible Americas. But English judges are meant to be less susceptible to the sprinkling of stardust. Where was *Happiness*, the movie that truly took the lid off happy families? Or *Topsy-Turvy*, which did *Beauty* all ends up both as tragedy and comedy, laying hold of life and therefore loving it more as a consequence?

In the end, what's important is not that the British Academy got it wrong – right will never be watertight, anyway – but that it was unable to think for itself. The moral infection of seasonal like-mindedness had laid it low.

Uniformity kills. And uniformity is the price we pay whenever an argument is comprehensively lost. I almost wish Irving had acquitted himself better, though he could have done that only by being a better historian, in which event he would not have denied the Holocaust. As it is, I'm left wondering how it helps to have the field of conflict silent, and heaven hushed beneath its blanket, when we know that God Himself has always needed the devil to contend with.

MIND YOUR OWN BUSINESS

Watching the last episode of Peter Ackroyd's television series on Charles Dickens last week, I came over all queer suddenly with a thought. Not the thought that in the course of his researches into Dickens Mr Ackroyd had grown (I speak merely of appearance) to resemble someone only Dickens could have created – I had that thought the week before – but the thought that maybe we have no business being quite so curious about Dickens's or any other artist's personal life, and that historians of illustrious persons' privacy ought not to indulge or even excite that curiosity to the degree they do.

That the work's the thing, and the life a mere accidental irrelevance, is one of those truisms old-fashioned academics of my sort were wont to iterate in the days before intertextuality came along, refusing to see the work for the trees, and eventually finding the trees more interesting. There was a time we would have called such a position philistinism, but we chose instead to call it theory.

Taking the critic Sainte-Beuve to task for his attachment to the methodologies of history and biography – knowing everything about the writer as necessary preparation for knowing what he wrote – the novelist Milan Kundera observes that Sainte-Beuve 'thereby managed not to recognise any of the great writers of his time – not Balzac, nor Stendhal, nor Baudelaire'.

'By studying their lives,' Kundera goes on, 'he inevitably missed their work.' Since Kundera throws into the pot what Proust had to say on the subject as well, I will help myself likewise. 'A book is a product of a *self other* than the self we manifest in our habits, in our social life, in our vices . . . the writer's true self is manifested in his books *alone*.'

Thus, while perfectly understandable at the level of gossip and idle curiosity, the impulse to unravel a work in an attempt to discover the circumstances that occasioned it – to find the truth behind the fiction – is necessarily inimical to art.

I have no such complaint against Peter Ackroyd's telly series. Telly must do what telly does. And while the base metal out of which Dickens's great novels were made was of necessity Ackroyd's subject, he never failed to marvel over the transformation. Indeed, what made me go over all queer in that last episode was more humanitarian than aesthetical, not so much the Sainte-Beuve in Peter Ackroyd as the Miss Marple – in particular the sight of him excitedly going through old ledgers proving not only that Dickens was living secretly with the actress Ellen Ternan, but that he was doing so, because he was desperate not to be discovered, under a sequence of assumed names. What the writer has gone to great lengths to hide, let the biographer go to even greater lengths to uncover! Not on account of any sin against Dickens the novelist did that suddenly strike me as callous, but on account of the trespass against him as a man.

We do, of course, take it for granted now that the wishes of the living, let alone the dead, confer no obligation on us when we scent a scandal. This being the case, what some dead writer wanted is bound to cut no ice. Did not Max Brod, faced with Kafka's dying instructions that 'all this, without exception, is to be burned', refuse to commit 'the incendiary act' his friend demanded of him, and is not the world a richer place as a consequence? They know not what they ask, that is our justification. We know better what will serve their memory.

A person's squeamishness dies with him – that's our assumption. Dickens did not want to be found out, for reasons of local delicacy which no longer apply. Those he did not want to hurt are dead. The morality he wished to be seen to live by has changed. Therefore there remains no reason why the facts he chose to conceal should stay concealed. More than that, applying the model of political chicanery, we believe it is in the public good that everything should come to light. We have a right to know.

But do we? Dickens has not been shown, despite the zealousness of historians and biographers, to have whispered state secrets into the ear of a Prussian spy. So what end is served by our right to know? Not any understanding of the art, we have established that. And why should our right to know enjoy paramountcy over Dickens's right to insist we don't? Who are we to deny his wishes or to quarrel with the ideal of dignity by which he tried to live? Who are we to assert that shame does not live on beyond the grave? The heart must have its secrets, D. H. Lawrence said.

And now it's the turn of the other – not D. H. but T. E. Lawrence. Nice, for his shade, to be reminded whenever his name crops up (forgive the 'crop') of the scars across his buttocks, maybe administered, maybe not, by a Turk hell-bent on rape. Having experienced and even courted notoriety, Lawrence chose to live the second part of his life in obscurity. When a 'film merchant called Korda' proposed a biopic, he did what few of us would do today, and said no.

So what to make of the sensational news that during the time he was serving in the RAF under the name first of Aircraftman J. H. Ross, then as T. E. Shaw, he paid a Mrs Bryant of Newark

two of the three shillings he earned a week? A closet heterosexual after all, was he? Or just an indiscriminate masochist, not
fussy who did the flogging – a glistening Ottoman on a kilim in
a tent in Wadi Safra, or a powdered married lady strapped for
cash (sorry about the 'strapped') on the doormat of a two-up
two-down semi in Newark?

Secrets of the human heart? Let the dead fret about the dead,
the living don't give a damn.

THE EGOTISM OF THE TERRORIST

There's a moment in one's attempt to understand the mind of a terrorist, or, if you prefer, freedom fighter, secessionist, let's just say any active member of any armed resistance movement, when one's imagination falters. More than falters, fails. No matter how hard you try, no matter how conscientiously you clear your mind of the clutter of prejudice and partisanship, you cannot make the next step to comprehension. Intellectually, the experience is like walking into a door you hadn't seen was there. One moment you're proceeding, however gingerly and distastefully, the next you're on your back and everything is darkness.

The moment I'm talking about, of course, is when the terrorist or freedom fighter straps on his or her belt of exploding nails and boards the bus crowded with strangers, or kneels to hack off the head of a hostage – in the latest instance a Nepalese cook, but it could have been anybody – or promises, for even a promise can be an act of violence beyond our understanding, that 'For every one of us you kill, we will wipe out fifty children'.

Yes, yes, I know that when you have a cause to further there are no innocents. The stranger is your enemy if he happens to be sojourning in the wrong place; and if your enemy's child is his vulnerability then you must strike him there. This is no time for softness. The other party drops its bombs on children and you must fight fire with fire.

Such reasoning I can grasp. And you may say that if I can grasp the reasoning I must be able to grasp the deed wherein reason is converted into action. But I cannot. God withholds the hand of Abraham in the moment of his sacrificing Isaac. Of the many meanings of that story, one is that a line can be drawn between intention and fulfilment. There is a chance, even in the final instant, for anger to relent, for a different decision to be made, for consciousness of the sacredness of another life to strike you, no matter how sacred the cause in which you meant to take it.

That's the door I keep walking into – the otherness of the other person. How are you able to convince yourself, in the moment of the deed, that whatever grievance has been visited upon you, you are justified in visiting upon someone else? Must there not be a flash of illumination in that arc of the knife which God prevented Abraham from completing, not only of the mysterious inviolability of a life that isn't yours to take, but of the supreme egotism of your reasoning? Hold your weapon and think about it. Something terrible has been done to you. Let's not argue the toss about how terrible, whether you had it coming, whether you've misread history, etc. Let's grant you your outrage and even your despair. Something terrible has been done to you. Agreed, agreed, agreed. What must follow from that? That something terrible must be meted out in return? Why? Who are you to measure outrage against outrage? Who are you to say that your suffering is to have a higher value placed on it than someone else's? In that split second when you are eyeball to eyeball with the divine equivalence of human souls, might it not be logical of you to conclude – never mind compassionate, forget compassion – might it not dawn on you with the light of reason that there is no righting your sense of wrong, not by you, not ever by you, because you above all people cannot be the judge of it, because resistance, retaliation, revenge – give it what name you like – cannot ever be anything but a privileging, that is to say a sentimentalisation, of yourself?

That's a lot of reasoning, and perhaps reasoning never stilled any hand raised in murderous intent. But there is a distillation of reason that is meant to come to our aid at such a moment, a sudden impulse if not of beneficence then at least of self-disgust, whose very purpose is to turn us back from action. And before the idea of a person in whom such a distillation of reason is absent, my imagination fails.

To explain a blood-thirst we cannot otherwise get our heads round we point to religion. Indeed, the bloodthirsty often point to religion for us. Acknowledging responsibility for the behead-ing of the Nepalese cooks and cleaners, the Army of Ansar al-Sunna invoked their deity. 'We have carried out the sentence of God against twelve Nepalis who came from their country to fight the Muslims and to serve the Jews and the Christians . . . Believing in Buddha as their God.' Where one person's God restrains Abraham, another's spurs him on. And it's a giddy roundabout we jump on when we try to sort peaceful Gods from bloody ones.

Myself, I'm not sure I blame religion for busying itself with political resistance as much as I blame political resistance for enlisting God. Look for a universally fetishised figure and it is the freedom fighter not the priest. Cradle a child in the ideol-ogy of resistance and you will make him go where our imaginations cannot. Resistance is what closes the mind to reason. The assumption of a wrong, and the assumption that it is divine to fight it. Divine, today, to the tune of fifty children's lives for that of every fighter. And divine, tomorrow, by virtue of calculations we cannot yet begin to make.

Of course, if we see capitulation as the only alternative to resistance, there's no argument. We shoot traitors as a matter of course, and our heroes, whatever else we believe, are those who fight, hang on, resist with the last drop of their blood and that of whoever else happens to be to hand.

Don't ask me where between craven capitulation and blind resistance we should pitch our tent. But after the events of last week, with warriors in their own cause making the earth fit for no one, my hero is the man who says shit happens, and walks away.

YOU CANNOT HAVE A MARGIN UNLESS
YOU HAVE A CENTRE

So it's been decreed – the Commission for Racial Equality has spoken – multiculturalism is no more. *Requiescat in pace.* Except that to die you must have once known life, and for that you need a heart and brain. Multiculturalism had neither. It was always a word in search of a definition. A flag acknowledged by no country. Which you could argue was precisely its point. We waved it to say goodbye to the idea of country altogether. By this we stand: we stand for nothing.

We have said it often in this column – you cannot congratulate everybody on contributing equally to the family while you're also proclaiming there *is* no family. You cannot rejoice at what is happening on the margins if you have no centre. And loving everybody else is not a virtue but a pathology when you cannot love yourself.

Of the various nationalisms Orwell identified as incident to the British intelligentsia, the most germane to our times is what he called 'Negative Nationalism', a sub-branch of which he further identified as 'Anglophobia'. 'Within the intelligentsia,' he wrote, 'a derisive and mildly hostile attitude towards Britain is more or less compulsory . . . In foreign politics many intellectuals follow the principle that any faction backed by Britain must be in the wrong.' 'Notes on Nationalism' was published in 1945, but its characterisation of the Anglophobes has not dated. Perhaps 'mildly hostile' should be changed to 'virulent to the point of hysteria', otherwise the charge stands. To be a member of the liberal British intelligentsia in matters bearing on national identity is to be in need of a psychologist.

What did Daddy do to us that we should hate him with such vehemence? How did we come to feel so worthless in ourselves? Were we not applauded adequately for the productions of our bowels? Did the attention accorded to our siblings shape the shame that crippled us and made us liberal intellectuals in the first place?

And don't tell me this is cheap psychology. Of course it's cheap psychology. But that's our fault for succumbing to a cheap distemper.

It's possible, sick or not, that we could have bumbled along in this manner, disliking our own culture while marvelling at everybody else's, so long as everybody else kept marvelling at ours in return. Historians will one day note that what kept us proudly British for decades was the enthusiasm, not to say the gratitude, for things British shown by generations of immigrants. We might not have cared much for what we had, but they liked it well enough. A good argument for immigration, would you not agree? – that it is a means of importing patriotism. Or at least *was*. Things are not now as they were. Hence the about-face by the Commission for Racial Equality. Now the children of those who arrived with love in their hearts for us dislike us every bit as much as we dislike ourselves. What is more, our lack of self-esteem is adduced as one of the justifications for their contempt. We don't like us, therefore they don't like us – boom!

So it's back to Shakespeare and Dickens. That should settle things down. Always supposing, that is, that we can find someone who remembers who Shakespeare and Dickens were. Maybe we should try persuading immigrants newly arrived on these sceptred shores to teach us what they know about English literature. My own suspicion is that it will be more than we do.

But already the Commission for Racial Equality is under attack from the usual suspects, not for naivety but for promoting racism. Racism, it would seem, is a one-way street. If they blow us up there must be reasons in our society for their disaffection. If we teach them Shakespeare we are racist bigots. To these absurdities has the concept of multiculturalism reduced us.

In fact, it is not remotely racist to insist that citizenship entails a quid pro quo of obligation. Indeed, it is racist to argue otherwise. Racist to be indifferent to the culture which houses you. Racist to despise it. Racist not to accept that the act of incoming imposes an ongoing respect even when you cannot manage fealty or devotion.

There used to be a photograph on our mantelpiece of my grandfather and my great-grandfather in army uniform. Their gaiters struck me as particularly splendid, as did the bullet hole my grandfather used to show me, a neat little aperture below his knee, through which I could see the light of day. When people say go back to your own country, my parents told me, remind them that we fought and were wounded for this country in two world wars. As it happened, nobody ever did tell me to go back to my own country, partly, I suspect, because they didn't have a clue which country that was. But we were always afraid they might, and anxious to show that whichever hell-hole we had fled from, we now called England home. For which stroke of tremendous luck we gave a little prayer of thanks each night.

True, some among our parents found it hard to forgive us when we married 'out', making it hard for us in turn ever to forgive them. But no one says it is a simple business retaining the essentials of your culture when you are a minority. Myself, I hate an over-anglicised Jew, who changes his name from Levy to Baron de Vere

Leamington-Lysart and feels at home in the Athenaeum. But I am no keener on the Jew who thinks he should resemble a rhapsodic Polish tinker of the eighteenth century.

Get it right, boys. A little of this, a little of that. Don't apologise for yourself, but be discreet. Honour those who moved over and made space for you, irrespective of their unwillingness to honour themselves. Be curious. It is as odious to care only for your own culture as it is to care only for other people's. And remember that the racist in the equation might just be you.

GOD AND BLOKES

Much struck by the sadness of my sex this week. Poor George Best's hollowed cheeks the abiding image, an old man before his time, the eyes bearing more disappointment than one could bear to look at, not angry, not surprised even, just apologetic in their forlornness. Saying sorry to whom? Us? His family? The gods who showered him with gifts? Himself? How to be, how not to be, a man. Haven't seen it yet, but the film *The Libertine* depicts an even briefer life of what Dr Johnson called 'drunken gaiety and gross sensuality'. The libertine in question being John Wilmot, second Earl of Rochester, who died at thirty-three, having, again in Johnson's words, 'blazed out his youth and health in lavish voluptuousness'.

Well, who's to say? A blaze is better than a fizzle, maybe. Or maybe not.

I fancied a life of blazing rakishness myself when I was thirteen but lacked the application. And was probably too sentimental about myself. Sentimental men fall in love too readily to make it as voluptuaries. Whether you're falling in love with anyone in particular or just the vision of yourself saved by women who understand you better than you understand yourself is a question

I leave to professional psychologists. But both sexes collude in
this. Charlotte Brontë gives her Rochester – no accidental name-
sake – a second chance, redeeming him through fire and rewarding
him at last with the devotion of that dirty-minded minx, Jane
Eyre.

And Best was not short of women wanting to do the same.

So glamorous, these abbreviated lives, I'm not sure the women
(or the surgeons) do anyone any service by prolonging them. It
could be that Best would have been better, for his reputation's
sake at least, to have gone out in a blaze much earlier. A point I
decided against putting to the Scottish painter Peter Howson at
the opening of his new show at Flowers East the other day.
Howson, too, nearly drank and drugged himself to death, until
religion found him. A woman, a religion: same difference when
it comes to being saved. In the middle eighties Howson was one
of the hottest painters around – a real painter not a conceptual-
ist, a shouter not an ironist, producing great masculinist murals
of working-class vitality, Renaissance muscularity made phan-
tasmagorical and transposed to Glasgow. Then the drink, the
drugs and what he candidly describes in his catalogue interview
with Steven Berkoff as the 'debilitating and soul-destroying'
addictions of 'pornography and lust'.

Rejuvenated, cleaned up, but no less muscularist for being
found by God, Howson now transposes his gnarled heroic
Glaswegian faces back into Renaissance narrative. But because
I'm on male-sadness watch this week, I find myself drawn less
to the dramatic central figures of the damned who dominate his
new paintings, and more to those on the periphery, men hidden
in the crowd, free of the sway of the artist's grand intention,
anxious, otherwise absorbed, pausing, wondering, confused . . .
How to be, how not to be, a man.

Or, to put that question in another form, 'How many roads
must a man walk down / Before you call him a man?' Forgive the
second invocation of Bob Dylan in as many months, but it was

going to see him at the Birmingham Arena last weekend that started me noticing the sad transience of my sex in the first place. There's an example, if you like, of someone who might be said to have outstayed his welcome. Every time we thought he'd blazed himself out, there he was, rediscovered and newborn, now as a rocker, now as a Zionist, now as a Christian, and now as someone who plays a keyboard in a blues band and turns his back – I mean literally turns his back – on his audience. Not that I have strong attitudes to Dylan's metamorphoses. You have to have been more interested in him than I was in the first place to care what he has become. The fans, though. Explain them to me – the fans. The tens of thousands of men my age as rapt as groupies, rushing to the stage to get a close look at their hero regardless of who they push out of the way and whose view they block, because nothing else matters, nothing else *is* except Bob and his music. Men! These are men I am describing!!

You acquire a measure of tolerance with maturity. That young girls must be allowed to scream and rend their clothing when they see a boy fingering his crotch to repetitive music I now accept. In the past I would argue that it wasn't considered necessary for girls to behave like that in Jane Austen's day, but someone was always at hand to point out to me that the absence of such release was precisely the reason Jane Austen's heroines fainted whenever the sun came out. So now I understand that a passage of psychotic self-subjection to such mass-hysterical impudicity as would make the second Earl of Rochester blush is not only perfectly acceptable in a girl child but actually facilitates her progression to that condition of wisdom and propriety we expect of our wives and mothers. But to see grown men – men not only my age but who looked and dressed like me, men in beards and with sad eyes for God's sake – clawing at the air, lost to themselves, all but prostrate before a scrawny arthritic guy who is bored with his own songs and doesn't even fiddle with his penis – this I found shocking.

After the show I met an accountant who had been to see Dylan earlier in the week in Nottingham and was planning to see him again a few days later in Brixton. 'It's a passion,' he told me, though he owed me no explanation. 'Other men have football.'

'Yes,' I said, 'but they don't go to watch the same game every week.'

His face shone. I recognised the refulgence. God. 'Dylan is never the same,' he told me.

Well, he was an accountant. But they couldn't *all* have been accountants. So what excuse did the rest of them have – the irrational ecstatic devotees who turned the Birmingham Arena into a sort of church? I mean no disrespect to the music. Were Dylan, Keats and Schubert rolled into one there could be no justification for such extravagance of appreciation. A man is but a man. And men at their peril worship men.

What's to be done about us? We don't know what to do – blaze long, blaze briefly, or warm our hands at someone else's fire. Where, as Besty used to joke, with a champagne glass in his hand and women lolling on his bed, did it all go wrong?

THOU SHALT NOT KNOW WHAT ONE IS TALKING ABOUT

Dawkins has been done already, and we like to think that what's done stays done. There is intellectual justification, sometimes, for breaking a butterfly on a wheel, but to break it twice is sadism. Which said, Dawkins's rewriting of the Ten Commandments in his latest blind foray into theology, *The God Delusion*, cannot be allowed to pass without remark.

We will take just one Commandment. The Seventh. 'Thou shalt not commit adultery.' Leaving aside the retributive consequences if you do commit adultery – the small print, as it were – the Seventh is a Commandment that has a lot going for it. It is unambiguous. It is sonorous. It tells you, should you be thinking of taking up adultery but feel in need of further guidance, everything you ought to know – DON'T!

Unlike several of the other Commandments, such as remembering the Sabbath day to keep it holy, and not taking the name of the Lord thy God in vain, it has gone on finding resonance with human experience in most parts of the world and throughout centuries of fluctuating faith. Of course it hasn't stopped us committing adultery; but we rarely – swinging, dogging and daisy-chaining notwithstanding – believe we are unequivocally right in our adulterousness. We pause on its threshold and think twice before we enter. And even when our last compunctions capitulate before a seemingly irresistible force, that is seldom the end of it. A Commandment can have a retrospective urgency. I committed adultery but I should not have done. Or, I committed adultery and in the same circumstances would commit adultery again, but I acknowledge the misery and havoc I have caused.

Actions have their consequences, that too is what a Commandment teaches. And in those consequences we need not, if we do not care to, see the unsmiling face of God. Let a man be the most confirmed atheist who ever held a chair in the Public Understanding of Science, he will still know the anguish of adultery if he is its victim, or the alternating joys and woes if he is its instigator, unless he is without feeling altogether. God, it seems to me, need hardly enter into it. Paolo and Francesca, the adulterous lovers whom Dante comes upon in the fifth canto of the *Inferno*, entwined in an embrace of eternal weeping, are in a hell of their own making, not God's.

'*Amor condusse noi ad una morte*,' Francesca tells the poet – 'Love led us to one death.' Forever together – that is the consequence of their adultery; not a finger coming out of angry clouds, but their consummation itself, repeated and repeated and repeated. Not only is this not a story of divine retribution, it is not a morality tale either. Adulterous loves works out its logic, that is all there is to say. And before the sadness of it, Dante falls, '*come corpo morto cade*' – 'as a dead body falls'.

A solemn business, then, adultery. As is all fornication, no matter what the circumstances. Eroticism has a terrible potential for tragedy. We take it lightly at our peril.

So what is Professor Dawkins's take on these exhilarations and sorrows, their todays, tomorrows and eternities? What is his alternative Seventh Commandment, emptied of the interferences of a non-existent God? Reader, believe me when I say I have not made up the words I am about to quote. And do not think me callous: what follows is not my doing or my fault.

Here then – and you can always look away if you can't bear it – is 'Thou shalt not commit adultery' in Dawkinsese. 'Enjoy your own sex life (so long as it damages nobody else) and leave others to enjoy theirs in private whatever their inclinations, which are none of your business.'

As a reader, I look for one thing above all others in a writer, whether that writer is a poet, a novelist, or a scientist on a polemical errand. I look for language with deep roots. The better the writer, the deeper into the soil of thought and imagination does his language seem to reach. The poorer the writer, the more scattered on the surface, as though pulled out and discarded long ago, are his words.

This is not simply a matter of aesthetics. When Nietzsche – no lover of God himself – finds in the Old Testament 'men, things and speeches of so grand a style that Greek and Indian literature have nothing to set beside it', he is not admiring mere expression. 'One stands in reverence and trembling,' he goes on, 'before these remnants of what man once was.'

What is revealed in the grandeur of the writing is the grandeur of man's conception of his being. We don't have to like it or approve it, we just tremble. As we tremble before that dread injunction, brought down from a burning mountain – 'Thou shalt not commit adultery.'

Words strike us as commonplace when the thoughts they express are commonplace. Or when they are inadequate to the complexities of the subject. 'Enjoy your own sex life' might pass muster as an expression of easy-going liberalism in the company of unexacting friends, but as a guide to behaviour it dishonours us. It assumes there's nothing to us.

Do not mistake me. I am no more censorious of other people's inclinations or their acting on them than is the Professor. Indeed, the more outlandish their inclinations the better, I say.

So it is not in the name of divine prohibition or prudery that I diss Dawkins. His Seventh Commandment is feeble not because there is no God in it but because there is no human in it. The man writes as though he has never lived.

And never read, come to that. Would 'Enjoy your own sex life' (so long as no one gets hurt, naturally) have been helpful advice to Madame Bovary, who if anything enjoyed it too much when she could get it? Was an enjoyable 'sex life' all that stood between Anna Karenina and happiness? Is it true that our actions have neither value nor repercussion in themselves, but acquire them only by the harm we do or don't do to others? Does sex resist all philosophic and ethical enquiry beyond the requirement to have fun but practise damage limitation?

'Thou shalt not commit adultery' is a Commandment most of us will disobey. But it shakes us to the core. There is reverence and trembling in it. 'Enjoy your sex life' makes sex sound like a good breakfast. A thing necessary to our well-being but uncomplicated and soon forgotten, like Dawkins-man himself.

It is not God that Dawkins cannot find, it is us.

ALIDA VALLI AND THE EROTICISM OF
THE RAINCOAT

The death of the Italian actress Alida Valli, obituarised in this newspaper last week, compels me to confront a long-dormant preoccupation, if you will allow that a preoccupation need not be a constant burden to the conscious mind. There is something my soul appears to have been busy with, let's leave it at that, and the name Alida Valli has awakened it. That something is rainwear.

Alida Valli, for those who can take rainwear or leave it, played the part of Anna Schmidt, lover of Harry Lime, in the film *The Third Man*, directed by Carol Reed and written by Graham Greene. She did not, in that film, have a lot to do – by and large Graham Greene's women don't have a lot to do – though what she did no one who saw it could forget. Essentially she had to look empty of feeling or passion. It was from Alida Valli's portrayal of a woman empty of feeling and passion that I formed my earliest impression – my mother and my grandmother aside – of woman in general.

That this was not unconnected with Anna Schmidt's being Czech, having to survive the Russian quarter of an edgy post-war Vienna, and being the lover of Harry Lime who lived in shadows and only ever showed his face when he could be certain there would be no light on it, I understood. Even at the early age I saw the film I grasped its cold-war cold-heart politics. But I nonetheless believed it depicted something eternal – allow me to say eternally irresistible – about women: they were disillusioned and unhappy, and they never looked better than when disillusioned and unhappy in a raincoat.

If it did depict something eternal there is a question to be asked, I accept, as to why women, at least as represented by film stars, are unable to look that way now. Tailoring is one explanation. The youth cult is another. You cannot be disillusioned and unhappy when you're dressed in a rah-rah skirt. But I suspect the real answer to the question lies in aerobics. The whole point of Alida Valli in *The Third Man* is that she has no zip. Get women bouncing about and that's their desolation shot.

Though Alida Valli, as we have said, does not have a lot to do but look beautifully unhappy in a raincoat, it is not for nothing that she is given the film's final say, that's if you can have a say without saying anything. I will let Tom Vallance, Valli's obituarist for the *Independent*, describe that famous finale. 'After Lime's funeral, Anna is seen in the distance walking towards the camera down a long lane in the cemetery. [The long lane in the cemetery of my soul, reader.] Waiting to one side is Lime's former friend Holly who has fallen in love with her. [As of course had I.] Her face emotionless, Anna continues walking straight past him with no acknowledgement as, to the accompaniment of Anton Karas's zither music, the film ends.'

That a zither never failed to play in my head every time I fell in love thereafter, I ascribe to the power of that scene.

But something is missing from Tom Vallance's description. The raincoat. How, in his otherwise attentively detailed account, can he leave out the most salient detail of all – Alida Valli walking towards the camera and then past it into a loveless future in a *raincoat*?

Whatever It Is, I Don't Like It

So puzzled have I been by this omission these last few days, yet so unwilling am I to see the film again, for fear it will not stand up to memory, or that someone has airbrushed Alida Valli's raincoat and put her in jeans and trainers, or worse, left the raincoat but made her wear something under it – for surely we were always to understand that she was naked beneath that raincoat, that having to go without hope had reduced her to actual no less than spiritual nudity, that desolation in a lovely woman expresses itself in a raincoat and nothing else – so fearful of the distorting hands of censorship and time was I, in short, that I consulted an Internet site called, succinctly, Rainwear Films.

As Rainwear Films is specifically for those with a 'rainwear interest' I did not intend lingering long in it. It is one thing to like an unhappy woman in a raincoat, it is another to have a 'rainwear interest'. I did, however, expect the site to yield what I was looking for. But guess what? Though it mentions Lana Turner in 'yellow storm gear', Pier Angeli 'inside a period trenchcoat', Anita Ekberg in 'translucent plastic', Sophia Loren in 'British style rainwear', Suzy Parker in a 'Burberry', Greta Garbo in an 'oilskin slicker', Joan Crawford in a 'wet, shiny cape', Myrna Loy in a 'white rubber', Virginia Bruce in a 'typical 1940s cut semi-transparent knee-length hooded mackintosh', and countless more, there is not a word of Alida Valli in *The Third Man*. It is only when I come upon reference to *Les Yeux Sans Visage*, a film about a surgeon who transplants faces, and whose leather-coated assistant Alida Valli plays – in one scene dragging a dead girl, nude in a man's mackintosh, across rough terrain – that I wonder whether my unconscious has been transplanting raincoats unbeknown to me.

I am not aware of seeing *Les Yeux Sans Visage* but men my age are not aware of most things. Could it be that in *The Third Man* Alida Valli is simply wearing a coat full stop, and I have, so to speak, undressed and transposed her into a belted skin-grazing raincoat for reasons my psyche alone can understand?

Alida Valli and the Eroticism of the Raincoat

It wouldn't surprise me. We misremember and misplace what we read and see routinely. Because art is collaborative, our engagement with it is a species of interference. We cannot read or watch anything without new creating it. There is no reason to get excited about this process as a contemporary phenomenon, the way Mark Thompson, Director General of the BBC, did in a speech last week, frothing about the new audience that 'doesn't want to just sit there but to take part, debate, create, communicate, share'. Portals, platforms, interactivity – these are just punch-drunk terms for what we've been doing since we sat in circles and moved characters from the *Iliad* to the *Odyssey*. You make the programmes, Mr Thompson, our imaginations will do the rest. All your techno brave-new-world-speak, confusing matter with mere medium, is hooey. You can dress up your unculturedness in all the jargon of electronic opportunity you like – we know when someone is naked under their rainwear.

DOTT AND SYMPATHY

Been feeling very sorry for my sex again this week, what with one thing and another. Rooney, Prescott, Clarke, Dott, even Zacarias Moussaoui denied the satisfaction of being executed by his enemies and having to face his own angry company for the rest of his life instead. It isn't easy being a bloke.

It was Dott who started me off. It's possible not every reader of this column knows who Dott is. Only some of us sat up until the early hours of Monday or was it Tuesday morning watching Dott grind out the World Snooker Championships. Seems a lifetime ago now. The year dot. And that's why I am sorry for him, having the name Dott when a dot is exactly what he looks like. Wee Dott they call him in his native Scotland where all the snookers players come from who do not come from Wales, and he is truly the weest of men. I gave up watching snooker on television four or five years ago precisely because of Dott. His name, his wan appearance, his fragile self-esteem, the way he barked like a seal before every pot, blowing chalk from his cue tip – my life was ebbing away and there I sat in the familiar telly-snooker stupor for hours on end, watching a dot. Enough. And then last week I got hooked on him again. Don't ask me

·why it's him I'm sorry for. He's just become World Snooker Champion. The person I should be sorry for is me, staying up to will him on, counting every frame, the attention of my soul concentrated on a dot.

And while I'm worrying for the dot my mother-in-law is fretting over Rooney's metatarsal. She rang me the morning after the dot's triumph to say she believed Rooney would be well advised to abandon all efforts to get fit for this World Cup and to conserve his strength for the next. She had broken a metatarsal herself a few years earlier and knew that the best cure was rest. 'But the nation wasn't hanging on your fitness,' I reminded her. She didn't see the relevance of that. 'Never mind the nation,' she said, 'it's the poor boy I'm sorry for.'

Me too. Poor Dott. Poor Rooney. Poor Charles Clarke even. I know, I know, but there's something about Clarke's face that has always appealed to me – that look as of a very rare breed of sheep, conscious, as rare breeds are often conscious, of the burden of their rarity, and of course lonely because no other sheep anywhere looks like them. And what has he done wrong anyway? Allowed a few criminals who shouldn't be here to disappear into the community, when it was only a few weeks ago that we were accusing him of not allowing a few criminals who shouldn't be here to disappear into the community.

Did I read that one of the prisoners who has been let back into the community to reoffend was not sent home to Somalia because Somalia was not considered safe? Is that possible? Though I'm sorry for anyone who has to bear the burden of being a bloke, I am not so sorry for a Somalian thug that I think we have a moral obligation to protect him from his own.

'I call that the fanaticism of sympathy,' says Will Ladislaw in George Eliot's *Middlemarch*. He is talking about Dorothea's inability to enjoy anything she feels others are excluded from. But he could be referring to our concern for the welfare of impenitent foreign criminals when we return them to the bosom of their culture. Myself, I see something shapely in their having to fear back home (assuming that they in honesty fear anything) the very violence they inflicted on us. Is that not the beauty of deportation when the deportee is a rapist and a murderer and the country to which we return him is similarly inclined – that we expose him to the brutality of values he recognises as his own? Is that not *just*?

Which brings me to John Prescott, or rather to John Prescott's mistress Tracey Temple for whom I am invited on all sides to feel sympathy. Not enough my heart bleeds for Dott and Rooney, I am now – though her metatarsal is, as far as I know, undamaged and no one, by way of comment on her stature, calls her Tiny Tracey – required to bleed for her as well. She has, in the words of Labour MP Geraldine Smith, been 'taken advantage of'. *Droit de seigneur* and all that. A boorish, fat old Labour goat reached out his podgy fingers and what they groped for, Wee Tracey in her toothy, cream-skinned innocence had no option but to give. 'She was poor but she was 'onest . . .'

Remind the outraged that she is a professional woman in her forties who chose to work for a boss by all accounts notorious for his lechery, who looked willing enough, in the photographs for which she plentifully posed, to be seen canoodling and otherwise galumphing with him – an equal party in whatever you want to call it, a modern liberated woman exercising her right to fornicate where and with whom or what she pleases – and they think you're advocating harassment in the workplace.

It is poor sociology to suppose no woman in a subordinate position ever chased her boss or saw securing him as a step up the ladder to her own preferment. And it is poor psychology to read sex only as a story of the strong taking advantage of the weak; or to think that because a man is not Orlando Bloom, or even Graeme Dott come to that, a woman will surrender to him only under duress and with the lights out. Not all women like to roll around with uncouth men, but some do.

Dott and Sympathy

Poor Prescott – there, you've heard it! Two words you never thought you'd see conjoined. Poor and Prescott. We employ him to be an incorrigible Old Labour sort of chap but when he gets embroiled in an incorrigible Old Labour sort of escapade – a bit of groping but also, let there be no mistake, a bit of being groped – we suddenly stop seeing the joke. What's he to do – turn New Labour overnight?

But yes, I am sorry for Tracey Temple too. I'm sorry for everybody. It isn't easy being a bloke and it isn't easy not being a bloke. You can't control your fate either way. That's the lesson of snooker: it's all to do with how the balls lie.

IT DON'T MEAN A THING IF IT AIN'T
GOT THAT SWING

A brief disquisition on rhythm this week. Occasioned by the wonderful Kandinsky exhibition at Tate Modern, by Harold Pinter's appearance on *Late Night Review* in conversation with the Scottish Person (it's bad luck, in my business, to speak her name), and of course by England's progress in the World Cup. Rhythm explains the success or failure of them all.

In Kandinsky, more than in any other painter, I think, you see why abstraction is the logical conclusion of painting. For the 'pure working of colour' to be felt – and these are Kandinsky's own words – a form of expression must be found that excludes the 'fable' we are always so keen to read in a painting – its ostensible references to objective reality – in favour of the 'inner meaning'. And for Kandinsky the inner meaning is the music of colour. Rhythm. Anyone who finds that hard to grasp should hurry on down to Tate Modern and take in Kandinsky room by room, then pause – for eternity, if you have eternity to spare – before one of the great *Compositions* of 1913 or thereabouts, in which feeling, thought and colour become indistinguishable by virtue of the rhythm that unites them.

You could say that Western art – Christian Western art anyway

– has always been abstract in the sense that the God in whose service art was made was never Himself paintably there. The artist can represent the symbols of belief, but not belief, or the reason for belief, itself. Remove even that abstraction and you have art with no subject or *raison d'être* but the spirituality of its own form. In a secular age the holy of holies becomes colour. And what unifies one colour with another is rhythm.

As is the case – to keep it brief – with the plays of Harold Pinter. Even as unmeaning is piled upon unmeaning, the rhythm of apparently ordinary speech, wrenched from its inconsequence, keeps us in the picture. Brutal, broken and more often than not malign, but ultimately pleasing, as art must be pleasing, by virtue of the harmony with which Pinter invests it. This is what strikes one about Pinter himself. Though to listen to him is often like being caught in the sights of a sniper – his delivery machine-gun abrupt, his thoughts flying about your ears like pellets – and though he sometimes seems to be in an argument he does not intend to lose with language itself, the overall effect of his speaking is minimalist-symphonic. Never mind the politics, which on their own are simplistic; just give in to the music, which is not.

The Scottish Person knew to do just that. Well briefed, skittish, neophytic, and now and then Hibernianly incomprehensible – try saying Hibernianly incomprehensible with an orange in your mouth if you want to know how hard pronouncing English words can be for her – she tended dutifully the fiery flame of Pinter's discourse. But Pinter wasn't put on earth to cosy up to television presenters. His conversation is with the unseen powers. Gripping to watch, for that very reason. And proof, were further proof needed, that what television does best of all is serious talk, though you wouldn't expect BBC executives, with their devotion to the tunelessness of demotic, to agree with that.

It is a pity no one has thought of sending Sven-Göran

Eriksson a tape of *The Caretaker*, even more of a pity there isn't time to fly him back to see the Kandinsky exhibition before England play their presumably final game today. 'Rhythm, Sven. You want to know why players who perform with such adroitness and athleticism for their clubs can't stay on their feet for you? – rhythm! You don't have any, so they don't have any. You're a man who loves fancy dining; you know what it's like when you find yourself in a restaurant that's badly managed. The individual dishes might be good but no course converses with another; the service doesn't flow; food comes at the wrong time; the wine doesn't come at all; waiters have no feel for what it is you want and when you want it. From first to last the evening is discordant. That the same holds true of an orchestra, I do not need to remind you, for you love music too, as I recall. No conductor with a sense of rhythm, no musicians with a sense of rhythm. Von Karajan on an off day and there was no Berlin Philharmonic. You on an off day and there's no England. The trouble is – you are always on an off day.'

You can tell Eriksson has no rhythm from the way he speaks. He has a staccato personality and presumably a staccato mind. He talks as though he is belching. For all I know he is belching. His is a job, after all, that would put stress on anybody's digestive system. But then what did we think we were doing employing a Swede as England manager in the first place?

I intend no disrespect to Swedes, a people I am otherwise disposed to admire, but rhythm is not their strong suit. I know there's Abba, but Abba is rhythm for the hard of hearing and credulous of tempo. It was Swedish gaucherie in the matter of rhythm that led them into the trap of supposing that sex could be uninhibited. This is the sixties I'm talking about, when Sweden was invented. And when I speak of rhythm in this context I do not mean whatever Swedes call jiggy-jiggy, or rhythm in the birth-control sense, I mean aesthetic rhythm – that coalescence of the material and non-material that Kandinsky aimed for and achieved. As in painting, so in sex – that which seems to come naturally is in fact the result of labour. Only a people with no instinct for rhythm would suppose that if you are easy and open about sex you will enjoy it.

What hell it was going out with Swedes in those days. My first Swedish girlfriend laughed before, during and after. My second Swedish girlfriend wept in exactly the same places. I accept that in both instances this could have had something to do with me. I was a dissonant boy myself. But none of my friends reported differently. Sex with Swedes was a washout. You banged into them, you fell over them, you interrupted each other's conversation, and in the end you interrupted everything else. No rhythm, you see. You might as well have been in bed with Sven-Göran Eriksson.

Next time we appoint a national coach, might I suggest an abstract painter. Or Harold Pinter, if he has nothing else to do.

IF IT'S 'READABLE' DON'T READ IT

I'm not usually in favour of electrodes. Not on the brain, I'm not. And certainly not on *my* brain. It's possible I'm frightened of what they will detect. What if it's not as busy in there as I like to think? What if everyone's asleep? Or what if it's a cesspit and the electrodes turn blue? But mainly it's a decorum thing. Like the grave, the brain's a fine and private place and I don't want strangers looking into mine.

I have, however, just learned something that changes my attitude to electrodes entirely. Vindication, I call it. For word is coming out of Liverpool University, where the distinguished English Professor, Philip Davis, has been working with a group of eminent neuroscientists, that electrodes prove what some of us already knew but had either lost the confidence to argue, or grown commonplace in arguing – namely, Shakespeare is good for the brain.

And not for any of the usual high-flown Coleridgean/ Arnoldian, Hegel/Schlegel/Schmegel reasons. Not because Shakespeare 'acts and speaks in the name of every individual', not because he is 'the Spinozistic deity – an omnipresent creativeness', not because 'Others abide our question / Thou art free', not because he makes his characters 'free artists of themselves'; nor, indeed, because, in the words of our less exalted, prole-mad times, he wrote bloody good stories and would have been at home writing a weekly episode for *EastEnders* had he been alive today. No, the reason Shakespeare is beneficial to the brain is that his syntactical surprisingness, to limit ourselves only to that, creates something like a neural flash of lightning, a positive wave or surge in the brain's activity, triggering a 're-evaluation process likely to raise attention' at the time and stimulate new pathways for the brain thereafter.

If I understand the science correctly, what happens is as follows. When electrode-fitted subjects are shown passages of Shakespeare in which, say, there are parenthetical distractions (e.g. 'that which angled for mine eyes – caught the water though not the fish –'), grammatical violations and compressions, nouns doing the job of verbs and vice versa (e.g. 'He childed as I fathered'), and other examples of apparent misshapenness of expression, the electro-encephalogram to which the subjects are wired notes modulations indicative of the brain's leaping about, quickly adapting itself to surprise, rethinking its normal processes, priming itself to look out for more difficulties, in other words performing, measurably, those very feats of intellection which we Eng lit people have always claimed, though in fancier language, to be what we go to literature for. Hoorah!

Forgive my jubilation, but I have been waiting for this scientific proof a long time, both as a teacher of books and a writer of them. Of all the attacks the common-minded make on any book that can't be started and finished on a Tube ride from Waterloo to Stockwell, the most usual is that it is 'hard going', that is to say fails to meet the contemporary criterion of unputdownableness. 'Then thank me for it,' I always say should the charge of 'difficulty' be levelled at one of my novels from the front row of a blowy tent in a muddy festival of letters field. 'Struggling with a book has more of reading in it than flicking through it at a predetermined rate,' I remonstrate. 'And laying it frequently aside to scratch your head does greater justice to a book's contents than never laying it aside at all. They also read who are not turning pages.'

Why people who gauge the quality of what they read by the speed and ease with which they read it always sit on the front row, I can only guess. Because they would find it too difficult to navigate their way any further back, is one explanation. Pertness, is another. The ruder readers of this sort mean to be, the closer they like to sit to you. It's as though they are half offering you sex. Beneath your imperspicuities, their dull eyes say, we know what it is you really want.

Now I can add science to my denunciations. Nothing will ever stop the pert believing that a difficulty unnecessarily clothes a simplicity, and that the hard writer therefore has something devious to hide. But at least they can now be shown that if they want to register some sign of brain life on an EEG machine they'd better knuckle down to grappling with what is not straightforward.

Do not mistake me. I do not value difficulty for difficulty's sake. *Ulysses* is sometimes harder work than it need be and *Finnegans Wake* too hard altogether. Our ears prick to self-indulgent obfuscation, or the out-of-touchness of a writer who has for too long kept company only with himself. And yes, there is merit in clarity. The Plain English Campaign fights a good fight against the jargon that means to disinform, or keep out those who don't share the ideology of the speaker. But what happens in a novel or a play is not subject to the strictures of Plain English. There is no clear external meaning to which a complex line of poetry answers. There is no arrival point of knowledge which the words delay our reaching. The meaning of a line of poetry or prose is found in the utterance that creates it and nowhere else.

'If it can be said it can be said simply' is an unctuous piece of flattery to the electroencephalogramically challenged. Some anti-elitist concept of 'communication' lies behind it, as though what the ear of the dunderhead cannot comprehend the voice of literature dare not speak. It is an assumption that lies close to those other reading-group inanities – 'I can't identify with the characters' or 'I don't find the hero a very nice person' – where the limitations of the reader's mind and expectations are paraded not in shame (in my day you kept your dwarf imagination a closely guarded secret) but exultation, as though the book in question is at fault, not you.

So, if an electroencephalogram can show how unexpectedness of syntax (and therefore meaning) will educate the brain into 'more complex variations and syncopations', to borrow a lively phrase from Professor Davis, will it also do the opposite? Can it measure the brain's inertia when fed utterly familiar syntax and the utterly familiar attitudes and emotions which utterly familiar syntax serves? It's not strictly necessary: whoever reads only what the ignorant find 'readable' has neural torpor inscribed across his countenance. But it would be fun to have scientific proof of what we know: that simple books make simpletons. And limpid prose is sure to leave us limp of mind.

HODGEPODGE

Another week, another inanity. If it's not Balls, it's Hodge. Not schools this time, the Proms. New Labour, New Culture. Only for New Culture, read No Culture. Alternatively, Hodgepodge.

'Collective Cultural Belonging' is what the Culture Minister (don't ask) has been banging on about, a phrase a wise person would think twice before using in the aftermath of Stalin and Pol Pot. But Margaret Hodge sips from a poisoned chalice. Terrorism, immigration, integration, assimiliation, identity, nationhood – all awaiting the salving balm of culture. If we can get everybody together – 'associating their citizenship with key cultural icons' is how she puts it, which sounds like having your photograph taken with Elton John and pasting it on to the back page of your new British passport – all will be well. By which standard, whatever fails of inclusiveness must be viewed with suspicion. Inclusiveness will always bedevil a Labour Party. Inclusiveness was the argument for getting rid of grammar schools. And now, in the begrudging hands of Hodge, it's an argument for getting rid of the Proms. Or at least for changing their character. Which amounts to the same thing.

'Ease' is suddenly the criterion. The problem with the Proms being that they're 'still a long way from demonstrating that people from different backgrounds feel at ease in being part of this'. I've tried counting the number of questions that broken-backed, shit-eating sentence begs, but this column is not long enough to enumerate them. So let's just stick with the begged assumption that a public event – we don't even have to call it a cultural event, just an event, cherished by some, not cherished by others – is obliged to put everyone, or even anyone, at their ease. What's sacrosanct about ease?

Nothing about this country has ever put me at my ease. I didn't feel at ease when processions of weeping Catholics passed my house carrying plaster saints. Didn't feel at ease at school when they sang hymns in assembly about famous men I'd never heard of, or accused 'some boy' of stealing toilet rolls. Didn't feel at ease at university where hearties in blue blazers ran up and down the towpath of the Cam shouting 'Olly, Olly, Jesus!' and moral tutors called me Abrahamson, Isaacson, Greenberg and Cohen. Don't feel at ease in the Athenaeum, or Glyndebourne, or the Courts of Justice, or any police station, racetrack, garden fete, rap concert or pole-dancing establishment.

Many are the ways a person whose family hasn't owned land on these islands for a thousand years might feel frightened, discomfited, embarrassed, or just not one hundred per cent at home. That will hold true for most of the population in one place or another, even those who do go back to the Domesday Book. There is always something to fear in the rites of others – whether older or younger, or of another class, religion or colour – but alongside the fear might exist, if we allow it, curiosity, admiration, and – why not? – the deep affection of the outsider looking in.

The experience of feeling ill at ease can be very powerful. A spur to emulation sometimes, but I don't doubt the cause of hostility, too, where the outsider is unstable. What doesn't follow is that, against such an eventuality, we are obliged to water down everything we do. Must a pole dancer dress herself to spare my blushes? Must Judaism, Christianity and Islam make changes to their practice and liturgy to accommodate any unease I might feel in the synagogue, the cathedral or the mosque? The one thing we do know is that religion never looks more contemptible than when it forgets it's for its own elect and turns populist. The disaffected do not scorn our institutions for their strength but for their tepidity. It is with culture as it is with the bringing up of children: a strong clear message is always best, however copious the bedtime tears.

Behind the ease and inclusiveness assumption lies a highly indulgent ideology of selfhood – the right of any individual to feel the centre of the universe, or, to borrow a phrase I heard at a dinner party the other night, to have his or her 'experience validated'. A teacher of French literature was telling me how the mother of one of his pupils had objected to his teaching her daughter French drama of the seventeenth century. The girl was uneasy reading these plays. They felt old and foreign to her. (Corneille and Molière – foreign!) Her mother agreed. How were these works, she wanted to know, 'validating her child's experience'? Because he was a charming man, the French teacher didn't tell her that the daughter's experience, if it was anything like the mother's, was the thing least worth validating in the entire universe. If her daughter felt at sea, so much the better. Study is meant to make you feel at sea. The self is not a precious entity that must be soothed and eased at every turn. Sometimes, the self is something you must learn to lose. Validation of the self, madame – again this is me speaking, not him – is what you might get from a finishing school, but not from a humane education.

I say something very similar to those pupils at a Jewish girls' school in London who recently refused to answer questions on Shakespeare in a national curriculum test as a way of protesting against the character of Shylock. Given the opportunity for some close textual analysis, I have no doubt I could persuade the girls that Shakespeare was not an anti-Semite, whatever that means in an Elizabethan context. But that's beside the point. Reading Shakespeare is not conditional on his loving Jews. The study of literature becomes no study at all if you read only writers whose attitudes chime with your own and with whom you therefore feel at ease. Encountering what is not you, indeed what might well be inimical to you, is one of the first reasons for reading anything.

So the Proms are more a problem for those who don't attend them, for whatever reason, than for those do. I wouldn't myself go to the Last Night of the Proms even if they offered to stand me between Cecilia Bartoli and Jitka Hosprová; but were I new to this country I would regard the Promenaders with the same degree of baffled awe that travellers experience when they behold a carnival in Rio, or Thasipusam in Kuala Lumpur. If cultural integration is the issue, there needs to be a culture to integrate with. And a culture that can't express its peculiar vitality without worrying how much upset it might be causing, isn't a culture at all.

TRISTAN AND ISOLDE

Thought my marriage was over last week. Or at least the free and open, disputatious, relishing dissent and disagreement part. The occasion was the BBC Proms concert presentation of Act 2 of Wagner's *Tristan und Isolde*, an opera I have long been in a dozen minds about but whose best bits I wanted my wife to enjoy as much as I did, Wagner having largely passed her by.

My being in a dozen minds about Wagner has nothing to do with his Jew-hating. An artist may hate Jews if he wishes. If it isn't Jews, it will be someone else. All you can ask is that the art itself rises above the hatred, harmonises all the ugly flotsam of single-mindedness that fed it. We make art to be better than we are when we are not making art. There is no more to say.

Which said, I've heard it argued that the Orphic inflexibility that made Wagner an anti-Semite remains residually there in the music; and I suspect anyone who goes to pagan saga for his inspiration, not because the stories aren't overwhelmingly wonderful, but because a pre-Christian heroising is the usual motive, an admiration for aristocratic man before what Nietzsche called 'the slave revolt in morals' was initiated by the Jews.

But all this is by the by, as we weren't watching *Der Ring des*

Nibelungen but Act 2 of *Tristan und Isolde*, a distinctly post-Christian legend, where what's imperilled is chivalry not Valhalla, and what does the imperilling is love or, if you prefer – because there can be a difference – sexual desire. Concert performances of opera are often thin gruel, but in the case of *Tristan und Isolde* there is something apposite about the principals just standing there, never touching, scarcely looking at each other, simply delivering their protestations of erotic abandonment as though to the unseen forces of the air. They aren't, you see, in the slightest bit interested in each other. Ask Tristan what Isolde is wearing and he wouldn't be able to tell you; ask Isolde to enumerate the personal qualities for which she loves Tristan and she'd be hard pressed to come up with any. This is not a complaint. I don't ask them to be lovers in the romantic-comedy mould. They are, after all, only in love because a love potion made them so. They have, in other words, no choice in the matter, so it's neither here nor there what either thinks of the other. Love strikes, and that's it. Which is sometimes, and maybe more than sometimes, the way of it.

I might be in a dozen minds about Wagner but I am sure of this: that the music of *Tristan und Isolde* celebrates an erotic transport that is entirely impersonal, and that this superbly orchestrated swoon of self-consummation describes love better than it is comfortable for us, in our twenty-first-century sentimentality about affection and the family, to admit.

Isolde does not want Tristan's baby. Tristan does not want to introduce Isolde to his friends. All Isolde hopes for is to vanish from the world while protesting her love of Tristan. He the same. Though the music is orgasmic, even sex isn't really what it's about. Death is what it's about.

I don't mind admitting that I am swooning to the music. When Tristan and Isolde finally and as it were in the abstract get it together, calling on love to 'free them from the world', I am a goner. Death can free me from the world as well. My wife is motionless in her seat, barely breathing. She irradiates love's tragedy, the great paradox at the heart of desire – loss in plenty, plenty in loss. Has death claimed us both?

It's at this point that I believe she has begun to judge me – not as a man, not as a lover, but as an artist. Why am I not Wagner? More specifically, why have I not sought to make tragic art as uncompromising as this? There is no comedy in Wagner. One laugh and that's the trance blown. But I have always argued for the primacy of comedy; comedy is what makes Mozart greater than Wagner. I don't mean jokes, I mean the illumination of another way of seeing, the sudden turning of an action on its head, not to make light of it but to enrich it, in such an instance as this, for example, to show the lovers why life has more going for it than death. Hence my own practice as a novelist, which is to take comedy into the very heart of desolation, to affirm life when it is most threatened.

At the end of an exhausting day at the theatre, watching tragic heroes putting out their eyes and tragic heroines murdering their children, Greek audiences would be treated to the wild burlesque of a satyr play – the invigorating comic obscenity of man as beast sating his lusts and never mind the consequences being what they finally took home with them. In the satyr play I have seen my own justification. Once upon a time I just wrote the satyr play, leaving the preceding tragedies to others. Now I try to create the whole cycle, but always going for that final invigoration of comedy. But what if I am – what if I always was – wrong?

There's no trace of satyr play in *Tristan und Isolde*. Of all lovers, Tristan and Isolde would be the last to admit that they share concupiscence with a goat. They own no allegiance to life in any of its robust forms; their medium is night, far from 'day's empty fancies'. They seek to be beyond corporeal existence, bodiless, obliterated, distilled into nothingness. They are satyr-proof. And I am lost in the music that celebrates them. As is my

wife. And how can she be thinking other than what I'm thinking – that *this*, Wagner, unremitting, exhausting, serious to the
point of annihilation, is what art's about?

We leave the Albert Hall in silence and walk home through
the park. I am wondering if she is thinking about leaving me for
a writer who doesn't revere comedy, a true artist who never
deviates from the sacred task of life-renunciation. After half an
hour of walking I dare to look at her. 'Well?' I ask.

'I don't know how to tell you this,' she says. 'I know how
much it's moved you . . .'

'And?'

'I really don't want to say this to you.'

'Go on.'

She breathes hard. 'I hated it.'

I gather her up in my arms. 'Thank the fuck for that,' I say.

NATURAL-BORN KILLERS

What would we do if we didn't have America? Invent it. Because without America we wouldn't feel half as good about ourselves as we do. And that isn't because America is now the only country left on earth that can't beat us at cricket. Without Americans we'd have no one to whom we could feel morally superior.

Guns again. Though our own kids are learning the trick of homicide fast, and can do pretty well with knives if knives are all they can lay their hands on, you strictly speaking need a gun to pull off a real spectacular. Hence our moral superiority. Because we make it that little bit harder for a college student without underworld connections to obtain a gun, we are able to shake our heads and wonder when those damn Yankees are ever going to learn.

I'm not saying they don't make superiority easy for us. When the executive director of Gun Owners of America, Larry Pratt – a man whose name I promise you I have not made up – describes the massacre at Virginia Tech as an opportunity for the gun lobby, arguing that if only every student had been armed fewer of them would have died, we all but give up on Americans. Arm everybody then nobody is a victim; kill before you can be killed – only in a universe of the insane is this a blueprint for a good society. Ask Pratt if it wouldn't be safer if no one could get a gun period, and he'll laugh in your face, that's if he doesn't shoot you in it first.

Americans!

What an orgy of righteousness we've enjoyed this week, accusing the Americans of glorying in gore, observing with a sneer that the only freedom they value is the freedom to pull a trigger. How many more? How many since the last time? Every paper had a journalist on hand to tell us. In the last ten years fifty-seven college kids plus eight of their teachers have been mown down in episodes similar to this. When, oh when, will America relinquish its love affair with the gun?

So what, I ask in return, about our love affair with the motor car? When, oh when, will we relinquish that? And if you wonder what the one has to do with the other, let the figures talk for themselves. Even as we were counting the American dead, articles were appearing in the same papers, often on the same pages, counting our own. Not victims of the gun, but victims of the car. In the last six months alone, 840 people killed or maimed by drivers under twenty.

You can't, I accept, measure tragedy in numbers. The thirty-two dead of Virginia Tech do not become less dead because we lose as many to boy racers every week. Nor do I embrace the gun lobby argument that if a madman wants to kill he will find something else to kill with if he can't easily obtain a gun. A gun might not in itself make someone mad, but its allure will always empower and intensify the madness. So no, I do not raise the question of the killer car to distract attention from the question of the killer gun.

But we might seize this opportunity to turn a little of our moral outrage on ourselves. Cars kill. Since we know that cars kill as surely as do guns why do we not do more to keep them out of the hands of those most likely to kill with them? You are too young at seventeen to drive. I drove at seventeen, and though I pootled along like a tortoise, hated engine noise, and never found a car a glamorous or potency-inducing object, I was still a menace, crashing three times in my first three months on the road. Mind elsewhere, that was the problem. Sex. Literature. Gina Lollobrigida.

The Association of British Insurers – not normally a body we turn to for ethical guidance – recommends putting up the minimum driving age to eighteen. Too modest a proposal. If the minimum age is to be determined by a brain unbefuddled by lyric poetry, eyesight unclouded by sperm, and an adequate imagination of disaster – that's to say a recognition that not only yours but every car coming towards you is being driven by a killer – then fifty should be the minimum age. But as society is probably not yet ready for that, we could settle, with enormous benefit to ourselves, at twenty-one.

Age is not the only issue. No car should have a speed capability, or an aesthetic denoting a speed capability, over what is legally permitted and what is legally permitted is already too high. Beyond sixty miles an hour we know not what we do. It's not just our bones that shake: the vibration of travelling beyond sixty miles an hour can cause our synaptic cleft – the space between the terminal button of the presynaptic neuron and the membrane of the postsynaptic neuron – to widen, confusing the flow of signals between one neurotransmitter and another. With young men this neural malfunction can occur even in anticipation of speed, as witness any crowd of them gathered jibbering around a Ferrari parked in Sloane Street.

What they will argue, of course, is that it's the beauty of the car not its intrinsic violence that renders them incoherent with admiration. I don't doubt it. Gun lovers, with equal justification, argue likewise. There is a terrible beauty in a weapon of destruction. Men are creatures built to kill, and whatever will facilitate that killing or add to the splendour of the ritual of causing death must necessarily excite their senses. Sport, the gun lobbyists call it. Drivers and rallyists ditto. Legislate against the gun or against the car, they cry, and you take away our fun. Tough. Find some other way of whiling away your time. Take up curling. Embroider. Knit. And if those won't give you the odour of deadly risk and slaughter you cannot do without, try dressing in ladies' underwear with an orange in your mouth and hanging yourself from a hotel doorknob.

For starters, then, no one under twenty-one to be allowed behind a wheel, and whoever breaks that law, or drives recklessly at any age, to be banned from driving for life. Not a fortnight, life. For our lives are their playthings. And should we catch them driving after that, we cut off the foot that presses the accelerator.

If you find this too draconian, fine, that's your human right – but you cannot now occupy the moral high ground when it comes to Americans and their guns.

WHAT IF JOSEPH K. DID IT?

Does literature serve us ill sometimes? Or, to put that another way, do we sometimes learn the wrong lessons from it?

What if Joseph K. was guilty? 'Someone must have been telling lies about Joseph K.,' is how Kafka's great novel *The Trial* begins, 'for without having done anything wrong he was arrested one fine morning.' But what if no one was telling lies and Joseph K. really had done something wrong?

Part of what makes that opening so chilling is its understated menace. The morning is fine. Terrible things happen in storms, in literature as in life, but at least you get a bit of warning with a storm. Our greatest dread is catastrophe striking when we least expect it. When the weather's good, all seems right with the world, and our defences are lowered; unprepared, we are at our most vulnerable.

And more vulnerable still when the attack comes not only from a clear blue sky but through an agency unknown. *Someone.* An unidentified person or persons, acting we don't know where or when or why. It's all surmise. Not 'someone was telling lies about Joseph K.' but someone 'must have' been telling lies about Joseph K. A deduction, in the dark of day, working backwards from the inexplicable arrest. Inexplicable, because the man is innocent.

Assuming that he is.

No wonder this novel has been speaking eloquently to our fears for eighty years. I am not sure whether we can talk of the last century yet, because the last century is by no means over. We shop side by side in Harrods now with Russians, but we'd be fools – as recent absurd and sinister events have proved – to think the Cold War has been amicably settled. It's been given a moneyed makeover, that's all. The spies are still busy, if in slightly better suits, and therefore so must be the secret police. The *some-ones* remain out there, somewhere, telling lies. Last century or this century, ours is the age of the faceless state, policed we do not know by whom.

Though it is history, Florian Henckel von Donnersmarck's remarkable debut film *The Lives of Others*, about the humanising of a Stasi agent, works partly because it somehow doesn't feel like history. The Stasi have been dismantled yet the apparatus of continuous surveillance looks familiar to us. The Wall fell, but we haven't stopped living in a world that punishes us when we believe other than we are meant to believe, no matter how liberal what we are meant to believe appears. Say the wrong thing about race at a British university, for example, and you can kiss goodbye to your career. If you happen to be the ruined academic, you will think, with reason, you are living in a police state. Someone has been telling lies about you. For it is a lie that some things are unsayable.

That we can fear the monolithic state in one context and be its agents in another is one of those paradoxes to which human nature is subject. Universities are bulwarks against tyranny but at the same time practise ruthless tyrannies of their own. Imaginatively, though – regardless of our being spies and inform-ers in reality – we are all so many inmates of the Gulags, each our own lonely warrior of individualism standing up against authority and those who do its dirty work. Thus we slip at once into the person of Joseph K. about whom someone has lied and who is arrested one fine morning for an unnamed crime he has not committed.

Simply to be lied about is enough to make a hero of us. The Advocate in *The Trial* tells Joseph K. about Leni's weakness for accused men. 'She makes up to all of them, loves them all . . . It doesn't surprise me so much as it seems to surprise you. If you have the right eye for these things, you can see that accused men are often attractive.' We are not, of course, to take this diabolic needling at face value. The Advocate and Joseph K. are rivals of sorts for Leni's affections. But we recognise a version of the condition he describes. Sexually and ideologically, we love a victim of what we take to be injustice. And conversely we assume an injustice where we sexually or ideologically have decided to love.

So have we decided too soon to love Joseph K.? Or, if you like, to love the prose in which he makes his first appearance? 'Someone must have been telling lies about Joseph K.' It's a brave and sophisticated reader who will resist the blandishments of that opening sentence, though it's entirely possible that the super-subtle Kafka is leading us into a trap of gullibility, for in a world where truth is hard to come by, how foolish of us to suppose we have so easily come by it.

Don't mistake me: I am not saying the innocent and the guilty are interchangeable. There is guilt and there is innocence and to pretend otherwise is, as Primo Levi says, an aesthetic affectation or a moral disease. But the siren call of literature, enticing us to identify without question with whoever insists he is innocent and has been lied about, can land us in trouble in the real affairs of life. So deeply implanted in us is the idea that the state must always be wrong and the individual always right, that we do not notice subtle supersessions in that conflict. But it sometimes happens, as in the case of terrorism, that it's the individual and not the state who is our enemy.

What IF Joseph K. Did it?

Old habits of allegiance die hard. Thus, though we don't usually smile on judges, we cheered them when they substituted control orders for imprisonment where there is evidence in plenty of malign intent but not evidence of the sort judges like. Normally we castigate authority for not protecting us from perceived danger. Why wasn't that paedophile arrested when his intentions were apparent? The long-time stalker and demented serial-strangler on parole, ditto. But when it comes to men with declared ambitions to be human bombs, we think that keeping half an eye out for them is enough – until they either run off or blow us up, and then we wonder why they weren't in prison.

Whether Joseph K. is innocent or guilty, the term Kafkaesque answers to a deep anxiety in us about power wielded cruelly and irrationally. Though the anxiety is psychological, it is justified by history. But the world isn't only Kafkaesque. Sometimes an accused man is guilty of a crime, even if the agencies who accuse him are shadowy, and the crime is one he hasn't committed yet.

BE VERY AFRAID

So now we know where the destruction of Western civilisation is being plotted: not in the madrasas of Karachi and Lahore, not in the Taliban training camps of Helmand Province, not even in the eschatological fantasies of Mahmoud Ahmadinejad, but in Crawley, West Sussex. I am not of course suggesting that we rule Karachi and Tehran out of the topography of terror altogether, only that we adjust the range of our apprehension and learn to grow afraid of the loathing for the way we live that's being brewed just around the corner, in the suburbs, in the green belts, in the new towns of our fair and pleasant land. Crawley, West Sussex – never did sound fun, but never did sound dangerous either. But there you are, nowhere's safe, now we all know how to make explosives out of aftershave, from the menace which is certainty.

Call it Islamic certainty, but what emerged in the course of the fertiliser bomb trial was such a hotchpotch of prejudice, ignorance, sexual immaturity, woman-hating and theology, that the only one murderous component we can identify with confidence is the absolute conviction of right. Most of us have horrible attitudes and wouldn't mind putting a figurative bomb under something or someone or other; what stops us is that we think differently the next day. If we want to get to the bottom of why some young men don't feel differently the next day we need to understand why one brain freezes and another doesn't. Disaffection is not an explanation, it is a consequence. Blame religion if you like, but a half-baked university education can have exactly the same effect. It isn't straightforward, charting the progress of fanaticism.

But the trial has thrown up matter which should embarrass more people than it can console. Good that we got the hateful little bastards, but lives might have been saved had we got them earlier. Much has been made of this, calls for a public inquiry into our policing and our security services etc., but I wonder how many of those calling for this inquiry were busy telling us not all that long ago that there was no terrorism for our security services to police. An invention of our respective governments – Blair's and Bush's – the lot of it. An inveigling us into fear for the purpose of controlling us.

In America the voice of the hour was Michael Moore's – 'There is no terrorist threat, somebody needs to just say there is.' Over here a BBC2 series, *The Power of Nightmares: The Rise of the Politics of Fear*, spoke of the 'dark illusion that has spread unquestioned through governments around the world', and in order to show that judges were not so easily made fools to an illusion, Lord Woolf warned us we had more to fear from violations of the Human Rights Act than from terrorists.

So is that a 'sorry' I hear amid the accusations that we have not been sufficiently vigilant? A sorry from those who thought vigilance was uncalled for and sinister?

Among the reasons to mistrust the rhetoric of human rights – not to be confused with our inalienable entitlement to freedom – is its politicisation. We most volubly declare the inviolability of the Human Rights Act where we deplore the government in power. Here is the danger of an incompetent and ignominious administration: it makes us incompetent and ignominious in our detestation of it, believing that whatever proceeds from it must be erroneous and whatever discomfits it worth praising. Our enemy's enemy must be our friend. So we jeered when a Labour Home Secretary ordered tanks to patrol the perimeters of Heathrow, and we allowed partisans of the ideology of terror to win the day when they complained of police in protective clothing charging for no good reason through their neighbourhoods of peace. Terror? What terror? Bombs in Crawley, West Sussex? Who would make a bomb in Crawley, West Sussex?

Thus does hating Blair turn us into self-harmers. We would rather be wrong about what is necessary for our basic safety than wrong about him. Shame on us!

And when we weren't accusing Blair of inventing terror for his own ends we were accusing him of fostering it – an extraordinary act of doublethink in which we clamoured for a person to be charged with a crime which in another part of our minds we didn't believe had been committed. The terror whose existence we denied was the consequence of our invasion of Afghanistan and Iraq, the consequence of our neglect of the Palestinians, the consequence of a stream of attitudes and policies which it was impossible to construe as anything but anti-Muslim. And what was our evidence for this? Why, the terrorists who were not terrorists told us so. And for what reason do you do what you do? we asked – a question which any psychologist will tell you cannot possibly elicit the truth. And back came the answer: Iraq. Investigation closed. As though a person capable of planting a bomb cannot be capable of telling a lie. As though an ideologue of violence will not have worked out a self-justifying narrative of his actions.

So it is good if in other ways alarming news that the Crawley bombers were animated as much by disgust for what they saw in their own backyards as by anything we were doing in Baghdad.

The words of Jawad Akbar in support of targeting the London nightclub the Ministry of Sound – not the Ministry of Defence, note, not the Ministry of Tony's Lies – have rightly become famous. 'No one can turn round and say "oh they were inno-cent", those slags dancing around.'

More than one commentator has noticed a certain home-grown quality in Jawad Akbar's language, something that has more in common with disgusted of Tunbridge Wells, or even amusingly appalled of Notting Hill, than Osama bin Laden. We should take the point. There aren't many of us for whom the sight of pissed-up brides-to-be spilling out of stretch limos in skirts up around their tushes is an occasion for national pride.

Disdain is not a fertiliser bomb, but it is still a good idea to remember how much we once liked getting pissed ourselves, whether in, or in the company of somebody in, a skirt up around the tush. There is nothing like recalling we have two attitudes to everything to stop us drifting into terrorism.

But a closed mind has its allure. And disgust can feel like power. That is why we should never stop being afraid. Just because a government we don't like tells us life is dangerous doesn't mean that life is safe.

ART FOR US

Though we abhor metropolitan self-engrossment in this column, we turn our attention today to an event that has brightened that dusty little corner of humanity we call the West End of London. The National Gallery's decision to hang full-size reproductions of great paintings from its permanent collection on walls all over Soho and Covent Garden is what I'm talking about. And while you could argue that a National Gallery should live up to its name and distribute its largesse to the whole country, better somewhere than nowhere.

When they first went up, one at a time – a Caravaggio here, a Joseph Wright of Derby there – it was like waking to find that the malicious urban fairies who come and go unnoticed, scrawling and fly-posting while we sleep, had been busy again in the night. Except that this felt the very opposite of vandalism or malice. Not knowing how they'd got there initially I took them to be the charitable offering of some local millionaire eccentric. Then explanatory plaques began to appear alongside the paintings and the hand of the National Gallery and its sponsor Hewlett-Packard was declared.

Clever PR for both – 'See what we've got,' says the National

Art For Us

Gallery; 'See what we can reproduce,' says Hewlett-Packard –
but the intention remains benign. A long way from the demented
desecration of the graffitist.

I've never got on with graffiti, even when it's higher order
graffiti. The thought for the day above my column a few weeks
ago was Susan Sontag's famous remark, 'Interpretation is the
revenge of the intellect upon art', and that's how I understand
the impulse to make graffiti – as interpretative in the sense that
it doesn't come about of itself, as art does, but must impose its
will, parasitically, on what's already there. It doesn't matter
whether that something already there is a train, a doorway, a
sculpture, or quite simply the existing fabric of society, the graffitist will exact his critical revenge on it. He cannot leave alone
what came before him.

This explains why we always read a sort of alienated envy in
graffiti. Whereas the Vermeers and Fragonards which descended
as on the wings of angels in the night . . . Yes, I know the coun-
ter-argument. Does turning Soho into a museum for showing
work long accepted into the canon – turning it into a street
version of a National Trust gift shop – do any more for art than
giving it over to someone raging at contemporary life with an
aerosol can? Might be prettier, but who ever said art had to be
pretty?

The National Gallery attempts to tread the line between
complacent connoisseurship and discovery. There's a tour map
you can download, showing you where every painting is sited
– though you have to be careful not to get trapped forever in
the version that requires a flash plug-in, because then you're
into installations that don't install and boxes telling you that
there's no default application to open what you would install if
only they'd let you install it. Better just to print out the one that
doesn't flash or show pedestrians and cyclists moving like Mary
Poppins across the West End skyline.

On top of that there are audio-guided perambulations that

can be downloaded as Zip files which you can drag into the software for your MP3 player. The first of these calls itself the Grand Tour and takes in the entire offering of forty-five paintings. It was marred for me when I tried it, first by the rain, then by the sun, and finally by my discovering that though the paintings are numbered they are not numbered in any intelligible geographical sequence, so that you've dashed there and back ten times between Putrefaction Alley in Soho and Kitsch Court in Covent Garden and still only got to painting number three.

The second walk is called the Heavy Hitters Tour which doesn't shilly-shally on the margins of greatness but takes you straight to da Vinci and Van Gogh. And the third, the Lovers Tour, guides you past the more sophisticated sex and tea shops in this part of London via Bronzino's *An Allegory with Venus and Cupid*. If I have one complaint about the latter it is this: it shows, I think, a lack of nerve to suggest rounding this tour off with a bowl of noodles at Wagamama, but not come up with the name of a nearby hotel. Bronzino's *Allegory with Venus and Cupid* for God's sake! – that's the one where Cupid holds the head of Venus with one knowing boyish hand while with the other (between his index and middle finger to be precise) he rolls her rosy nipple. Small wonder that to the left of Cupid a grey-green figure, variously interpreted as Jealousy and Despair but which I like to think of simply as Deranged Desire, tears his hair and howls. Now tell me a bowl of noodles will do you as a sequel to my description, let alone to the work reproduced in all its grand salaciousness.

In the time it has taken me to write this column so far, four new tours have appeared on the National Gallery's website, so we must assume the idea has taken off. Good. I approve the project unreservedly. I love running into a Rubens when I'm nipping out to buy the papers. Love having a Holbein to look at when I'm hailing a taxi, rather than a handbill or a road sign. And everyone I talk to feels the same. Even the most difficult to please of

London's bloggers report obediently downloading maps, charging their MP3s, getting on their bicycles, and marvelling over the sometimes fortuitous, sometimes brilliantly engineered juxtaposition of art, architecture and life. Snap a hooker hanging around Caravaggio's *Salome with the Head of John the Baptist* in a puddle of urine and the devil knows what else outside a Lithuanian whorehouse in Peter Street, or a couple of pisspots slumped in front of Rembrandt's end-of-the-world *Belshazzar's Feast* on the wall of the theatre where they're showing *Les Mis*, and you've made a sort of art yourself.

Credit where credit's due: this has turned out to be everybody's idea of a good time. Art, you see. And not just any art, not another fatuous shop-window installation, but painting. By universal consent, the Grand Tour has turned a pig's ear of a summer into a silk purse.

Now let's start seeing the great paintings in our possession on walls all over the country.

VENGEANCE IS MINE

Another day, another killing. They get younger both ends – the killers and the killed. And we, meanwhile, we the wise ones, tear our hair, caught between calls to meet violence with violence, and calls to hold fast to our liberal ideals.

'Vengeance is mine; I will repay, saith the Lord.' We forget sometimes that that was more a bargain than a threat. If we restrained the vengefulness intrinsic to our natures, He'd take care of the justice side of things on our behalf. In this way God fulfils the same function civil society entrusts to the judiciary. He does the dirty work with which we, in our boiling wrath, cannot be entrusted.

That, of course, is if He notices or remembers. Of all God's promises this is the one we find it hardest to forgive Him breaking. And when at last enough crimes go unavenged, we become unbelievers. Thus our disappointment in God becomes the model for our disappointment in the judiciary. We might not like a hanging judge but a judge who cannot bring himself to hang at all we feel betrays us. And that's because we've ceded anger to him and when he does not adequately honour the outraged morality of which our anger is, so to speak, the spokesperson, it is left without a voice.

The problem with a liberal society – an impassioned defence of which was mounted by this newspaper last week – is that it can fail to take account of how dearly we attach ourselves to our anger, how many of our frustrations in an unjust world it speaks for, and how reluctantly we part with it.

Hence the bitter arguments that have broken out as a consequence of Learco Chindamo, killer of Philip Lawrence, winning his appeal to stay in England after his release. To near universal sympathy, the murdered headmaster's widow has voiced her 'devastation' on learning that Chindamo will not be deported to Italy, the country of his birth. For this paper, Mrs Lawrence's devastation, though entirely understandable, cannot be the final arbiter of justice. Whereas for the 'gutter press', as it pleases us to call it, her distress mirrors a greater sense of disillusionment with the way we punish crime in this country. It is an opportunity to rail against asylum laws, the EU, the Human Rights Acts, and whatever else seems to favour foreigners against nationals, and the criminal against the victim. What about *our* human rights? they shout, and we are off.

There's no doubt that the legal and liberalist arguments for Chindamo's staying here have been made. A good prison system must rehabilitate; a just society allows the criminal to pay his debt; Chindamo is a citizen of the EU and free to move within it; his staying violates no one's rights. All reasonable and true, but an objection still remains: such reasoning doesn't stop another killing on another day, and is cruelly deaf to the blood that crieth from the ground. A liberal conscience is a fine thing, but a liberal conscience isn't all we're made of.

It's hard to believe that what really matters to Philip Lawrence's widow is the country in which the boy who widowed her will spend the rest of his life. At the heart of this is the question of whether Learco Chindamo should have any life left to spend. 'Vengeance is mine,' saith the Lord, 'I will repay.' 'Then repay!' saith we back. Chindamo was fifteen when he knifed to death a headmaster trying to break up a fight. A boy but not that much of a boy. You know, at fifteen, what a knife can do, which is why you choose to carry one. If he is released next year he will have spent twelve years in prison. Not much, twelve years. An eye for an eye was the recommendation of that vengeance-bearing Lord from whom the Jews, the Christians and the Muslims learned justice. No more than an eye for an eye, and no less. Twelve years for a life is not an eye for an eye. Twelve years for a life is the nail of a little finger for an eye.

Already we're wondering how little time in jail the killers of Rhys Jones will get. And how little that will deter the next ones.

Mrs Lawrence feels that someone has broken his promise to her. Someone has. We were all promised when we plumped for a more civilised society and abolished the death penalty that soft sentencing would not be the consequence. Play about with tariffs and you play about with the value of the life the killer took. It is not querulous of Mrs Lawrence to ask, 'What about our rights?' A profound disordering of things takes place when we feel that the dead, and those who must go on living in the icy shadow of the dead, are not given justice, for justice is all the dead ask at any time, and when the dead are the murdered dead their unanswered cries are terrible, not only for those who loved them, but for us all. Any unrequited crime unsettles us. An unrequited murder deranges us.

This is why the Furies in Aeschylus' great trilogy, *the Oresteia*, are never stilled. With every humane advance a liberal society appears to make, there is an answering retrogression. Take the concept of redemption – a noble idea, but profoundly unjust. For by what presumptuous logic of the soul do we grant a person who has knowingly taken another person's life the right to redeem his own? Perhaps this, more than any other issue, divides us. To some, the criminal's willingness to own and expiate his crime is the proof that good exists. The God of redemption is civilisation's answer to the God of vengeance. But to others, redemption is a spiritual impertinence and a travesty of justice. 'Only the overweening spirit takes on itself to dole out forgiveness,' D. H. Lawrence wrote. 'But justice is a sacred human right. The overweening spirit pretends to perch above justice. But I am a man, not a spirit, and men . . . can only live at length by being just, can only die in peace if they have justice.'

That liberal society to which we all aspire demeans us when it disavows the force of human feeling which its liberalism cannot contain. The popular press will seize on the distress of Mrs Lawrence and the parents of Rhys Jones, and in the process whip the old gods into fury; but we make a grave mistake if we consign this to the 'gutter' and call it mischief. The old gods speak for sacred necessities and will be heard.

'A GENTLE VACANCY OF SPIRIT'

Discovered a new pleasure: lying on the beach reading writers describing lying on the beach. It's awkward reading on the beach if you're not sufficiently flexuous to get the right degree of shoulderly twist to read the words, or the right degree of cranial lift to turn the page, and if you don't have the bodily or astronomical savvy to work out how to get the sun on the book but not on you. But that's the joy of reading about someone who manages it no better. Reading is never more satisfying than when you feel allied with a writer in discomfort. So lying in agony on a beach with a book that excels at evoking the agonies of lying on a beach is the most perfect reading experience of all.

Simon Gray got me through the holiday from which I've just returned, or least he got me through the beach part of it. I'd been saving *The Last Cigarette*, the third volume of his *Smoking Diaries*, to take away with me, knowing that his masterfully comic dyspepsia would be just the tonic in the heat. But I hadn't realised that he too would be on holiday in it some of the time, so that I would be able to lie there, so to speak, and let him fulminate for both of us.

'Listen to this,' I say to my wife, who is lying next to me.

Though she has a back injury, and no more wants to be exposed to the sun we've just paid thousands of pounds to lie in than I do, she still manages to find a graceful way of curling up and reading. Women, of course, have more adaptable bodies than men. Something, presumably, to do with childbirth. Come the hour, they have to be able to bend themselves into positions impossible for a man. Not that we're here to have a baby. We're just here to escape the sun. And read. Which sometimes means reading to each other.

'Listen to this,' I say, interrupting her and Philip Roth. I am not entirely happy, I have to confess, about her lying there with Philip Roth. The one consolation is that he doesn't find life funny any more, so at least I don't have to listen to her laughing. It's not quite a rule between us but it's understood that I would rather she didn't laugh at another man's prose – laughter in a woman denoting erotic appreciation – particularly when she's in the prone or semi-prone position. For some reason we make an exception of Simon Gray. This is not because I don't find him masculinely threatening – he is, actually – but because he is not a marriage-breaking writer, as Roth most definitely is. I can only explain that by saying that Simon Gray doesn't raise the ire of either sex against the other. On the stage sometimes, maybe, in earlier days, but in his diaries, no.

The passage I want to read aloud to my wife, who has already read *The Last Cigarette* but doesn't mind hearing it again, describes the diarist lying on a plastic bed on a cement beach in Greece, surrounded by bodies he doesn't find attractive ('little strips of material between their legs'), listening to voices he loathes ('voices you could grate cheese on'), a cigarette jammed into his mouth, 'the sun pouring through my straw hat like a molten headache'.

A wonderful image, a molten headache, partly because it enacts the condition of becoming molten which is continuous – the sun continuing to pour, the hat continuing to provide no adequate protection, the head continuing to melt. So you can go on reading and rereading the sentence, the ache getting worse with every read. Indeed, when my wife wonders why I haven't interrupted her with another favourite phrase or paragraph for at least fifteen minutes I have to tell her that I'm still on the molten headache which is beginning to pour like liquefying gold out of my own skull now.

That is partly the actual sun's fault as well as Simon Gray's. It has crept under the umbrella while I've been busy laughing but I can't work out which side it's coming in from. There are diamond-shaped patches of intense light on my arms and chest, caused partly by gaps in the material of the umbrella. I could climb off my bed to fix them, and at the same time work out where the sun is, but it's so hot out there that if I quit the shade for more than ten seconds I will grow a melanoma. There is also, to be considered, the difficulty of rising from a sunbed at all at my age. How to get the leverage? Apply too much force to the bed and it sinks into the sand, grab hold of the umbrella pole with your weight and you'll topple it – and that's a melanoma each in the time it takes you to put it up again – which leaves only your wife's shoulder to reach out and press down on, and she won't appreciate that given her injury and the intense absorption of her concentration on Philip Roth's *Exit Ghost*, which has patently reached a crisis, that's if there's anything in late Philip Roth that isn't crisis.

It's crisis time for Simon Gray, too. Best friends dead and dying, his own tobacco health no great shakes, the body reluctant and unwieldy – for which, as I try covering up the triangles of killer light, first with what's left of a sandwich I've been eating, then with *The Last Cigarette* itself (a manoeuvre that involves balancing it on my ankles and bending double to read the words), I have considerable fellow feeling. 'Not exactly serenity, more a gentle vacancy of spirit,' Gray writes, describing that 'suspended mood when you know there's much to worry about but you can't remember what it is'. All we have to look forward to now – a gentle vacancy of spirit, which is a great thought because it admits its impossibility, or at least its fleetingness, in the utterance.

But no, there is something gentler about this volume of Gray's diaries. No dilution of the rage, no minimising of despair, and certainly no false comfort – but a great suffusion of warmth, especially in the man-to-man, eyeball-to-eyeball descriptions of his friends Alan Bates, Ian MacKillop, Harold Pinter. Astute portraits these, but infinitely touching, too, in their acknowledgement of love. You have to be of an age to write like this. It's not only the wit but the time-dyed tenderness a younger man could never manage. I console myself with that thought as I lie dying in the sun.

WHAT ARE THEY SAYING?

Made a Polish waitress cry last week. I must stop doing that. This time the ostensible cause was teapots. My tea arrived as a perforated bag floating corpse-like on its back in a cup of brown soupy-looking liquid, which is not how I like it, and when I asked what had happened to the teapot she told me there'd been an incident. 'Incident or accident?' I asked. I suppose I didn't need to know, since knowing wasn't going to get me a teapot, but if you're having a conversation, you're having a conversation. It is a species of impoliteness to go on speaking to a person when you aren't certain what they're saying.

Her eyes filled like my teacup. I didn't see what I had said or done to occasion that. I hadn't been aggressive. I had even essayed a smile. It is comic, after all, in a serious restaurant, to be served tea which you would no more think of drinking than you would an open sewer. 'All usualised teaposies incriminated in unaccountable Nietzschean engineering catastrophe,' she said, before scurrying away with her apron to her face. Now I know she couldn't possibly have said that, but it was what I heard. So whose fault is that?

Suddenly I can't understand what anyone's saying. I don't

mean intellectually, I mean I can't distinguish the words people are using. Can't harmonise the sounds with any I already know. I've had my ears tested. They're not perfect – I've been using them too long for them to be perfect – but taking one thing with a bugger, the ear specialist told me, they're not too bag.

It's not only in restaurants that I have this problem. Shops the same, telephones, television, movies. Especially movies. I've been going to a lot of movies recently in company with a person who's close to me and happens to be a member of BAFTA. At this time of the year she has to see every movie made since the BAFTAs of the year before. I make no attempt to influence her judgement. I just go along when I'm allowed and try my best to hear what's being said.

Usually I'm lost within the first ten minutes of the movie starting. *The Bourne Ultimatum* had me floundering in five and with *American Gangster* I didn't make it past the credits. *No Country for Old Men* (overrated, in my opinion: violence stylised for intellectuals) had a mumbly beginning and got more mumbly from there, whereas *There Will Be Blood* was unintelligible initially before clearing itself up in line with Daniel Day-Lewis's marvellously mad theatricality – and there is that to be said for the theatre: you can hear it. Even Sidney Lumet's *Before the Devil Knows You're Dead* had me baffled for long stretches, which doesn't alter the fact that its failure to pick up a nomination is a scandal. Too Shakespearean, I can only suppose, in the playing out of its ineluctable morality. Too hot. Coen Brothers cold is the temperature of the hour. We like our existentialism ironic just now, perhaps as a relief from the childish ardour of our politics.

I have no doubt that subject matter has a lot to do with what I can and cannot hear. The majority of this year's most successful films are about killers, hitmen, gangland members and other assorted scumbags, and I have never penetrated what gangland members say to one another in the movies. It's a matter of the conspiratorial pitch of their voices, partly. But also of what in my polytechnic days we used to call their aims and objectives. Not everyone is interested in the whys and wherefores of rubbing people out; and if the vocabulary of skulduggery doesn't grab you, you don't listen. Let Marianne Dashwood lose her heart to Mr Willoughby and I follow every syllable of every palpitation. For love and its trials I am all ears. But the minute there's a criminal plot in the hatching I go to sleep. Even *The Sopranos*, to which I am a late and obsessive convert, is far more engrossing when Tony commits adultery or buys his wife a bracelet (the two are usually connected) than when he beats someone to a pulp.

And I suspect I am not alone in feeling this. Certainly every time I whisper to my companion to get her to explain what's happening everyone in the cinema turns around to tell me to shut up, which I take to be the proof that they're having trouble following as well. So I must assume that the fault is not in me but in the movie-makers, who want us not to comprehend because incomprehensibility is now the measure of cinematic authenticity.

This can't be the case in actuality, of course, because if criminals had as much trouble understanding one another as I have understanding them no crime would ever be committed. But then crime for cinema buffs is not crime as it is for criminals. Why we are so keen on watching killings from the comfort of our cinema seats at the moment is a subject for another day, but there can be no question that there's some *nostalgie de la boue* in the wind, a hankering for the brutalities which, for most members of BAFTA, daily life does not provide. And concealed in this hankering for brutality is a further hankering for a time before language. It is as though we have entered an anti-evolutionary period in which we wish to roll back civilisation and with it the words that mark us out as civilised.

However you explain what's going on in America, I date the

demise of verbal communication in this country to our rejection of received pronunciation. Rather than be spoken to by a snob we understood, we chose the Babel Tower of warring regional accents – a trade-off of intelligibility for equality. Now we live in an anti-elitist dialect-democracy where no one knows what the hell anyone else is talking about. A godsend for the capitalists who can with good conscience locate their call centres in places where nobody can assist you or otherwise purposefully take your call because you can't understand them and they can't understand you. Recently a person from the deep north-east of England attempted to sort out inconsistencies in my mobile phone account. 'Aylike Baader–Meinhof mullhi mead ya doont you cal coolate Gloria Steinem, anything else I can help you with?' he said.

'Forget it,' I told him. 'I might as well be talking to a Dutchman.'

'You calling me a douche bag? I won't be spooken to like that,' he said.

I'd have had him rubbed out, had I only known how to communicate with criminals.

LEONARD COHEN IN CONCERT

These have been a serious few weeks, our country locked in profound moral debate about aesthetic judgement versus popular appreciation, the boundaries of good taste, the rights and wrongs of telling radio audiences whose granddaughter you've been knocking off, the case for universal suffrage when it comes to deciding who should win *The X Factor* or remain on *Strictly Come Dancing*. Anyone just landed from Mars watching John Sergeant's farewell dance to a standing ovation of solemn tears and eulogy would have supposed we were saying goodbye to a leader who had led us through war, famine and the plague. Certainly Sergeant spoke to the nation as though he'd done that and more. Those whom the television gods would destroy they first make vain.

What Sergeant forgot was that he'd entertained us because of what he couldn't do, not because of what he could. Incompetence is a great virtue to the English, but only so long as it's wedded to modesty. Imperfection with no delusions is what we like.

'Ring the bells that still can ring' is my motto. 'Forget your perfect offering – there's a crack, a crack in everything.' I have, of course, stolen those words from Leonard Cohen. Why not? In complex moral times we need whatever guidance is on offer.

Leonard Cohen isn't somebody I'd put my mind to much until the other week when I went to see him at the O2 arena in Greenwich. I and fifty thousand other people, not doddery exactly, but not of an age to pull a knife whenever someone disrespected us by breathing in our direction. Not the same audience, in other words, as attended the Urban Music Awards the night after. Trouble waiting to happen, if you ask me, the minute you call someting Urban Music. What's in a name? Everything. Urban is a moral anagram of armed. But who's going to come jingling weaponry to an evening entitled *Leonard Cohen*? You would as soon take a gun to a bar mitzvah. We, anyway, were just there for the words, the music and a dollop of nostalgia. Is that why the urban young are so jumpy – they don't have enough to remember? Certainly there's less room for knives if you're loaded down with recollection. And of course you move more slowly.

I read Leonard Cohen with passing interest, in the sixties. I liked a number of his poems whose names now escape me and was aroused by his novel *Beautiful Losers*, described by someone as the 'most revolting novel written in Canada', a compliment it's hard to gauge until you know what other revolting novels have been written in Canada. I could suggest a few but this isn't a provocative column. After Leonard Cohen I'm in beautiful loser spirits – 'Dance me to the end of love' spirits, decadently moony, feeling it's all over but still hoping for another chance, 'For flesh is warm and sweet.'

Sound a bit 1960s? Well, there you have him. And there you have me too. After the sixties, when he started to put his poems to music, I fell out of interest with him. Singing, singing, singing – why had everyone suddenly burst out singing? Thereafter, since I wasn't a buyer of albums, I lost track of his career, didn't know if he was dead or alive, couldn't remember a line, even of the most revolting novel written in Canada, and never expected to think about him again. Now here I am in his audience, and now here he is, a devilishly attractive man in his middle seventies.

Some men do old age better than they do youth. Especially melancholy-sensual men who can't decide whether they're happy or not. The not knowing, like the not eating, keeps them lean. He is fascinatingly attenuated, as laconic as a snake on grass, with a face lined by a lifetime's amused and desperate indulgence of the appetites, by which I don't just mean wine, women, infidelity and betrayal, but also rhapsodic spirituality alternating with ecstatic doubt. A meanings man. It's corny in its way, as well as beautiful. All existentialism when it's life style is corny. But there's a crack, a crack in everything. And you won't be popular unless you're corny.

I like it that he doesn't jig about. Such a change to see someone on a stage, immobile – as still as thought. We have the attention span of children. A thing will interest us only if it sparkles and moves. Madonna, Michael Jackson – people come back from their concerts raving about how well they move as though moving is a virtue in itself. I don't get it. If you want moving ring Pickfords. Leonard Cohen barely stirs, limiting himself to crouching over his microphone into which he whispers with hoarse suggestiveness. When he does essay a ghost of a dance he gets an affectionately ironic cheer for it.

I would have wished the audience to follow his example. It's all a bit cultic for my taste, fans whooping and waving like born-again Christians at a hymn-singing hoedown whenever he starts a song they recognise. I'm thinking about this, wondering if they'd be whooping if he hadn't put his poetry to music, wondering why the words alone won't do, when I hear those great lines from the song 'Anthem'. Ring the bells etc. Forget your perfect offering. There's a crack – a crack in everything.

It's like a reprimand to people of my temperament – life's

complainants, eroticists of disappointment, lovers only of what's flawless and overwrought. Could he be singing this to me? You expect too much, mister. You are too unforgiving. Not everything works out, not everything is great, and not everyone must like what you like.

I've been taught this lesson before. I remember reading an essay by the novelist Mario Vargas Llosa in which he argues for the necessity of vulgarity in serious literature. Thomas Hardy said a writer needed to be imperfectly grammatical some of the time. Mailer told an audience that not everybody wanted to ride in a Lamborghini. And now here's Leonard Cohen saying the same thing. *Forget your perfect offering. There's a crack . . .*

And then comes another, still more wonderful, clinching line – 'That's how the light gets in.'

Savour that! At a stroke, weakness becomes strength and fault becomes virtue. I feel as though original sin has just been re-explained to me. There was no fall. We were born flawed. Flawed is how we were designed to be. Which means we don't need redeeming after all. Light? Why go searching for light? The light already shines from us. It got in through our failings.

Had I known how to whoop I'd have whooped.

NOE-BEAVER

Omitted mention, in last week's panegyric to San Francisco, of a lovely little park, the size of an apron, situated in the gay suburb of Castro at the junction of Noe and Beaver Streets. You heard me – Noe and Beaver Streets! What chance of finding – in the heart of this predominantly male homosexual Shangri-La – a well-tended, spiky-shrubbed community garden (with locked gates) called Noe-Beaver? – beaver being, as I don't have to remind my raffish readers, American slang for the female pudenda.

Odd, in that case, that the gay women of Castro haven't sought to change the name of the junction. To Yess-Beaver, say, or Moore-Beaver. Or Noe-Schlong.

Could be, I suppose, that they are all too grown up in San Francisco to care or notice. But while I am standing there, one foot in Noe and the other in Beaver, marvelling at the happy conjunction, I overhear a gay man, who happens to be wheeling a small child in a pushchair (children in pushchairs being must-have items if you're gay in San Francisco), discussing quinoa on his mobile phone. I am able to deduce – don't ask me how – that he is talking to another gay man who also has a child, and neither is sure how many quinoa cookies make an adequate breakfast for a two-year-old. 'So where are you speaking from?' the father on the other end of the line must have asked, because the reply comes back, 'Noe-Beaver', followed by a laugh.

So it isn't just me.

People think you make these things up. Tell them it's novelist's serendipity and they look at you suspiciously. Which is inconsistent of them considering how biographical everyone is in their reading today, convinced that the only story you have to tell is the story of your life. Until, that is, you stumble upon Noe-Beaver. Then they think you're fabricating.

Coincidentally – except that there is no such thing as coincidence if you're a novelist – I was interrogated on just such writerly matters at Heathrow airport en route to San Francisco. One of those random security spot checks. Not the sort that goes 'Has any terrorist packed your case for you? Are you carrying a samurai sword? What about nail scissors? Enjoy your flight.' No, this was the business. Cases on the table, security guards with surgical gloves sliding their fingers under the collars of your shirts, even your cufflink box examined for secret compartments. I approve of exhaustive baggage searches. Better if they're happening to someone else, but as a person of vaguely Middle Eastern appearance I submit to them philosophically when stopped, because if they let *me* past without a second glance who else might be slipping through?

As far as I could tell, though you can never be entirely sure, the writerly interrogation had nothing to do with airport security. It was more about the Sikh security man's ambitions to write a novel himself one day. How he knew I was a novelist I can't imagine, unless that's just something you can tell from a person's wardrobe. Novelist's shoes – maybe I'd packed a few too many pairs of those. What he wanted to know, anyway, was how you start. 'Where do you get the words from?' he asked me.

A tough one, that. 'You immerse yourself in words,' was the

best I could manage in the circumstances, 'and at last they come to you. Words are your medium. If you don't have those, you might as well forget it.'

Not true, of course. There are countless successful novelists who have no words. But I took the liberty of assuming he wanted to be a good novelist.

And I was right, because his next question was one only a good novelist in embryo could have asked. 'But you must employ so many words,' he said. 'Don't you worry you might one day use them up?'

He was a charming man with impeccable manners and teeth worth about a million dollars apiece where I was going. If you sell your teeth, I wanted to tell him, you'll make far more than you will writing novels which evince concern for words. But I could see that the other security staff were losing patience. They hadn't stopped me so that their literary colleague could start a conversation about the exhaustibility of language. There were things of more suitcase-associated importance they needed to discuss, such as the number of ties I'd packed for a three-day trip to San Francisco. Almost as hard to explain the ties as where words come from. I just happen to be a word and tie person. Even though it's unlikely I'll wear one (a tie, I mean) where I'm going, I like to travel with a variety, one for each shirt – and I travel with a multiplicity of shirts (hence the boxes of collar stiffeners) – just in case.

A nutter? Maybe. But they can't stop you from flying for being a nutter. So it was thank you and have a good flight, or it would have been had the indefatigable Sikh not found a final question for me. 'And the stories? Where do they come from? Do you sit at your desk for years on end and make them up?'

'No,' I told him, 'I catch planes.'

Funny, but they never believe you. Walk the cliffs from Eastbourne to Beachy Head and you'll find a proliferation of wooden memorial benches, all facing out to sea, all bearing melancholy inscriptions, all heartbreaking if you're the memorial-bench fanatic that the hero of my latest novel is. Some reviewers have doubted their existence. Too unlikely. Too convenient. Too much of a coincidence that he should find them while out walking, looking for sorrow. But the truth is that's exactly when I found them, while out walking, looking for sorrow. God is good to novelists. He puts things where they hope to find them. Such as Sikhs with literary ambitions at Heathrow. Or a place called Noe-Beaver, plumb in the middle of homoerotic San Francisco.

THE LAST CIGARETTE

I feel there must be some Shakespearean line out there, to the effect that death does not come singly, that when one person dies another person dies, by association, with him. I'm not thinking of the Donne metaphor, that we are none of us islands, that any man's death diminishes us because we are involved in mankind. It's not the universality of loss I'm speaking of but of the way a living man might stand in, in some way, for a dead one, and that we only finally register the death of the first with the death of the second. Forgive the clumsiness. It is possible I am seeking consolation in abstruseness because I cannot bear to write what I feel.

My friend the writer Simon Gray died last week. Though he had been ill and had written about his illness without illusion, his death was unexpected. It was to me, anyway. We have been reading Simon Gray's *Smoking Diaries* for some years now; the damage caused by his excesses has become part of our experience; we look forward to each new volume, fully expecting him to be clinging perilously on, for us, for the joy and relief that making merry with calamity brings, for another thirty years. But he won't be.

The Last Cigarette

The person whose death he has reawakened – making me relive it, if that's not a tasteless paradox – is Ian MacKillop, academic, author, biographer of F. R. Leavis. We were, you see, all Leavisites together, though MacKillop and Gray were five or six years older than me, friends of each other at Cambridge, beyond my reach when I encountered them, in the way that prefects are out of reach when you first turn up at grammar school. To my jealous northern eye they had an air of aloof sophistication, to do partly with their being handsome, tall, southern, well spoken, fiercely articulate and attractive to other men – no Mancunian was ever attractive to other men, not even to fellow Mancunians. Simon appeared the more worldly of the two, partly because he was a bachelor, on the qui vive, and Ian was married young, with a baby that cried while he was supervising Leavisian neophytes like me at his home. The minute the crying started he would turn pale and tear his hair, sometimes pulling himself up by its roots, like a character in Dickens. But conversationally, out of the house, he shared with Simon Gray an edge of wit which I took to be disdain – I had always wanted to be disdainful myself – and an intellectual curiosity that gave the lie to the supposed narrowness of the Leavis cult.

In time, the influence of F. R. Leavis will be appraised more generously than it is today. He stifled his pupils, critics who know nothing say of him, consigning them to a cramped evaluative hell of mean-spirited judgementalism and non-creativity. Here is not the place to list the diverse achievements of Leavisites, but the briefest look at Simon Gray's output alone disproves the charge of narrow unproductiveness: over thirty plays for stage, television and radio on the most diverse subjects – the spy George Blake, the relationship between Duveen and Bernard Berenson, Stanley's rear column left behind in the Congo in 1887, academia, language schools, etc. – plus five novels and seven volumes of those magnificently splenetic but tender memoirs which won him a second and more than ever devoted audience. Ian, too, though he was less prolific (unless we allow that teaching is its own prolificacy), wrote with extraordinary variousness – a book on *The British Ethical Societies*, a study of the real-life trio of lovers that inspired Henri-Pierre Roché's novel *Jules et Jim*, the biography of Leavis, essays on all manner of non-canonical subjects such as new wave French cinema and Kingley Amis, whom he taught me how to appreciate, and a sadly unfinished annotated edition of Keats's letters.

Simon wrote touchingly about the span of Ian's interests in his recent volume of diaries, *The Last Cigarette*. 'He knew so much about so many unexpected things – horror films, pulp fiction, westerns as well as thrillers, early Agatha Christie, every poet alive writing in the English language . . . He seemed to have a completely uninhibited mind. I can't remember him being shocked by any subject or event. His curiosity was limit-less, willing to go through endless byways for the pleasure of the journey.'

It takes one to know one. Simon's mind was no less uninhib-ited. Read him on Hank Janson in *The Smoking Diaries,* Vol. 1, and then, to get his range, turn to what he has to say about the novels of Mahfouz in *The Last Cigarette*. As for 'the pleasure of the journey', that, in a nutshell, describes what it was like to know and read both men. You never knew where they were going to take you, only that the articulateness would be all the company you needed. It was briefly fashionable to berate Simon's plays for their 'cold detachment'. Articulacy is not always in favour. It frightens people. But the mistake was to confuse it, as I had confused it in 1962, with disdain. In fact, articulacy is the tragic core of his most famous plays – *Butley*, for example, and *Otherwise Engaged*, which depict men trapped in the dazzle of their own intelligences.

Ian MacKillop died four years ago. Again, suddenly. The night before he died he rang to say he could not make it to a publica-tion party I was giving. I was disappointed. I wanted him to be there. It would be wrong to say he was a father figure to me – he was a touch too spectral to be that – but I did seek his approval and admiration. He told me he was not feeling well, but not to worry for him. It struck me as a strange thing for one man to say to another. 'Don't worry for me.' It was almost feminine, like a caress. And those were the last words he spoke to me.

'He made a calm comedy,' Simon wrote, 'out of the worst events in his life.' Simon the same. Calm comedy bound them. I wanted to make them both laugh, though Simon said his smoke-ruined lungs were making laughter difficult. 'Anyone who wanted to murder me,' he wrote, 'would simply have to say three funny things in a row.' I hope I didn't want to murder him.

His last words to me were as a caress too, though they were for my wife. 'A protective hug for Jenny.' He didn't say what he was protecting her from. The sadness of it all, I suppose – our calm comedy.

SAVAGE TORPOR

We don't use the phrase 'dumbing down' in this column. We believe it exemplifies – maybe even connives in and encourages – the very sin it offers to decry. Say 'dumbing down' and you're dumbing down. There are other words beginning with 'd' to describe the will to destroy a culture. Denigrating, disparaging, dishonouring. And then there's defeatism – the faint-heartedness of intellectuals in that battle for language and meaning in which they have a sacred trust, if not to lead the charge then at least to man the battlements.

I am sitting on a pretty hotel terrace (speaking of battlements) looking out over Windermere (where I have come to unwind), still fuming about a Radio 4 programme I listened to about ten days ago. *Word of Mouth* it was called, and its subject was, in that fair-minded Radio 4 way, 'dumbing down', for and against.

Since there is no 'for' I am not sure why I went on listening. Fair-mindedness on my own part perhaps. Or maybe I was unconsciously calculating that I'd be winding down in Windermere shortly and would need something to fume about. I don't recall whether someone on the programme mounted the usual defence of complacency: namely that people have been complaining about falling standards since the beginning of time – as though the longevity of a complaint proves its falla- ciousness, or the fact that someone said we were getting sillier three thousand years ago must mean that we aren't. But if no one actually said it, I could hear it in the voices of the guests hauled in to dumb up dumbing down – Angela Leonard and Ziggy Liaquat, a pair against whom, like the would-be Tarzan Dudley Moore's one leg, I otherwise have absolutely nothing.

Both Ms Leonard and Mr Liaquat are employees of Edexcel – the former being chair of examiners for history, the latter managing director. Of what again? I believe you heard me the first time. Edexcel – a privately owned examination board, the concept of which I find hard to grasp, though I guess I'm going to have to get used to it now that we have a government that believes in the virtue of privatising everything. But it isn't just the 'private' I'm having trouble with, it's the barbaric compound. *Edexcel*. Oughtn't that to hurt the ear of anyone for whom educational excellence (I assume that's what they're getting at) is a priority, and to whom linguistic euphony therefore matters? Edexcel. It sounds like a cross between a laxative and a substance for sticking stuff to stuff; all right, a substance for sticking stuff to stuff in a specifically educational context, say for sticking presentation accessories to whiteboards, or pupils to their desks.

That something that goes by the name of Edexcel can assess and mark, offer qualifications and award certificates, make judgements and set standards, bothers me to the degree that the word 'Edexcel' is itself a barbarism to anyone for whom language has dignity. I can't imagine Angela Leonard or Ziggy Liaquat, however, having time for such verbal squeamishness, their first concern being clarity in the setting of examination questions, or what they call 'keeping the threshold low'. The great obstacle to keeping the threshold low, in their view, is unnecessary difficulty or 'inaccessibility' of language in the examination question. One example of this was the

Whatever It Is, I Don't Like It

word 'salient', which reputedly floored an examinee with its
obscurity, thereby preventing him from showing what he knew,
though I would have said it made a very good job of showing
what he didn't. Another was 'expediency'. And a third was
'perfect'. Come again? *Perfect.* Is that the verb or the adjective?
Well, there, reader, you have the nub of the problem, if nub isn't
too great a bar to comprehension.

Let me set the scene as Angela Leonard set it. The subject is
history and there is a question relating to the trial of the
Rosenbergs in the 1950s. The question cites the ruling of Judge
Irving Kaufman who told the Rosenbergs: 'You put into the
hands of the Russians the A-bomb years before our best scien-
tists predicted Russia would perfect the bomb.' Clear enough if
you read it out, Angela Leonard conceded, but picture the
consternation of the candidate who 'probably' – her word –
would read the verb per*fect* as the adjective p*er*fect. In order to
avoid which confusion the examiners changed 'would perfect'
to 'would be able to perfect'.

If it says little for the candidate that he'd be unable to work
out how that word 'perfect' was operating in the context, it says
even less that the chair of the examiners for history positively
expected him to flounder. But that might be the consequence
of years of sitting Edexcel exams if you're the candidate, and
years of working for Edexcel if you're the examiner. Low
threshold expectations all round.

How a person ignorant of the different ways of reading the
word 'perfect' can pass an exam on any subject requiring a
working knowledge of the English language – as history assur-
edly is – I do not know. But more bizarre still is the idea that he
will have grasped the political and ideological subtleties of the
Rosenbergs' defection. Presumably he will have been spoon-
fed the requisite information and the accompanying received
opinions. Spoon-fed by Edexcel itself, I don't doubt, which
won't want its efforts stymied by some pesky little word that is

314

both adjective and verb. It was at this point in the conversation that Ziggy Liaquat reminded us there had been a great deal of investment in education, 'so you would expect a return of some kind'. Chilling words, the only meaning of which I could deduce was that examinees have to pass as a matter of economic necessity, which amounts to saying that the only thing that is actually being tested is Edexcel's ability to create the conditions for passing, and whatever stands in the way of as many examinees as possible getting through – such as ignorance of the most basic English vocabulary and word usage – has to be Edexcelled out of existence. Thus does dumbing down, though we don't use the phrase, brazenly declare itself to be the handmaiden of commerce.

The last I heard was Angela Leonard citing another difficulty-in-waiting – 'wicked'. A word we must be careful of using because it no longer means what it used to mean. So that's the end of 'Richard III was a wicked bastard – discuss'.

Looking out over Windermere, I think of Wordsworth writing about 'the multitude of causes' combining to reduce the human mind to 'a state of almost savage torpor'. Now why would I be thinking of that?

PINTERESQUE

I have just come across a story in the papers describing my rift with Harold Pinter and its subsequent repair. This flatters me. A rift implies an earlier state of friendly relations, and until very recently – I wish now it had not been so recent – we had not by any definition of the word been friends.

My first encounter with him was at a party given by Simon Gray who, as far as I could tell, had mischievously alerted Harold to a joke I'd made about his work in one of my early novels. A couple living in Cornwall and starved of culture, but in a sort of war with what passed for culture at the time, would drive to London each weekend, go to one play after another only to walk out at the interval, unless the play was by Pinter in which case they walked out at the first pause. Trust me, it's funnier on the page. But there was no reason Pinter should think it funny in the least. And no reason – I did not suppose he was reading me – for him to have come across it. Indeed, I'm pretty sure he would not have but for Simon Gray, in a spirit of absurdist high jinks, fancying the spectacle of a couple of his friends squaring up to each other.

Pinter, anyway, approached me in what I took to be a

pugilistic manner and told me who he was. I told him I knew who he was. He told me he knew what I'd been writing about him. I told him I was surprised but honoured. He told me that what he was thinking did not honour me. I told him I was honoured to be dishonoured by him. He looked me up and down as though calculating how many blows it would take to floor me. One is the answer but I didn't tell him that. And so it would have gone on had Simon Gray not interrupted us. 'You two met each other then?' he asked.

Looking back I wonder whether Pinter really was being menacing to me. Could he just have been making merry? You don't always know in his plays whether one character wants to kill another or just have fun with him. That's Pinter's subject – the borderline, the uncertainty, the hair-trigger moments when joking turns to violence and vice versa. We are powder kegs and clowns, and it's hard to know which makes us more dangerous.

I wasn't a great fan of his plays. Surreal minimalism leaves me dissatisfied. I like amplitude and excess. Of course he could do hyperbole, but it was the hyperbole of less, and I'm a more man. Maybe his work rattled me. What if I was wrong? What if less was more and more was less? The other reason he rattled me was that his screenplays were so good – *The Servant* and the *The Go-Between* I loved – and he spoke so compellingly about his work in interviews, that I could see he had a genius I couldn't find in his stage plays. At the edges of my professional life he nagged away at me. I was always thinking about him. Then came a decisive incident. I was chairing a *Late Show* Booker Prize panel, being rude as I was hired to be, when a courier on a motorbike delivered a hand-written missive (I almost said missile) from Harold Pinter – believe me when I tell you it was still blazing hot from his hand – saying he hoped never to see me discussing literature on television again. It felt like a threat to the entire edifice that was the BBC, never mind to me.

Thereafter, when we found ourselves in the same room, we

took up positions in opposite corners. Or at least I took up positions in opposite corners. When he became a more overtly political figure, railing against America, I poured scorn on him. What a waste of a linguistic gift to expend it on so banal a cause, saying exactly what men with no gift for thought or language whatsoever were saying. How could a masterly writer of ambiguities sink to the same level of crude one-note commonplace as Ken Livingstone and George Galloway? How could he bear to share the air with them let alone a platform?

Perversely, that made me think again about his plays. Such subtlety there, such crassness on the soapbox. Then a second decisive event. Quite out of the blue he approached me, again at a party, and extended a hand. 'There has been a certain froideur between us of late,' he said. I didn't reply, '*Froideur!* Harold, it's been glacial.' I simply took his hand and melted. He could do that when he bent his gaze on you, he could turn you to jelly.

I am unable to account for this sudden gesture of goodwill. Perhaps it was Simon Gray's influence. Or perhaps Harold's wife had said something. He was becoming ill, maybe she thought he ought to be settling accounts, or needed a nice Jewish boy for a friend. It's my belief that what's unspoken in Pinter's plays – the great mysterious lacuna at their heart, the object of all those apparently motiveless interrogations – is his Jewishness. Maybe Lady Antonia thought that too and wanted him to fill the space, at least in life.

Not that we talked Jews. Or, thank God, America. What we talked on the single occasion we lunched together was literature and sex. He had invited me out to discuss my new novel which he had read in proof and was generous enough – more generous than I had ever been to him – to say he liked. The novel is about jealousy, husbands and lovers, the elusive transference of erotic power – Pinter territory in fact. Without realising it, I'd written a Pinteresque novel, Pinteresque in subject, I mean, not in form. Less I still won't do. Or can't do.

He knew screeds of James Joyce by heart, which I listened to in wondering rapture. An observer would have picked us for master and acolyte, hero and heroiser. And so it felt. Ill and angry, he was still a great talker and, to my guilty surprise, a great listener too. His deep beautiful brown eyes swallowed me whole. I was in love. No other word for it. Bewitched. I skipped home like a boy. We'd agreed we would do it again. Then Simon Gray died and the time for conviviality passed. And now Harold. So there was and will be no second lunch and I am desperately sad about it. I would have liked more of him, not less.

WASHINGTON I

Here's a line I never thought I'd hear myself employ: I caught the last plane out. In fact – if only prosaic fact will satisfy you – it was just the last plane out of Heathrow to Dulles International, all later flights to Washington having been cancelled because of the snow forecast to 'bury' the city.

There was even some question of whether we'd be able to land at all before the snow began to fall in earnest. But we made it. There's another line I never thought I'd hear myself employ: We made it.

By a whisker. We weren't only the last plane out, we were the last plane in. It was like landing in some hellish Eastern-bloc state before the Communists decamped. Not another plane in sight, nothing moving, all the runways vacant, no understanding where the snow was falling from because there was no sky. In such places snow would fall as a kind of ironic commentary on the political system: behold the spiritual nothingness to which ideology has reduced you. But this was Washington – bright, pushy, free-enterprise, illuminated Washington! Snow belongs as though by its intrinsic nature to Communism. Capitalism, one feels, should by now have found a way of dispensing with it. But it was about to close Dulles International Airport.

So how long, I wondered, before the American middle right, the Tea Party folk, would blame the most violent blizzard to hit the capital in living memory on Obama's socialist agenda?

Expect more of this political savvy over the next few weeks. I am in Washington being a visiting professor. Seemed like a nice gig when I was offered it, but that was before the snow fell. Let's not be churlish: it still is a nice gig, or it will be if George Washington University ever reopens. The minute we landed, the city's institutions began to close their doors. You've never seen so much snow. Lock yourself in your room and don't come out is the advice on radio and television. Which is all very well if you're in your own home and have a freezer stuffed with pizzas, but an apartment hotel with a complimentary sachet of coffee, two tea bags and a packet of chocolate chip cookies – the difference between civilisation and barbarism is the difference between an English biscuit and an American cookie – is no place to be holed up in for a month.

Rather than unpack my summery shirts – the weather had been unseasonably mild in Washington in January; I've even brought shorts in expectation of paddling in the Potomac – I head straight out into the blizzard and make for Trader Joe's, a grocery store which the woolly-hatted porter tells me is just across the street, that's if I can get across the street. Trader Joe's, he adds, is organic. Like I care – to speak the way the locals speak – whether Trader Joe's is organic. I am about to be immured in the worst snowstorm in Washington's history and I am supposed to be pleased that I can get unsalted sunflower seeds and reduced-guilt (I kid you not) tortilla strips grown with consideration to Mother Earth. In weather like this it's impossible to show love to nature, and I know the argument that says it's lack of love for nature that's got us into this mess. Without going so far as climate-change denial, I don't hold with quid pro quo explanations of natural events. This blizzard is an act of motiveless malignancy and there's an end of it.

As luck would have it, Trader Joe's turns out to be the best grocery store with principles I have ever shopped in, and that isn't just desperation talking. Yes, you can get your slivered seeds if you want them, but you can also get salamis soaked in red wine, puttanesca sauce made with red wine, excellent red-wine vinegars, red-wine mustard and, best of all, red wine itself, organised not only by country but by grape. Suddenly I don't want the siege to end; God willing I won't have to do an hour's teaching and can sample every Pinot Noir the state of Oregon can produce before I fly back home again, assuming a thaw, in March.

But this isn't all that's raised my spirits. Reader, they are panic buying here. All the bread has gone. All the eggs have gone. Bottled water's running low. (Don't ask me why they're just not buying wine.) And the queues stretch out into the street. And why does this please me? Because it shows it's not just us who go to pieces in extremity. I passed more and bigger snowploughs between Washington airport and the city than the whole of our impecunious country can rustle up from Land's End to Gretna Green. I drove by mountains of grit as high as Snowdon. This is the way to do it, I thought. This puts us to shame. But the roads remain unploughed and ungritted and they're panic buying in the shops.

What is more, when I turn on the television weather hysteria is all I can find. Channel outdoing channel with 'wall-to-wall coverage of the bad stuff' – 'Snowmageddon', Obama is calling it; 'snowpocalypse' is another popular coinage – hour upon hour of footage of deserted roads, stranded vehicles, scenes of people fighting one another over the last snow shovel in Wal-Mart. And we Brits are the ones who are said to fall apart when winter strikes. True, it only takes a snowflake to bring our railways to a stop, and here, so far, thirty inches have fallen, but still and all, snow's just snow.

Having seen an item about panic buying in Washington on the BBC News, my mother calls. 'I hear they're running out of toilet rolls,' she says. When I was a child my mother never let me leave the house without a hundred yards of toilet roll tightly folded in the back pocket of my trousers, 'just in case'. Now she isn't here to look after me the catastrophe she always dreaded has arrived. 'I might still have a wad,' I tell her, trying my back pocket.

At school the other boys laughed at my wad of folded toilet paper. Who's laughing now, sucker?

In fact, before you start sending parcels, I have plenty of everything I need, especially self-satisfaction. Last plane out, last plane in, a storm to end storms ravaging a strange city, egg riots at the organic grocery store – and I am unfazed. My wife runs me a bath. After a long soak I crack open a Sonoma County Zinfandel and watch television report more closures. Schools, museums, churches, and now the federal government. Wimps.

WASHINGTON II

A small American in a small art lover's beard – a small art lover's beard on an even smaller art-loving American would be a better description – greets us at the door to the permanent collection and asks us to leave our coats in the cloakroom.

I let him know we would rather not; our time is limited and we don't want to spend it queuing for cloakrooms when we could be looking at the Rothkos and the Bonnards for which the Phillips Collection is renowned. May we keep them on? He shakes his head politely. Washington is a polite town. 'They look pretty heavy anyway,' he says, as though he's insisting on this only for our convenience.

I don't say that the weight of my coat is my business, that no one tells me how many clothes I may wear at Tate Britain, and that this is pretty rich all round given the fuss America is making at the moment about state intrusion into what Brits call civil liberty and Americans free enterprise. If free enterprise means anything doesn't it mean I may look at Rothko in a coat if I so choose?

In fact, if he'd had his way, Rothko would have determined not only how many clothes people looking at his work should wear, but of what colour and what weave. There's a small Rothko room at the Phillips Collection, chapel-like according to the painter's stipulations, an environment in which, in his words, the walls are to be 'defeated' so that the space can be 'saturated with the feeling of the work'. Myself, I think the artist should leave feelings of saturation to the person looking. Which is what Bonnard does. Look if you like, Bonnard says. My colours will work on you or they won't. Very French. But not Rothko, who is very American. With Rothko you don't look at the work, you submit to it.

Call this art as tyranny. First the gallery dictates your wardrobe, then the artist commandeers your mind. So is this an American paradox or another instance of American schizophrenia? Free the individual and then tell him what to do with his freedom; entangle him in red tape and then raise the roof if anyone mentions socialism.

The shock jocks of American television are defining socialism as the government invading your home with a shotgun and stealing your furniture. The Mad Hatter's Tea Party, whose patrons include Sarah 'Read My Hands' Palin – otherwise described by the comedian Bill Maher as 'the Nudnik from Alaska' – is making inroads into popular opinion with a mix of perfectly explicable loathing of the banks and perfectly inexplicable anxiety regarding health-care reforms which they are convinced will lead to the elderly and the sick being left to bleed to death in the corridors and waiting rooms of filthy hospitals, as they are in England, rather than on the roads as they are, if they happen to be uninsured, in the USA. (Don't bother to correct me on either score. I am infected by the new adversariality of American politics. Someone attacks you with unreason, you strike back with more unreason still.)

You would think that what has happened in Washington this last week would have finally disclosed to Americans the overwhelming truth about free enterprise: namely, that it doesn't work. It's the snow I'm talking about. Not who was responsible for making it fall, but who is responsible for clearing it away. Questioned by snowed-in citizens on the matter of uncleared sidewalks, the Mayor of Washington, Adrian Fenty – a man with an unnervingly over-polished bald pate – explained that responsibility for clearing a path outside a house or shop falls to the individual whose house or shop it is, and not the city. Interrogated further as to why he hadn't used his powers to compel people to fulfil these responsibilities, Mayor Fenty raised a hand and did to his glistening head what he will not do the city sidewalks. 'I prefer the carrot to the stick approach,' he said.

Meaning, we don't hold with telling people what to do in these parts, unless they're wearing too many clothes to look at art in.

So the situation is this: some stretches of sidewalk appear passable, because owners of property have been out with their shovels, but these you can access only by leaping the hummocks of filthy snow, or fording the roaring rivulets of freezing sludge, left by owners of property who don't give a shit. The consequence of which is that the cleared sidewalks are of use to you only if someone helicopters you in.

Now wouldn't you think that if you were clearing your own two feet of pavement you would clear the two feet on either side of you while the spade was in your hand, no matter that the persons charged with that responsibility can't or won't? If not as an act of common courtesy, then in order to make your own coming and going that little bit easier? In socialist England where the government steals our furniture and leaves us to die where we fall, we shovel away snow and ask who the snow belongs to later. But in free-enterprise Washington this apparently is not possible. What's mine is mine, what's yours is yours. So go break your neck. But it's said politely.

I could have the sidewalks cleared in minutes. I'd invite government intervention. That's what governments are for. To make us do in a body what we are cussedly incapable of doing as individuals. Individualism is a fine ideal; it's only a shame individuals suck.

Bill Maher, to whom I've already referred, made the same point in an interview with Larry King the other day. 'The people stink,' he said, alluding to the illogicality of the popular disillusionment with Obama for not doing what would, were he to do it, disillusion them still more.

There, in a nutshell, is the case against empowering the people. They stink. But how can you not love a country where someone will say that on television? We Brits might shovel one another's snow but we haven't the courage to insult the Demos. Love is what our politicians and comedians crave. They want the people to adore them. Cry a little over them. Feel their pain. Not even Paxman will tell the British public they stink.

So, thanks to Bill Maher, I approach the great democratic experiment which is America from an upside-down position. It doesn't work because the people stink. But in a country where you can say the people stink, the people can't stink. So it does work.

It's convoluted, but you can get there. Which is more than you can say about the sidewalks.

ELITISM FOR EVERYBODY

Here's a little test for you. Who said of Samuel Beckett, 'His appeal lies in his directness – the sparse, unembellished prose that can make his meticulous stage directions unexpected'?

No, not Terry Eagleton. Guess again.

I'll put you out of your misery. Nick Clegg.

Let's not get carried away. I wouldn't have given that an A+ had it turned up in an essay at Wolverhampton Polytechnic. He who would avoid cliché must not put 'sparse' and 'unembellished' together. And 'directness' is not a noun that quite winkles out what's distinctive or, as Clegg has it, 'disturbing' – another cliché – in Samuel Beckett. Mrs Thatcher had 'directness', as did John Prescott, if you remember him. The quality makes neither of them Beckett. But never mind. The wonder of it is, that asked to choose his hero, Clegg chose Beckett.

Whether Cameron will come round to any of Clegg's tastes in the long nights of slinky rapprochement ahead remains to be seen. His own stated preferences have always been strategically populist. As, of course, were Blair's and, latterly, Brown's. In Blair's case I believed them. Blair was superficial to his skin. In Brown's I didn't. We will never know now whether Brown would have fared better had he been allowed to speak in his own native sparse, unembellished prose, but it would have been worth a try. The lesson should not be lost on Cameron. The British might despise elitism but they quickly see through cultural sycophancy.

Though I don't doubt the sincerity of his passion for Beckett, Clegg is not what you would call an intellectual. No more than is – or maybe just a little bit more than is – Cameron. We wouldn't want it otherwise. In this country the intellectual life and the political life are inimical. We don't do philosopher or poet leaders. That keeps us tepid but it also keeps us safe. Clegg admits himself 'unsettled' by Beckett's idea that 'life is just a series of motions devoid of meaning'. A little flirtation with emptiness in the front row of the orchestra stalls is one thing, but we would rather our politicians didn't embrace nihilism.

It doesn't, however, have to be a choice between being an intellectual or being a dickhead – the choice Old Labour made when it came up with John Prescott, as did New Labour when it came up with Ed 'Give 'Em a Laptop' Balls. Seeing both of them popping up in news programmes as power changed hands last week was like watching a person age before one's eyes. The world was new and they weren't. The thing they vowed to go on fighting for nobody any longer wanted – not in those terms anyway. The new language being spoken belonged to men – neither dickheads nor intellectuals – whose time we thought had passed but who suddenly were here again: public-school boys unabashed by the privileges education had conferred on them, unapologetic, burnished by advantages of birth and money. That such an old reality could present itself as a new one has been the most fascinating aspect of this election. What are they still doing here, such men? They were supposed to have been superseded long ago. We thought we had cleared the way for people of another sort entirely.

Noting its predominantly private-school make-up, Lee Elliot

Major of the Sutton Trust – a charity whose aim is to promote social mobility through education – expresses concern that the Liberal Conservative Cabinet 'is highly unrepresentative'. So whose fault is that? Ought the Tories to be less representative of themselves? Are the Lib Dems now shown to be as self-serving as their new partners? Or are we to blame – still servile in our souls, still doffing our caps to gentlefolk?

Or – and this is the explanation I favour – isn't their reappearance the final proof of a self-defeating contradiction at the heart of socialism itself? After thirteen years of Labour, and many more years of grievously misguided tampering, not only with grammar schools but with the very principles of a humane education, relativising knowledge for fear of privileging truth, denying children an education in the name of not imposing one on them, have we not simply left the field open for Clegg and Cameron's return? They are not in power because they are monsters of deviance – the attacks on Clegg for acting politically this last week have been as absurd as anything in Beckett – nor are they in power because they are throwbacks for whom we entertain a sentimental hierarchical regard; they are in power because we have not come up with a sufficient number of people educationally equipped to seize it from them.

Social mobility through education is a wonderful ideal; but first we have to provide the education.

The irony is that the Tories, with or without the Liberal Democrats, are far more likely to facilitate this mobility through education than Labour in any of its guises. Michael Gove is the new Education Secretary. I confess to a liking for Michael Gove. He is a cultivated man and looks the way a cultivated man should look – always just a touch unkempt, cross-toothed and with a bit of a headache (I'm talking of impression, not fact), ironical, intellectually impatient, not quite inhabiting the space, as the two Cs occupy space, carved out for him by privilege. He is also, against all the prevailing orthodoxies, Arnoldian.

Education, he said recently, is about 'introducing young people to the best that has been thought and written'. And you can't get much more Arnoldian than that.

Think of it – 'the best'. And no 'Who are you to be telling me what's best, sunshine?' To which the answer should always have been: 'Your teacher, you little bastard, so sit down and listen.' The fear of teaching 'the best' because it is an expression of canonical authoritarianism that will ultimately stultify pupils is rooted neither in reason nor experience; the history of educated man shows that it does the very opposite, equipping the well taught to disagree, to resist, even to overthrow, from a position of independence and strength. Myself, I hold the root-and-branch changes in educational thinking promised by Michael Gove to be every bit as as important, in the long run, as bringing down the deficit. Make of Clegg and Cameron what you will, but they persist against the odds because they are in possession of a culture which is no more theirs than ours, but which, thanks to a wicked ideology of principled self-disinheritance, we have ceded to them. Whoever would empower the disadvantaged must give them back 'the best'. Only then will we see men and women who don't look quite so archaically deserving in power.

GLUE STICKS AND HUMAN RIGHTS

Let's be clear: I didn't vote tactically the other day to keep Labour in by voting Liberal Democrat to keep the Tories out which was itself a ploy to get Labour out by voting Liberal Democrat to put the Tories in, on the off chance that we'd get a Liberal Conservative coalition which would collapse so quickly that the Tories would have to form a second coalition with Labour which would strengthen the Liberal Democrats, thereby ultimately keeping both the Tories *and* Labour out – reader, I didn't tie myself in these electoral knots just to wake up two weeks later to hear that al-Qaeda operatives are alive and well and being looked after in the country they can't wait to blow apart, or to hear Nick Clegg assert that 'The law is very clear, that it is wrong to deport people for whom there is serious concern that they could be seriously mistreated, or tortured or indeed killed'.

Groundhog Day. The same what's right and what's wrong and what the law is clear about, as though the law was ever clear about anything, the same giving largesse with one hand while taking with the other, the same claptrap of hand-me-down compassion we've been hearing for the past thirteen years of unexamined holier-than-thou human rights assumptiousness.

What I want to wake up and hear from a new government is that the law is an ass and we intend to change it.

Whatever Cameron's thinking, Clegg is thinking same old same old. 'We, like any civilised nation, abide by the very highest standards of human rights,' he continues, but we will stop him there. We cannot argue with someone who asserts what he's offering to prove. You don't defend human rights legislation by invoking it. For it is not evident beyond disputation that we have a duty to worry what happens to those we send back to their own countries, when they only left their own countries to destroy ours. Nor is it evident beyond disputation that to show such concern for those who show none for us is the mark of a civilised nation. Loving our neighbours certainly belongs to civilisation, but loving our neighbours more than we love ourselves belongs to pathology. As for loving our neighbours more than we love ourselves when those neighbours' idea of neighbourliness is a kiss with a stick of explosives, I'm not sure that the psychology of human self-destructiveness can supply a word that does justice to its derangement.

Nor do I know many people who see the matter differently. You may think this merely shows I hang around with right-wing thugs, but I ask you to try this test with your nearest and dearest: sit them down somewhere convivial, look them in the eyes, and ask them whether, in the great spirit of human consciousness, man and woman speaking to man and woman, honestly now, in that non-ideological part of themselves where justice and humanity reside, they give a shit what happens to a deported terrorist.

Two things, in my experience, will now happen. Firstly, they will leap at the opportunity to say what at other times they feel they cannot, which is that they couldn't care less, absolutely couldn't give a monkey's – an expression of indifference which only a fool or a knave would condemn, for indifference is to humane concern what hate is to love: you need to feel the one to feel the other. Secondly, they will revel in the delicious irony of sending back to where they learned their violence those who would bring their violence here. Not only, in other words, are they indifferent to the suffering to which the would-be bomber might be subject, they long for it in their souls.

And if you don't believe this will be the response, again I urge you, try it. But be prepared for a fun night. The genie of mischief, long bottled-up but at last released, is a great lightener of spirits.

There is, I concede, an argument to be made against following the dictates of our heart. Ideally, the law exists to express our best selves, free of partisanship, passion and self-interest. It is impersonal because we cannot be. But it's a hair-trigger negotiation: now the law is too like us, now it is too little, now too much the brute, now too much the angel. So we dare never let it out of our sight. Least of all human rights law whose justification, paradoxically, is that it is removed entirely from the experience of being human – humans being punitive, vengeful, mischievous and on the whole against it.

This much we know: that society is a rough-and-tumble affair, and that whatever legislation would, in the ether of high-minded abstraction, make the person inviolable in all circumstances, is legislation that cannot work.

Lynda May, the art teacher charged with assaulting a pupil with a glue stick, has just been cleared. Three cheers for that. But why was the case ever brought? Why was she charged by the police? Why was a prosecution allowed to proceed to the level of the High Court? Why did the pupil, whose finger bled a bit, think he'd been hard done by? Why was he encouraged to pursue his nothing grievance by whoever it was at home that should have given him an Elastoplast and locked him in his room?

Human rights, that's why. The culture of the inviolability of the individual which has permeated society and found a particularly congenial, not to say opportunistic, resting place in our schools. Schoolchildren now think they have a human right. Here's your big chance, Mr Clegg – tell them they don't. By every account, the boy whose thumbnail Mrs May was alleged to have assaulted had a mouth so foul he spat asterisks. 'F★★★ off,' he told Mrs May when she welcomed him to class. And this was art class. You could understand had it been geography or gym. I wish I'd said 'F★★★ off, Hargreaves' fifty years ago when he tried to hang me upside down from a wall bar after a lunch of braised tongue and sago pudding. But art class!

'F★★★ off', anyway, was what the boy said to Lynda May, for which vileness she would have been within her human rights to glue his lips together with a Pritt Stick and then send him somewhere he was certain to be tortured.

Only in heaven is there inviolability of person. Only in heaven do we enjoy the human right of not suffering the cruel consequence of cruel action, and that's because in heaven we have ceased to be human.

DAD SKILLS

According to James May, a person who drives fast cars on television, men are not what they once were. Myself – though I am definitely not what I once was – I never trust anyone who puts the word car and the word man in the same sentence. I just have, I know, but only in reference to James May. We have lost our 'dad skills', he's been telling us. That's three, no, four words I don't care to see in the same sentence: man, car, dad and skills.

In support of his thesis, a poll has been conducted in which men who want a quiet life admit to not being able to bleed a radiator, unblock a sink, change a fuse or hang a picture. I suspect most men can do all these things well enough, but in their own time. If there is one essential difference between men and women it is that women cannot live for more than five minutes with a blocked sink whereas a man can survive a lifetime indifferent to it. He just runs the taps less often. Doesn't notice the smell (only women notice smells). And tackles the problem of washing-up by not doing any. This is a skill I learned from my dad.

His laissez-faire attitude to blockages apart, my father was a man of the sort James May laments. He could paint, he could

336

wire, he could seal, he could grout, he could tile, he could install concealed lighting – to this day my mother is still looking for some of the concealed lighting he installed – he could wallpaper, he could lay carpets, he could fit a lock, but most of all he could make a hatch. Hatches were my father's passion.

That there must be some psychological explanation for my father's love of hatches I don't doubt. Always look for the pun, Lacanians tell us. Knowing to look for the pun is as far as I've got with Lacan, but it could be far enough in this instance. To hatch is to bring forth from the egg by incubation. My father was hatched as a twin. His twin survived the hatching but died tragically a few years later. Could it be that my father went on 're-hatching' into adulthood, making holes in walls in the unconscious hope of 'breaking through' and finding his lost self on the other side?

We were the beneficiaries, anyway. No sooner did we move into a new house than my father began knocking through from the dining room into the kitchen. No other job came first. The windows might be broken, the walls might be damp, gas might be coming in through the plug sockets, but still the hatch had precedence. I say we were the beneficiaries, but the benefits were not always immediately apparent.

'Remind me why we need this,' my mother felt it behoved her to ask before the first brick was removed. My father would laugh away her puzzlement. 'We need it to make life easier for you – so that when we're sitting in the dining room you don't have to carry food in from the kitchen.'

'Max, we don't sit in the dining room. We've never sat in the dining room. We don't *have* a dining room.'

'So what's this room for?'

'It's where you will fall asleep in front of the television.'

'And where are we supposed to dine?'

'Dine? Since when did we *dine*? We eat in the kitchen.'

He would turn from the wall with his club hammer in one hand

and his stonemason's chisel in another and throw us all a look of supreme triumph. 'Precisely. That's why we need a hatch.'

Though it began quickly, the hatch usually slowed down sometime towards the end of the third week. It wasn't that he would lose interest – though it's true his passion for knocking through cooled a little the minute he saw into the other room and presumably had to face the fact that yet again he had not found the missing half of his divided self – but little niggling problems would arise and put a dent in his fervour. The wall would start to crumble, necessitating a bigger beam than he'd anticipated. The house would turn out to have been built on a slant or a mudslide, so that while the hatch was at an ideal height in the dining room, it was either too low or too high in the kitchen. ('Should have used a theodolite,' he admitted once.) And on one occasion he knocked through only to discover that he'd come out over the cooker. 'That will save you even more carrying,' he tried to persuade my mother, but conceded that a hatch you could reach only at the risk of going up in flames had a serious design fault.

'Snagging,' was how he described these problems. From which we were to assume that they would soon be fixed. But no hatch was ever finished or put to use. Unless you call having a shelf on which you could pile magazines from either room useful. Eventually, as the magazines and unread mail accumulated, the hatch vanished altogether and was never referred to again until we moved house and his enthusiasm to knock out another revived.

I see now that we should have been more grateful to him. Whatever the initial psychological compulsion, he was only trying to make our lives more comfortable and sophisticated. But in this he suffered as many men have suffered before and since. Though a woman claims she wants a man around the house who can 'do' around the house, the truth of it is she will deride him for half the work he does, and not notice the rest.

Dad Skills

An old girlfriend of mine sent me spiteful letters after we broke up, complaining that the bookcase I'd built when we were together was so flimsy it fell down the minute her new boyfriend rested his aftershave on it. Another wrote letters no less unpleasant cursing me for putting up a bookcase that was so sturdy it could not be dismantled without the wall it was on having to be demolished.

This is why men eventually stop trying. I, for example, can lay new floorboards, retile a roof and plaster any surface. But I'm damned if I will. The floor has only to subside, the roof let in rain, the plastering look as though a bear on heat has rubbed up against it when it was damp, and there's hell to pay. Better to affect a practical incompetence and let the women call in James May.

MAN BOOKER

I am in the garden of a house in far, far north London. So far north London that it might as well be Manchester. It has been a day of immense sadness. We are just back from a burial. My wife's uncle Gerry died three days ago. He was ninety-two and so there has not been that sense of tearing tragedy that makes the burial of a young person unbearable. But he was greatly loved. And precisely because he has been in people's lives for so long, it is already hard to imagine life without him.

On the way to the grave the black-hatted official leading the mourners stopped intermittently and held us up. This is a Jewish custom. It denotes our unwillingness to part with a person we have cared for. We would rather stop for eternity, but of course we don't have eternity on our hands.

Back in the house people are drinking tea and eating bagels filled with smoked salmon. Call that stereotyping, but what am I to do? They truly are drinking tea and eating bagels filled with smoked salmon. Jews don't throw down alcohol on such occasions. And they like food that tastes soft. In another column we might put our minds to why.

In the garden, which is big enough for me to stroll through

on my own, I decide that it is all right if I turn my mobile on. I am waiting for an important message regarding an article I'm writing. No one thinks this is unfeeling. The living must return to life. There are an unaccountable number of texts and emails waiting for me. This is when I discover that my novel *The Finkler Question* has been longlisted for the Man Booker Prize.

I don't want this news to intrude upon the family, but I know my wife would want to know so I go back inside and whisper into her ear. She is excited, and moved, as I am, that we should learn of such a thing on such a day. *The Finkler Question* is partly the story of a man not much younger than Gerry who is trying to hold himself together after the death of his wife. He has loved her for sixty years. The assumption is sometimes made that the old are people of diminished feelings, husks of confused recollections and barely remembered desires. Well, Gerry was no such thing. He was a man entire. Libor, the broken-hearted widower in my novel, is the same. He burns still with a love for his dead wife which is as intense as any youth's. No, he burns with a love that is more intense. The terrible thing we have to face about old age is that there is no release from longing in it, that we go on with our passions blazingly intact. Terrible and wonderful.

We have been so involved in the last few weeks of Gerry's life, in hospital visits and finally in the paperwork of decease, that we haven't thought about literary prizes. This is the first time in eleven novels I haven't waited to see if I am on a Man Booker list. I make that confession with some embarrassment. I have always argued against prizes. My ambition to be a writer dates from infancy. 'As yet a child, nor yet a fool to fame, / I lisped in numbers, for the numbers came.' I wanted to make sentences, not win prizes. The sentences were prize enough in themselves. Let others be fools to fame, I cared only about the quality of the work. But, as Alexander Pope knew, the opinion of the world matters, and the quickest way to gain its notice as a writer is to win a prize, and of all prizes to win for a writer of fiction in English, the Man Booker is the biggest and the best. So my protestations of scorn for it were inevitably mixed with covetousness. In a perfect world, where the words you write are immediately found and lauded by those you write them for – the whole of humanity, no less – a prize would not be necessary. But since humanity is deaf, or just too busy to give a damn, and since there seems to be a disconnect between those who want to read a good novel and those who write them – as though the world of reading is one big lonely hearts club waiting for a matchmaker – there must be prizes to bring us together. In which case, yes, thank you, I would like to win one.

And so, with every novel I published, I knew to the day, knew to the hour, when the list would be announced, grew abstracted for weeks before, and waited for the phone to ring. It didn't. It didn't for nineteen years. And then, in 2002, it did. Longlisted. First euphoria, then a quiet relief – for isn't victory simply the absence of defeat? – followed, of course, by the second phase of anxiety and abstraction. After the longlist, the shortlist. Knowing the very hour, the very minute, you wait again for the phone to ring, and when it does it's your publisher or your agent, depending who draws the short straw, telling you what you don't want to hear and they don't want to tell you, though you know it from the first jeering trill of the accursed phone.

After decades of this, the inside of your brain becomes like one of the novels you have never wanted to write: a seething, muttering melodrama of corruption and crass cowardice, peopled by sinister forces of mindlessness against whom you plot the bloodiest revenge. You know their names, the judges of the Man Booker, you know where they live or where they teach or where they practise whatever dark arts of indiscrimination are theirs. One by one, when you are ready and when they least expect it, you will pick them off.

Not to have been thinking about it this time, therefore, not to have known when these judges were deliberating, made the good news doubly sweet. It felt like a last blessing from Uncle Gerry. I owed it to him, I thought, to rejoice in the thing itself. And hope for nothing further. That would have been his advice to me, as it was my mother's: enjoy the now. An intelligent panel of judges had liked the book sufficiently to nominate it with a dozen others. Enough. Be grateful.

But you might as well ask a river not to flow. Five weeks later I am sitting by the phone. And this time it rings with a different tone. The shortlist tone. How do I recognise it? Twenty-seven years of waiting has prepared me. I know how the shortlist tone sounds because it is unlike all the others. It rings like a fanfare. Now, surely, surely, this will be enough. Five judges, exceptional for their discernment – judges such as there have never been before, paragons of acuity and good taste – have narrowed me down to six. I promise myself I will ask for nothing more. This will do. This will more than do.

Come the the night of nights, I hear, to my astonishment and wonder, the name Finkler read out. Finkler! Don't tell me my own character has stolen the prize from me. Am I in yet another novel of the sort I don't write? But I am propelled towards the stage. It's me. I've won.

So is that sufficient now? Is the summit reached? Ah, reader, reader . . .

A NOTE ON THE TYPE

The text of this book is set in Bembo. This type was first used in 1495 by the Venetian printer Aldus Manutius for Cardinal Bembo's *De Aetna*, and was cut for Manutius by Francesco Griffo. It was one of the types used by Claude Garamond (1480–1561) as a model for his Romain de l'Université, and so it was the forerunner of what became standard European type for the following two centuries. Its modern form follows the original types and was designed for Monotype in 1929.

IN THE LAND OF OZ

The *Sunday Times* bestseller

On what he calls 'the adventure of his life', Howard Jacobson travels around Australia, never entirely sure where he is heading next or whether he has the courage to tackle the wild life of the bush, the wild men of the outback, or the even wilder women of the seaboard cities.

In pursuit of the best of Australian good times, he joins revelers at Uluru, argues with racists in the Kimberleys, parties with wine-growers in the Barossa and falls for ballet dancers in Perth. And even as vexed questions of national identity and Aboriginal land rights present themselves, his love for Australia and Australians never falters.

'A marvellous read ... he is a comic explorer in the grandest mould'
FINANCIAL TIMES

'The most successful attempt I know to grip the great dreaming Australian enigma by the throat and make it gargle'
EVENING STANDARD

'A wildly funny account of his travels; abounding in sharp characterization, crunching dialogue and self-parody, it actually is a book which makes you laugh out loud on almost every page'
LITERARY REVIEW

BLOOMSBURY

THE FINKLER QUESTION

Winner of the Man Booker Prize 2010

Julian Treslove, a professionally unspectacular former BBC radio producer, and Sam Finkler, a popular Jewish philosopher, writer and television personality, are old school friends. Despite very different lives, they've never quite lost touch with each other – or with their former teacher, Libor Sevcik. Both Libor and Finkler are recently widowed, and together with Treslove they share a sweetly painful evening revisiting a time before they had loved and lost. It is that very evening, when Treslove hesitates a moment as he walks home, that he is attacked – and his whole sense of who and what he is slowly and ineluctably changes.

B L O O M S B U R Y

ZOO TIME

Novelist Guy Ableman is in thrall to his vivacious wife Vanessa, a strikingly beautiful red-head, contrary, highly strung and blazingly angry. The trouble is, he is no less in thrall to her alluring mother, Poppy. More like sisters than mother and daughter, they come as a pair, a blistering presence that destroys Guy's peace of mind, suggesting the wildest stories but making it impossible for him to concentrate long enough to write any of them.

Not that anyone reads Guy, anyway. Not that anyone is reading anything. Reading, Guy fears, is finished. His publisher, fearing the same, has committed suicide. His agent, like all agents, is in hiding. Vanessa, in the meantime, is writing a novel of her own. Guy doesn't expect her to finish it, or even start it, but he dreads the consequences if she does.

In flight from personal disappointment and universal despair, Guy wonders if it's time to take his love for Poppy to another level. Fiction might be dead, but desire isn't. And out of that desire he imagines squeezing one more great book.

By turns angry, elegiac and rude, *Zoo Time* is a novel about love – love of women, love of literature, love of laughter. It shows our funniest writer at his brilliant best.